The Waterbearers

THE Waterbearers

A MEMOIR OF MOTHERS
AND DAUGHTERS

SASHA BONÉT

ALFRED A. KNOPF

NEW YORK

2025

A BORZOI BOOK
FIRST HARDCOVER EDITION
PUBLISHED BY ALFRED A. KNOPF 2025

Published by Alfred A. Knopf, a division of Penguin Random House
LLC, 1745 Broadway, New York, NY 10019.

Knopf, Borzoi Books, and the colophon are registered trademarks
of Penguin Random House LLC.

Grateful acknowledgment to reprint previously published material
can be found on page 295.

LIBRARY OF CONGRESS CATALOGING-IN-PUBLICATION DATA
Names: Bonét, Sasha author.
Title: The waterbearers : a memoir of mothers and daughters /
Sasha Bonét.
Description: First edition. | New York : Alfred A. Knopf, 2025.
Identifiers: LCCN 2024042047 (print) | LCCN 2024042048 (ebook) |
ISBN 9780593536087 (hardcover) | ISBN 9780593536094 (ebook).
Subjects: LCSH: Women, Black—Biography | African American single
mothers—Biography | Single mothers—Biography.
Classification: LCC HQ1163 .B66 2025 (print) | LCC HQ1163 (ebook) |
DDC 306.874/32092396073—dc23/eng/20250408
LC record available at https://lccn.loc.gov/2024042047
LC ebook record available at https://lccn.loc.gov/2024042048

penguinrandomhouse.com | aaknopf.com

Printed in the United States of America
1st Printing

The authorized representative in the EU for product safety
and compliance is Penguin Random House Ireland,
Morrison Chambers, 32 Nassau Street, Dublin D02 YH68, Ireland,
https://eu-contact.penguin.ie.

for my daughter, my mother, and my grandmothers

SHE SAW HIM DISAPPEAR BY THE RIVER,
THEY ASKED HER TO TELL WHAT HAPPENED,
ONLY TO DISCOUNT HER MEMORY.

WATERBEARER, LORNA SIMPSON, 1986

If you don't understand the history of African American women, you don't understand the history of America.

—TONI MORRISON

Here is your truth and vengeance against you . . . Masters of towns and dachas, be afraid of the Sender of the Wind, fear the breezes and drafts because they give birth to hurricanes.

—SASHA SOKOLOV, *A SCHOOL FOR FOOLS*

MATRIARCHAL TREE

Lilly

Rose

May   Righthand   Junior

BETTY JEAN   **CONNIE**   **SASHA**   **SOFIA**

Gone   Shannon

Artemis

Red

Daddy's
Girl

The Baby

CONTENTS

/ / / / / / / / / / / /

NOTE ON TRIBUTARIES

Tributaries are branches of a main-stem river. Branches start small at the headwater source and gradually grow as gravity pulls them and they join more streams, increasing the force and speed of the flow. Eventually this network of tributaries creates a collective river that flows toward a single end point. Geographers and potamologists list a river's tributaries starting with those closest to the source of the river in ascending numerical order.

THE Waterbearers

Prelude

Listen.

When I say waterbearer, I mean carrying all that weight. With calloused hands, dry mouth, split ends, and a back that don't bend, except to pray. I'm talking about balance; flat-footed strides grounded so deep into the earth look like she sinking when she actually sprouting. 'Cause she of it. Sure of a path nobody but God can see. I'm talking about no map, no paving, no clue where to find it, but, somehow, she gone get it. I'm talking sweat above her lip and mud beneath her nails. You know who I'm talking about. Big Mama 'nem, Grandmama 'nem, Mother Dear, Granny, Nan, Buela, T. Lady, Meemaw, Mommi, Motha. Your nanny, your mammy, your punching bag, your liberator, your organizer, your siren, granter of your manhood, affirmer of your masculinity, the soft warm pink place for you to deposit your darkness. Go in broken and come out whole. When I say water, I mean life force. I mean ancestral inheritance. The water of the womb. All that Mama tried to shield you from, but you got it honest. I mean bloodline. All that she dare not say, and you bet not ask, came to you through that water. Water so pure it don't tell no lies. That water damn near broke her back, but she'd die before she let somebody take what belongs to her. That water's all she has to call her own, and she'll give it all to you and won't even burden you with the tale of how she made it cross the valley. Not nobody can imagine what she saw, what she felt, what she stepped on and over to get there. Feet so swole look like they might bust. Hardened soles tender to the touch, still sensitive enough to feel moisture's gesture, subtle as a whisper, certain as forsythia. Before you can even smack your lips and suck your tongue, she's already at the mouth of the river. She's carrying all that heavy. Parsing out what you need from what you thought you wanted. Taking a whole bunch of nothing and making it enough, all you gotta do is trust her with your whole throat when you lean your head back and open up wide.

And then maybe, if you live long enough . . .

One day, on an ordinary day, after all those yesterdays, you yourself will try to find your way to that well, to that river, to that delta, and only then will you be able to look to her and ask:

Mama, are you thirsty?

My grandmother Betty Jean tells me I look like she did when she was my age. In a photo I keep of her on my desk, she sits on a bed, her golden-brown skin shimmering with red undertones, as if she had swallowed the sun whole. She is in her twenties, about ten years younger than I am now. Her brown eyes are black and deep. Wearing shorts and a summer blouse, her body appears relaxed, her legs are crossed, and she leans back, arms spread out like wings. Somehow, she appears weightless and immovable at once. There is a man on the bed, not too far away, his blurred face and body partially cut from the frame. He could be anyone. Who he is, is of no consequence. But who I am, and who *you* are, and who America is, has everything to do with what's hidden behind the smile she is only half committed to.

. . .

Every morning back in 1955, after migrating to Houston from Louisiana, Betty Jean would walk to the 44 bus stop in Acres

Home where she would meet a man with skin like midnight. She walked slow but this was not an indication of indifference, she simply did nothing with haste. Sometimes, all she could see were the whites of his teeth and eyes in the predawn darkness. Still, his beauty was evident. He greeted hers each day without subtlety. And for a short while, at the top of each day, they opened up to let the soft insides show, the insides they'd spend the rest of the day shielding, kept tender in its shell like sweet young scallops.

They were both domestics on their way to hotels downtown. Elevated on concrete overpasses, they traversed buildings that seemed to touch the sky. Betty Jean listened as he lied to make himself bigger, more than just a country Creole Nigga from Grand Coteau, Louisiana. They both valued the autonomy that Houston offered in its vastness, the opportunity it afforded them to shed their pasts. They'd both migrated from rural farmlands in Louisiana. Him the south, her the north. As they constructed new selves, Louisiana became only memories. He stopped speaking the French that was his mother tongue. And she never put her hands in the dirt to feel the insides of the earth again. Their intimacy was forged in reminding each other of home despite their insistence on forgetting. They never spoke of the past, but their calloused hands and the cadence of their breath told the stories they had laid to rest inside themselves.

Betty Jean hadn't known the midnight man for more than six months before making a father of him; this guy with a French surname she couldn't pronounce. She named my mother Connie, after her cousin, Laconia (Connie) Walker Cain, a willful community organizer and educator who helped Black folks from Louisiana transition from the backwoods into urban life in Acres Home. She was a lighthouse of a woman. A bridge of a woman, and in time, like her namesake, my mother's back became one, too. My mother Connie was born at night in early spring; her skin shone like a polished plum. Betty Jean says she resembles her father—he is said to be beautiful, and he knew it.

I wonder if Betty Jean ever loved him. Or would she see this as weakness? I wonder if he is the blurred man on the bed in the photo I keep. I wonder if, at the bus stop each morning, he would hold her hand. At night, did she lay her head on his chest and hear their hearts beat in unison? Did she love him in the moment that he released a piece of himself inside her, which she'd hold forever? Did Connie's father, after he'd left Houston, ever think about returning, walking by her apartment after my mother was born, peering into the window, yearning to hold the child?

Betty Jean never mentioned why she left my mother's father, but she let it be known that she left him—just as she had left the men before him. She never elaborated on what any of them had done to be dismissed, but once she was gone, there was no coming back. When she became pregnant with my mother, she stopped taking the midnight man's calls. She took an earlier bus into downtown. There was no romantic farewell or goodbye kiss. He stopped by their home once, after he'd heard that the child had come. He looked into her eyes and saw his own. Those eyes that questioned him. Shamed him. The eyes of his firstborn. Eyes that he would only see when he closed his to pray for forgiveness at Mass. He was gone within weeks. The midnight man stopped in Houston, only to crash with his sister while he worked to make enough money to continue his migration to the Bay Area by train, where his mother had gone ahead and established a place for him to land. He did not plan on the collision at the 44 bus stop. Perhaps there is no gravity mighty enough to hold a Negro intent on escaping the South. My mother was evidence of the wreckage and would spend the majority of her life wondering why she wasn't enough to keep him.

· · ·

Where I come from, you're not a woman until you're a mother.

I grew up on the water in Houston. The bayous remain mystical to me still. There was always mythical lore surrounding what lived beneath the brown surface. Snakes, spirits, crawfish, catfish, gators, and largemouth bass. The stories we children told

one another about the creatures that lived within those mysterious winding canals invoked anxious temptation while the adults
insisted that we stay clear so that the water doesn't take us, as if
it might simply slurp us up. It was my earliest memory of adults
admitting the limitations of their power. Because the water is so
unpredictable, there is no telling where it may take you if you let
it devour you.

The bayous appear to be still, stagnant waters without a destination. But they are deceptive as they move steadily toward larger
bodies. The bayous carry the water and its memories from the
city into the Gulf of Mexico, which flows into the Caribbean Sea
and on into the Atlantic. A reverse migration of the souls of Black
folks. Water flow that reminds me of my inheritance. The way my
mother and grandmother pour into me, and I into my daughter;
the valuable and the harmful, the minerals and the mud. Each
generation shifting, little by little, closer to freedom without ever
defining it aloud. The shape of freedom, like the shape of water,
is difficult to define as it is ever shifting but so elemental that it
can't be mistaken. It is understood that water takes on the shape
of its surroundings, but if you stay a while, observe a little longer,
you'll notice its patience. Never not pushing back on its environs,
like these women I come from, the water redefines everything it
encounters. And if it cannot, water can simply change its form
entirely. Each generation of women in my family seeks to transform realities, voyaging varied and sometimes cyclical routes, but
we somehow always find our way back to what we know. And we
come from a long line of Louisiana women who traversed these
troubled waters of the South. These waters that can tell you the
true history of America, how it all really went down, if you just
ask.

My grandmother Betty Jean left the cotton plantation in Louisiana but brought the whip in her satchel on the train to Houston. My mother rode off to suburbia from the hood in a Benz and
told me that she would never call me a heifer the way her mother
did, but she told me I was *the type of girl that everyone wrote about*

on the bathroom walls. She told me she would never backhand me across my mouth the way her mother did, but she tore me up with Italian leather belts until my body was covered in welts. And when it was time for bed, I'd bathe and feel that burn when my flesh dipped below the surface. I still remember the way I'd clench and hiss between my gapped teeth as the water submerged my fresh wounds. Afterward, my mother would say, *This hurts me more than it hurts you.* Insisting on the old master's tools that suggest to grow a Black child up in God's image, they must first be knocked down, stripped to the bone, and then only the hand that holds the belt can bestow upon them their dignity in return for obedience. For protection's sake, so the White folks don't get ahold of you, because they're ruthless. *I whoop you 'cause I love you.* To raise a child everybody can love. So by the time you're good and grown, you don't go looking for mercy, but you damn sure gone find misery and you'll tell him you love him because he feels like home.

So when it was my turn, I ran away from all that familiar. I ran to Manhattan, where me and my daughter woke each morning to seagulls singing songs I didn't know the words to. I didn't realize all I sought to escape was already inside me. *Wherever you go, there you are.* I didn't realize home is nowhere and somehow everywhere at once. Before learning new ways to love, the harm comes first. The harm flows naturally. Unless you become the bend in the river that turns just so, then breaks away, becoming a new body, still informed by those from which you derive.

. . .

My country tells me you're not a mother if you're not a wife.

I'd always known that I would be a mother. Everyone around me that had power had given birth. But in my daydreams, there was never a man there. I never imagined being married or having a wedding or walking down an aisle in a gown with my father beside me. Perhaps it seemed too fantastical, the concept of a man I could trust with my life. That I could sleep beside with both eyes shut and my daughter's bedroom door open. Nothing goes untouched, our subconscious is impacted by our social circumstances. Even a dream has its limits. I was surrounded by reliable women. The men were peripheral—inefficient and fickle. All I had ever been taught about men was to be cautious of them. Never sit on a man's lap, family or otherwise. Don't come out in your pajamas as that may be cause for provocation. If a man offers you candy don't take it, *Ain't shit free.* They always want something in return. I couldn't comprehend the need for a man in a domestic capacity and no space was afforded them in my imagination. But as a girl, what was made legible through these warnings was that there was something powerful between my thighs. Something that needed protecting yet seemed to have little to do with me as an individual, however, if trifled with, could classify me as a certain *type* of person. Or worse, usurp my personhood, leaving a little puddle of waste in its wake. These women who raised me were never more attentive than when a man was in the room. Every gesture of the girl is studied for suggestions of sensuality while the grown man's impulses are foreseeable. This small moist crevice could make a man lose his mind, abandon his family, risk it all for this religion between my legs. Although not my family's intention, I understood where the power was. And I thought everyone else just wasn't using it right. My grandmother could read the arrogance all over me, perhaps because I am her mirror, as she herself has played dangerously with the pleasure principle. After all, she did have eleven children with nine different men, with no one to answer to but God.

· · ·

When you get pregnant, they think they own you.

My grandmother has always been both my anchor and my compass. She was warning me, but she was also instructing me to take hold of myself. She was telling me I was something worth keeping. To her, freedom can only be realized through self-possession, because we come from a lineage of people who had been owned. When she told me this, I didn't belong to myself yet. Can you imagine? Just giving your whole self over to any old fool with their hand out? I thought value was in what I could purchase, or that my value was determined by what was purchased for me, I didn't know the value was *me*. When Betty Jean warned me, I was already pregnant by a White man, more than twice my age, an oil-man with oil money. I didn't yet connect myself with the history as old as America of White men with dirty money who liked to own and impregnate Black girls, but my grandmother had seen the product of that equation on the face of her grandmother back in Louisiana, in her pale skin and the sorrow in her green eyes, she knew how it ended. She knew that just like my mother, and my grandmother, and my great-grandmother, I, too, would raise my daughter alone. But you can't tell no girl in love how the game go. She just let me play my hand.

I thought *the oilman* loved me when he asked me to have his daughter. Betty Jean didn't tell me that just because a man says he wants you to bear his child that he actually means it. Foolish girl. I wrapped my long brown legs around that little White man, and he was seized so by the warm wet waters, that his body quickly clenched all over and I clenched back, to hold him still until he fell asleep inside of me. Afterward, I lay on my back in the bathroom against the cool tiles and lifted my toes to the ceiling, squeezing my pelvic floor until my body absorbed every drop of him. We did not plan to marry, but he gifted me a diamond ring, because all mothers should have one, he said. The same way my father didn't raise me but gave me a diamond ring at twenty-one because every woman should have one, he said. The stone signals to other men that the woman is kept. Her flesh carries the precious stone to compensate for a heart worn thin by the burden of men's departures. His wealth was endless, the wisdom he bestowed would be everlasting. Introducing me to worlds beyond my imagination. But like my mother and my grandmother always advised, *Ain't shit free.*

Wherever there is water, there is mystery. And mystery breeds mythology.

Emerging

BETTY JEAN

///////////

For those of us who live at the shoreline . . .

—AUDRE LORDE,
"A LITANY FOR SURVIVAL"

I

50 10

My grandmother Betty Jean had a dream about the water when her daughter was pregnant with me. And she had that same dream when I was pregnant with my daughter. One afternoon in May we were packed tightly in my grandmother's home. There was something stirring in the living room. It was an unusual afternoon when you could clearly hear the tune of the ice-cream truck pass outside, more still, the children didn't beg for a dollar or run out to the street in pursuit of sweetness. There was, of course, the savory stewing smell coming from the kitchen. I sat on the floor with my weight resting on my palms beside my cousins while the grown folks took the seats. The solemn aunties' arms didn't graze but their hips kissed across the length of the sofa, shapeshifting women who spread upon being seated. Sometimes that living room felt consecrated. Other times tribunal. That day it was peculiar, and I couldn't place it. Betty Jean didn't even look away from her crossword when she said she'd been dreaming about the fish and the water. A room full of wombs and I knew she was talking about mine. After I gave birth, before going home alone with my baby, I stopped first at my grandmother's house so that she could hold her great-granddaughter. So she could bless her. My mother and I sat on either side of Betty Jean while she told my daughter that she was the one she'd been dreaming of, as if she had willed her here. And hadn't she? From that day onward,

I didn't sit on the floor anymore. The women moved over now, making space for me on the sofa.

. . .

We are deep. I am in the middle of about three dozen cousins. Not among the oldest, not among the youngest. As a child, I felt inconsequential at 5010 Chennault Road. The older cousins caused trouble, and the younger ones needed help with most things. I was merely a silent witness. This left me both excited to be there, because it felt like theater, and terrified because of the sheer size of the ever-expanding group. I was content if I got no attention at all. I would take a deep breath before entering because after putting my arms around my grandmother's neck, my mother expected me and my younger brother, Shannon, to greet every auntie with an embrace, and on rare occasions, an uncle with acknowledgment. Worsening my angst by confirming along the way, "You speak?" It was imperative that my mother's children be regarded as having home training. My heart would race as I pressed myself into them, becoming one. Each of them commenting on my body in some way. My hair was good, but why was it so short? I was getting tall, but why were my thighs giving my jeans hell? My hips were spreading, but I better be keeping my legs closed. My body belonged to the tribe, and they projected their insecurities onto me, and I held to them tightly. After all, this was my inheritance. It is from those closest to us that we learn how to love and how to hate ourselves too.

50 10 was our *haven. Our well.* A place for gestation. A place where big-legged women gathered with their troubles and sorrows tucked in their bosoms. The women came parched in search of answers and approval. They didn't concern themselves with justice, fairness, or peace, for those were never promised. But what they did receive between those walls would help them stand more erect along the way. Where the women spoke emphatically, and the men knew to keep quiet or stay away altogether. A realm that contradicted everything learned beyond its threshold. A place where nothing grew but the children, and they did so quietly as to be seen and not heard. Markings on the wall outside the bathroom charted their progress. Making a monument of Black children blooming, because this too was never promised. The living room was center stage for the women stuck between life's torments and the imminent threat of death, both of which kept them from wasting their time with the frivolity of dreams.

But despite it all, joy was at home there. The house, which never felt structurally rooted, would vibrate with the eruption of a chorus of laughter. The women's bodies would lean into one another, waving from top to bottom with their heads rolling back. *Substantial* women who breathed deeply in laughter, otherwise their bodies were clenched like fists, sipping only the air necessary to survive. Never taking more than their share. Yet still stepping through the world full-footed, like they had a right to be there. You can't erupt like this if you're not intimate with *tragedy*. If you haven't lain beside her and closed your eyes as she fondled your jugular. If you can't smell the blood before you taste it, you'll never know laughter like this. This joy was the kind you earned.

Conflict was not uncommon in the modern-day Greek tragedies that unfolded in the living room at *50 10*. Where both betrayal and forgiveness were exercised regularly, and everyone agrees to forget. The walls hold records and keep the score. The water lines ring the discolored walls and baseboards, marking the rise and descent of flood waters. The punctures formed from a release with nowhere else to land. The sticky ribbons that hold petrified pests. And Betty Jean reigned over it all, maintaining an order that only they understood to be true. She sat as a guardian in her chair near the door, a tower of photographs of her kids, and their kids, and *their* kids in the corner beside her like a shrine, the hum of the AC unit in one ear and her girls' stories ringing in the other. Listening and only speaking when she needed to be heard. It is here, and only here, that she feels most divine.

My grandmother's home is a small single-story structure with sky-blue siding punctuated with white shutters. The porch is a concrete slab extending from the foundation. The air conditioner pokes out over the porch from the living-room window and slouches toward hell, which is precisely what sweltering summers in Houston resemble. The wide yard holds a sole grand live oak tree in the middle that shields the children playing outside from the relentless Texas sun. Most of the time the door is not closed, but the screen door must always be shut. The latch is stripped, but no one bothers to repair it because people pass through end-lessly. Dropping kids, grabbing mail, taking naps. Recharging in the only place on the planet where they were always welcome.

Kids weren't allowed to run in and out of the house, else the humid heat seized the cool air inside. We chose the outside, as to not hear the women shout in unison, "Quit slamming the screen door." With the cicadas singing our favorite summer song, we felt most free out there. We listened to Screw tapes that seemed to embody the slow-motion rhythm of the heat waves we saw in the distance. If we were doing something we weren't supposed to, we just needed to get out of the view of that front window, but if we got too quiet, somebody's mama would peek her head out in suspicion: *Y'all must be doing something y'all ain't got no business.* When we weren't playing basketball across the yard's hardened dirt, shooting anything round we could find into a milk crate that we'd tied to the trunk of the live oak, or picking and peeling switches from the tree's limbs for Granny to welt our own, should we transgress, we were being embraced by its shade.

If you pull up to *50 10* and there is a car in the yard, then some-one is there. Someone is always there. It is rare for less than half a dozen cars to be in the wide yard at a time. There was no driveway, just a path that led to the lip of the porch. A well-worn engraving that says we've been here, and we'll be right back.

I never knew when we might end up at Granny's house. We could be going out for groceries, leaving a doctor's appointment, leaving church, killing time, or just escaping the tension of our own home when my mother would say, "Let's stop by Mama's." Sometimes she wouldn't even tell us, but when we took the MLK exit off of 610, and made that right at Calais Road, and a quick left at Burma, I knew where we were headed.

The kids always outnumbered the adults. Where your grand-mama stays is a social signifier that says you come from some-place, that you were raised according to a certain set of principles. Many of my cousins have lived with Betty Jean at some point in their lives. Everyone had their mail routed there. My driver's license had always listed *50 10* as my residence, I was registered to vote there, my passport was mailed there. Legally, it has always been my permanent residence. The phone number is everyone's emergency contact. It's the number used when someone was arrested and needed to call collect. It's the place where people slept off hangovers, of love and substances. The place where one healed and recovered from life's wounds. The place where the kids went after school and where they went when they were sick and their mama had to go to work. For the troubled kids and the ones that were a bit touched. It was the only place we could run to that would always be there to catch us.

. . .

Betty Jean's affection was not always visible to the uninitiated, but it was evident in the unspoken, in the gestures. *Go in there and git you summ'n to eat,* she'd tell me tenderly. I feared offend-ing her. But the dimly lit kitchen terrified me. Anything you overturned would reveal an army of roaches. Like motion detec-tors. They even survived the chill of the refrigerator, they were in the microwave, the faucet, the cupboards. There were hot days when I wanted a popsicle so desperately from the freezer but abstained. Or I discreetly asked my older cousin to grab one for me, only for him to raise his voice and say, *What, you too scared?* We learned young how to swat the roaches for our share. If you allowed them to swarm your plate, you would be shamed for your passivity. We exploited each other's fears to make ourselves seem brave.

I am tempted to recount these memories in the *we*. My younger brother, Shannon, and I, two years apart, were often treated as one. As twins. Although we couldn't be more different, everyone assumed we possessed the same interiority, perhaps because we shared an identical balance of the feminine and the masculine. Strangers squint in search of resemblance when we tell them we are siblings. Quick to ask if we have the same father. At *50 10* Shannon made everyone laugh with the timing of his absurdities. A naturally outgoing and charming Gemini with a slight, round, brown frame; everyone adored him. Anyone who has ever met him recalls that he gives the best hug they've ever received. I believe he acquired this skill in the living room of *50 10.* Where many lessons were learned. I learned how to repress my discomfort and smile through angst in a room full of people. If I was in trouble at school, my mother would force me to recount the story to the living room of *50 10* as punishment. A shaming device that would later prove useful for public speaking. It was at *50 10* that I learned about the complexities of relationships, that you can openly despise someone and still love them hopelessly. My aunts would talk about their lovers and husbands with such vitriol, reducing them to filth, and shortly after, the very topic of the conversation would walk through the door, and he would be greeted with lukewarm cordiality and the offering of a plate. *Niggas and flies,* they'd nudge one another and whisper. It would be many years before I understood that they meant that all men are maggots, feasting on you until they've satiated themselves enough to sprout wings and fly away. But I wondered if that would make the woman the corpse. The unalive. The sense of loss was ever-present. Someone was always losing something or someone, but somehow these women found ways to keep carrying on. It was heartbreaking to witness, even as a girl. It was in opposition to the tragedies I heard at *50 10* that I began to construct my dreams. I didn't want to become a woman whose life was a sequence of unfortunate events.

I learned about finances at *50 10* while I witnessed one of my aunties lose everything when her husband became addicted to crack cocaine. "He smoked up the whole house," my mother said, "and she sat there and let him." No one except Betty Jean would dare challenge my mother. When my mother spoke in the living room, everyone listened. Because she had a mortgage, and a husband, and three children who weren't illegitimate, she was always *right*. Even if they didn't necessarily believe in her message, her ideas were always considered. Rarely did her sisters take her advice. This frustrated her and created a tension that shifted between disappointment and disgust among them. These conversations led to monologues from my mother on the long drive home from the inner city to the suburbs where we lived. "Never give a man your all," she'd say while peering at me through the rearview mirror. I sat with her lessons and burdens in the backseat of our Mercedes-Benz. "Always keep something for yourself tucked away. These men will strip you to the bone if you let 'em. Just look at my sister, back in the poor house." And everything she said to me in the car, she had already said to her sisters in the living room. Some shaming, Betty Jean allowed. At least for a while, until she deaded it. All she had to mutter was, "*Aht aht aht.*"

Betty Jean was selective in what chaos she allowed to transpire at *50 10* and my mother was often at the center of it all, judging. Since girlhood, my grandmother has told my mother that she talked too much. "Yo mouf gone be da def a you," she'd warn in her slow deep Southern rasp. A voice without haste but not without thunder. There were times when she'd allow my mother to do the talking that she never could find the words to say. It was as if Betty Jean would let my mother off the leash on her sisters. And when she did, my mother was vicious, because she could bring you to your knees with truths and secrets that only she held. Secrets that her sisters had confided in her. The women were nonviolent, but one time my mother crossed the line and her younger sister snatched her up by her arm, leading to a mild scuffle. And then there are some moments that are too painful to ever mention, and even my mother honors those.

Once when my parents were newly married teenagers, my mother said something slick and took off running into *50 10* and locked the door. My mother knew his anger would have its limits there. We all had our limits there. Then my father kicked the door in. Betty Jean always favored my father, a too cool, high yellow fast-talker with a quick wit and bright smile. But on this particular day, she was there to greet him with her gun, the one I always saw under her pillow on her bed. She also kept a rusted old butcher knife on the dashboard of her small American-made sedan. I was never sure if it was there to threaten those inside or outside of the car. Whenever she made a turn, the blade would slide from one side of the dash to the other, sometimes falling between the legs of the poor passenger riding shotgun. We all knew to spread our legs so that it would fall between them to the floor. Even if it didn't cut you, which it never did, the metal was burning hot from the sun piercing the windshield.

No one doubted that she was capable of taking a life if her family was threatened. This was crystallized for me as a girl, when one afternoon a rat scurried across the living room of *50 10* while us kids sat on the floor watching cartoons. My grandfather was timid in his approach, Betty Jean sat still and unbothered until she grew weary of watching him flail so she rose from her seat, unrushed, commanding that he "Git out da way," before pushing him aside. She stomped the rat dead with her bare foot, killing the creature in three swift blows. Disgusted with the timidity of her husband, she walked flat-footed to the bathroom to wipe the residue from her foot before returning to her seat, insulting him all the way for the inconvenience. To me, she seemed to be a kind of warrior woman. To me, she was supernatural. Fearless. Working up the strength to kill a small mammal and returning to a crossword puzzle with calm. Now I realize that she was never without fear, rather she knew how to maneuver with this shadow at her back. And I wondered then, and still do, from where she sourced that power, and how can I harness my own.

2

Elm Grove, Louisiana

At *50 10* we all knew Betty Jean came from somewhere and had been through some things, but no one person knew the entire story, we each held fragments. There is an unspoken understanding that you do not ask elders questions about the past, because you don't want to dredge up all that hurt that comes with recollecting. And these women have a motive for wanting to forget. Which begets an assumption that no one has overcome or worked through those things, but that they have succeeded in their burials. Imagine a family, a tribe, a lineage with a cooperative commitment to forgetting. One cannot successfully forget all alone, it's a collaboration. Collectively not asking, or correcting, as a courtesy, an act of love. Until someone comes along and decides to puncture a tension pulled so tight, spread so thin, that all it took was a gentle poke to burst it wide open.

I was sitting on the sofa one day at *50 10*, it was one of those quiet times in the middle of the day when everyone was at school or work. I was between classes at the university that was actively gentrifying the neighborhood where my grandmother raised my mother and I had driven over to *50 10* as I often did. I felt so grown-up driving to my grandmother's house on my own. To pop in with a fish sandwich, fries, and a red slushy from Burger Park like I was one of the women. During these times it would just be the two of us, which I hadn't experienced at any point prior. And one day while I was laid out on the couch watching whatever she had the TV tuned to, while she was working on her crossword, I dared to ask. *Granny, what was your life like in Louisiana?*

And she looked up at me as if she had been waiting her whole life for someone to ask.

. . .

Betty Jean was a cotton tenant for twenty summers near Lake Bistineau in Louisiana in a small town called Elm Grove. She pronounces it "el-uhm." The town is named after the elm trees that grow alongside riverways and bayous. Just like my family, they can be found near currents, so the bark is conditioned to bend without breaking. In Greek mythology, Orpheus rescued his wife, Eurydice, from Hades in the underworld by enchanting and distracting the people by playing the harp. It was there, between notes of a love song, that the first elm grove was said to have blossomed. On the precipice of beauty and perdition. I like to think of my grandmother as both the man and the harp. Gorgeous and surreptitious. Among all the elms and all the cotton, she became a woman.

Betty Jean was the great-granddaughter of the enslaved, and the firstborn child of her mother, May. She was born Jessie Mae, but when they looked into her eyes, they said she had to be called Betty Jean. I wonder what they saw in her fresh out of the womb that made them think she looked like a derivative of Elizabeth. Perhaps there was a regality and determination in her gaze that suggested Jessie Mae just wouldn't do. She was brought to this side with the help of the local midwife in the plantation house where her mother was born in Elm Grove at the foot of Lake Bistineau.

. . .

Betty Jean's mother, May, was born in Elm Grove in 1915 on that same plantation where her daughter and son were raised. Because Betty Jean called her younger sibling *Brother*, when he was born five years after her, everyone else did too. His identity was established in relation to his older sister. He spent a lifetime trying to remove himself from the long shadow her light cast on him. May was a domestic, helping to raise White children in Shreveport while her mother, Rose, raised Betty Jean and *Brother,* a customary arrangement for Black families in the South. It was a practicality that began during slavery, the able-bodied would fetch the cotton, the cane, the indigo, while the older women cared for the young. A common professional progression for Black women leaving the fields that held the memories of their youth was into the homes of White people whom they would care for until their demise. The children they bore would take their place as sharecroppers with their grandmothers to make up for the lost hands. To free the flesh was a mere legislative act, but after two hundred and fifty years of slavery, it would take generations for Black folks to incrementally establish their own terms of liberation. Because free is nothing but a word when you and your mama and your grandmama and her mama have all lived lives in service to White people. Freedom is not given, it's taken.

May had grown up tending the cotton fields alongside her parents and a dozen siblings, as large families were essential to maintaining the impossible expectations of the sharecropping scam. For a spell there would have been four generations living in that small wooden house with the deep porch in Elm Grove. Inside the screen door the modest kitchen and dining area sat on the left side of the house and the bedrooms on the right. In the central living room there was no sofa, only a bed in the middle of the floor with a double fireplace that warmed both the living room and the bedroom with two beds for Betty Jean and *Brother* on the other side. There was little time for leisure, so a sofa had no function in the space, but the porch held an array of chairs and objects for sitting in the shade. The beds were occupied alternately by an array of family members. May's paternal grandmother withered away on the bed in the living room after her husband died. She had been what they called "contraband" during the Civil War. Union soldiers took enslaved people and kept them from their enslavers until the war ended. They were no longer considered slaves, but they still weren't considered freedmen, so they settled on contraband. The purgatory between bondage and freedom. The camps were in deplorable condition, filled with disease and famine. But protected from Confederates. She was kept at Milliken's Bend, Louisiana, a major site of defense for General Ulysses S. Grant. It's located in a bend in the Mississippi River that divides Louisiana and Mississippi. Northern Louisiana and Mississippi were Confederate-heavy regions, and the Union Army recruited the newly freed men to protect the camp and provided them with basic military training in return for rations and housing for women and children during the war. May's grandmother lived there with her daughter, whom she's said to have conceived with her former enslaver. She too was a child of such conditions. She assisted at the shanty hospitals that had been erected to repair the Union soldiers. Those Northerners had no clue how to traverse the swampy lands surrounding the Mississippi River and were at a disadvantage. The formerly enslaved women employed their knowledge of the healing plants and herbs growing wild in the region to help with the recovery of the Colored troops who were putting their lives on the line for them. It is unclear what happened after the war was over and how she ended up in Bossier Parish on a cotton plantation. Maybe she married one of those Colored soldiers. All May remembers is her grandmother telling her about a boat. The stories always come back to the water with these women.

Both of May's grandmothers were of the first generation of liberated Black folks. The liminal Black folks. The ones who had lived on both sides. Those born not having freedom, and those condemned to it. Both women had been sold and had lived in various areas of Louisiana. One lesson that echoed repeatedly throughout the house in Elm Grove was that she was never to trust White folks. "May," she'd been advised, "you can't trust 'em as far you can throw 'em."

Ona Judge

I have looked for my grandmother's lineage using ancestry web-sites, but I have yet to find evidence of her birth. It's as if she made herself appear one day in Bossier Parish. Instead, I discovered a different Betty Davis, the enslaved seamstress of President George Washington and his wife, Martha. Betty wove cotton, wool, and linen into elaborate clothing for the nation's first president; his blouses and buttons were threaded by slaves, even his teeth were taken from the mouths of Black men. His dentures were con-structed of wood, stone, and the extracted teeth from the mouths of Black folks. Every bit of their flesh belonged to him, and he was entitled to have what he pleased.

Between Mount Vernon and the executive residence of the United States, in New York and later Philadelphia, Davis lived the entirety of her life in servitude and conceived five children with different men at the estate, who would dedicate their lives to the Washingtons' whims. One of the White men Betty conceived with was an indentured servant and sometimes she was lent to visi-tors of the president seeking comforting after dusk. Something warm and soft to rest inside of. Davis's children were born under the same conditions as their mother. Motherhood during slav-ery dissolved the line between parenting and property expansion, through laws like *partus sequitur ventrem*, Latin for "that which is brought forth follows the *belly*," which meant that the child assumed the mother's social status; regardless of whether their fathers were slavers or freedmen, the children of enslaved women shall be in bondage as well. The mother was positioned as the only acknowledged parent. The man was of no consequence. It is peculiar that one of Davis's children, fathered by an English indentured servant and tailor named Andrew Judge in 1773, carried her father's name. Ona Judge escaped in 1796, leaving her mother and siblings behind. One evening in Philadelphia, before they were to all return to Mount Vernon for the summer, Ona slipped away while the Washingtons enjoyed their dinner. At this time, slavery had been banned in Pennsylvania, and the president intentionally witheld this from Ona and the other dozen-plus enslaved people that typically traveled to Philadelphia with him. But she had already begun making friends with free Blacks about town. The Washingtons searched with fervor and deployed all the resources of the executive office in pursuit of her. An ad was placed in the *Philadelphia Gazette* and word was put out to his local countrymen in pursuit of an *almost* White mulatto slave girl with bushy hair who had run off unprovoked. *Almost,* but not quite, White. These are the actions of the first president of the American empire, an establishment of the concept of enforcing federal policy to satisfy personal interests. Washington passed the 1793 Fugitive Slave Act, a law which protected the assets of slavers. It ensured that slavers could regain their property across state lines, even while venturing into states of liberation. It would not help Washington, however. He feared that crossing into New Hampshire, where Ona now resided, to capture her would provoke a riot and threaten his bid for reelection in the abolitionist states of the North.

The Washingtons' attachment to Ona went far beyond that of asset. Despite being consumed with the duties that come with governing a newly founded empire, finding Ona became a significant priority to the president. Martha wanted her favorite slave-in-waiting back as she felt she had reared her more like her own child than a slave. Even if her own children surely did not wash her back nor labor over her handsewn garments under the threat of a lash. The Washingtons were united in their pursuit of property. A shared feeling of grief, betrayal, and shame for the Negress that got away. Ona was never captured. She lived as a fugitive slave in New Hampshire until her death in 1848 at the age of seventy-five. She had spent most of her adult life in New Hampshire working as a seamstress and domestic—free, but not without her own grief in knowing that she would never see her mother again. She could not call on her for advice or write to her when in need of her wisdom when she herself became a mother. Legally the children that Ona Judge would have with her free Black husband belonged to the estate of President George Washington. She would forever be looking over her shoulder for the White man wearing the Black man's teeth.

Other than her other daughter Philadelphia, who married her way to freedom, Betty Davis and her other three children died enslaved to the Washingtons. There were sure to be prayers of praise and protection for her girls that brought Davis to her knees at night. I wonder what those days were like between Ona's escape and Betty's death, because if Ona were to follow the fate of her mother, would that mean the mother should suffer the consequences of her daughter's resistance? If Davis had any favor at Mount Vernon, it was surely diluted. Washington didn't seem to share the same affection for Betty that he did for her mulatto daughter. At Davis's burial at Mount Vernon in 1795, the nation's first leader would mock her: "It is happy for old Betty . . . that she is taken off the stage; her life must have been miserable to herself, and troublesome to all those around her."

If it weren't for Ona's escape, Washington's insistence on locating her, and her later interviews with abolitionist newspapers, we would know nothing of the life of Betty Davis. Even still, the story we have is rooted in motherhood. Sometimes stories left untold become the burden of our children. Sometimes stories become our liberation. Either way, these stories of the American project belong to all of us.

3

Shorelines

I was raised to believe that each of us is the sum of our grandmothers' prayers. We were never made to believe that we as individuals were mighty enough to stand on our own without the will of those who came before us. We were carried by their insistence. When you understand the price of life, and witness how quickly it can be taken, you understand that every act of preservation by your ancestors was a blessing. We were taught that death doesn't mean loss, as we are never not in communication with those who have passed. That death is not to be feared but expected. And sometimes beckoned. As a girl, something inside of me could depend on that, when there was nothing else. That somewhere, my grandmother is praying. A prayer is but a manifestation. And the thought of my life being willed by the manifestations of my grandmother always made me feel like she wouldn't let me lose. I've never seen my grandmother on her knees. But maybe she prays standing up, to be closer to God. In our family structure, she was, in a way, our God, or perhaps our connection to her. I would sometimes sit between my mother and my grandmother in the pew of our Baptist church. It was one of those megachurches with three services on Sundays and the pastor drove a G Wagon, had no kids and a beard. When some audio was leaked of him having an affair with a young man, most of the congregation fled, including my aunts. But Betty Jean was not bothered. When I asked her what her thoughts were she said, "That's his business and nobody else's. Ain't got na'an to do with me." She is always so sure but without judgment for others and doesn't bother with persuasion. And she expects the same in return. She sat in the same seat every Sunday and the pastor stopped to hug her after each service. On Mother's Day, he gave out hundred-dollar bills tucked inside a Bible to the mother and grandmother with the most children, and after the first few years when she won, he would just say, "C'mon get your money, Ms. Betty Jean."

One Sunday a woman named Helen "Little Helen" Baylor came to the church as a guest performer during praise and worship. On Sunday mornings my mother wasted time begging my father to join us, and he rarely obliged, so we were always late, but we'd arrived on time that day. Sister Helen started by saying she used to go to church with her grandmother in Oklahoma when she was seven years old. I was around seven at the time, so the story was more accessible to me than most sermons. She shifted between speaking and singing, with the pianist playing gently behind her. She had a testimony. That she had moved to Los Angeles and slipped into the devil's playground. Like it was one step that had landed her there, and it can often feel like this, but really, it's a series of moments, some of which had been taken before you even arrived. At twelve she was playing around in the night with drugs and sex. *But I had a praying grandmother,* she sang out, and all the women around me began to weep. Not Betty Jean. But everyone else. "Alright now," my mother chanted, "let him use you, let him use you, let him use you." With just that one line, *I had a praying grandmother,* Little Helen brought hundreds of Black folks to their feet.

Little Helen told us she had overdosed, but she never told us what exactly she was trying to escape. Her grandmother called from Oklahoma and told her that she was fasting and praying on her knees with her face to the ground. As Helen sang about how her grandmother had willed her back to herself, my grandmother placed her hand on mine.

I always felt uncomfortable in my body, but even more so at church. I wondered how everyone came to feel confident jumping and shouting around the sanctuary among strangers. There was a lady who kicked off her shoes so spectacularly that before they hit the ground, she had already taken off to run laps around the pews. And each week my mother delighted as if it were the first time, "We got a sprinter." The very behavior that we children were discouraged from doing in public. But this wasn't public. This was sacred. Many of my family members had been Catholics in Louisiana and I was only able to locate them through the archdiocese when the state didn't deem their lives worthy of record. After emancipation they converted to Baptists to distance themselves from their enslaver's rituals. As a way to reunite themselves with more inherent ancestral practices of praise that included using your whole body to speak in unison with the heartbeat of the drum to bring forth the spirits. This is when I began to understand that there were powers that existed beyond what I could see. Powers that made the room move.

. . .

That day at church Betty Jean's hand covering mine was a kind of silent prayer laid upon me. Perhaps the same way her grandmother who raised her had done. A long line of grandmothers before Betty Jean have been the anchor to steady the child in preparation for the storms that are sure to come. Even as far back as 1881, Frederick Douglass understood, as he wrote in his autobiography, *Life and Times of Frederick Douglass,* that to tell the story of slavery, he had to begin with his grandmother. Chapter one speaks of his birth. Chapter two is filled with what was to come next and be everlasting—grief. To illustrate his early introduction to mourning, the second chapter is aptly titled "Removal from Grandmother's." Douglass's earliest memories are of being beside his grandmother Betsey Bailey in her small home some distance from the big house. She cared for him tenderly but with strict discipline, in preparation for servitude.

His mother had been let out to a neighboring plantation to

discourage bonding between mother and child. Douglass had reason to believe his father was a White slaver whom he did not know nor seek out. But he carried traces of him across his face. His mother would walk twelve miles in the night to rub his back until he fell asleep. He recognized her only in the dark, a night woman. He can recall her brief but settling presence, the pulsing of her fingertips gently scraping across his back, the vibrations of her chest as she hummed him to sleep. I imagine her working all day, perhaps in the house, where she'd encounter the man who'd claimed her body like he'd claimed his land. And just as the land produced vibrant blossoms through conflict, so did she. Her feet swollen but still finding the strength to carry her weary body toward the child her breasts yearned to feed. The throbbing intensifying at dusk, pulling her as naturally as the moon pulls the tide. Twelve miles of sweet silver milk drops glowing under the moon's guidance. When he woke at dawn, she was gone. Twelve more miles back, without the moistened trail behind her.

About his grandmother, Douglass is less ambiguous. He recognizes her every crevice. Her hands calloused but still tender. He adores and worships her. With her he feels kept and safe. As a child he doesn't realize that she is only able to raise him until he is of age to work at the slaver's house. She was a confidante of the enslaver and was positioned to rear the children and ready them for their unfortunate fate. One can only speculate all that she sacrificed to gain the trust of the White man, so that she was able to have a private home to rear her grandchildren, if only briefly. Perhaps her daughter was the greatest sacrifice of all.

Douglass's first moments of intimacy are informed within the embrace of his grandmother, who would also be the one to take him on the twelve-mile walk to the Wye plantation on the eastern shore of Maryland and leave him there to labor beside his siblings and other Pickaninnies while she slipped away silently into the night. At the age of five or six, he was no longer a child and now tasked with using his small body to uplift the wealth of the plantation and, ultimately, the nation. Oh, what great weight for a boy to bear.

I wonder what the twelve-mile journey back home was like for his grandmother. I imagined she prayed for his survival. That she prayed all twelve miles that he never forgets that he was once loved. That six years of love would sustain him for a lifetime. That he remembers to love again. That he doesn't allow the White folks to take every part of him, that he saves a bit for himself.

Harriet Jacobs also wrote about her grandmother in *Incidents in the Life of a Slave Girl* (1861), which was one of the first autobiographical accounts written by a Black woman about the sexual harassment and abuse that was customary to enslaved women and girls. At the age of eleven, Jacob's slaver died and she was sold to Dr. Flint, who then proceeded to harass her relentlessly for sexual favors. Jacobs soon met a White lawyer and began a sexual relationship with him that led to the birth of her two children, whom Flint legally owned. This angered Flint, and Jacobs felt this to be a victory, "it was something to triumph over my tyrant even in that small way." It is no small thing to take control of the body you carry that does not legally *belong* to you. The not so small victory of choosing. And still, even in her choice, Flint would benefit by acquiring two additional Black children who belonged to his estate. Jacobs employs the very subjugation of which she is reduced to liberate herself. This is the perplexity and genius of destabilizing stereotypes of your sexuality by placing yourself in control of them.

The victory provided her with the courage and belief that there may be a life beyond the plantation. She ran away and hid in the swamp, waiting for the signal from her uncle before returning to Flint's estate, residing in the top of her grandmother's shed. In the chapter called "The Loophole of Retreat," Jacobs describes the crawl space as sweltering in the summer and biting in the winter. Rats and other insects would roam about her flesh, and she couldn't turn or swat them away without fear of falling and revealing herself and thus losing any potential for freedom. Imagine the mental dexterity necessary to dismiss the immediate pains in lieu of the consequential ones every day for nearly seven years. Seven years of a horizontal existence at the summit of a shed. Seven years of a grandmother risking her life for her granddaughter's freedom. Content with never tasting it in her lifetime just as long as someone in her bloodline breaks away. Her grandmother came in the night, whispering to her, feeding her, applying remedies to her insect bites. Affirming life for her, because this is what grandmothers do, assure us that we are alive and that we come from somewhere.

Her grandmother also looked after her two children, while Jacobs secretly watched through a small slit she'd carved in the shed—a loophole. She was able to look out at her children and sip fresh air. She eventually escaped the South and traveled to New York, and Flint continued to hunt her unceasingly. "The war of my life had begun; and though one of God's most powerless creatures, I resolved never to be conquered."

. . .

As generations move further away from the plantation, the role of the grandmother is shifting. The grandmother has taken on a more passive role, while the mother occupies the center. Even though I'm raising my daughter in New York, she still has a special bond with my mother. She calls her "Mama" and it is the only word in which I can hear that she has roots in Texas as she elongates it, letting her call to her grandmother savor on her tongue, *Mawwmuh*. When I hear her laughing in her room, unable to catch her breath, I know she's on the phone with my mother. In the summers and on spring breaks, there is no place my daughter would rather be than beside my mother, starting each day with walks along Buffalo Bayou and watching the Mexican free-tailed bats emerge in the hundreds of thousands to take flight above the water at dusk. Since my mother is retired, she is able to engage in leisurely activities with my daughter that she never could with me because back then, if she wasn't working, she was sleeping in preparation to return the next day. My mother scheduled a vacation for us each summer and took us to the rodeo every spring, but she was always on the sideline dozing off while we played.

Motherhood has introduced me to a version of my mother that had been concealed, that she herself had not known but that was yearning to be fed. And when the four generations gather at Betty Jean's home, and my grandmother hugs me and my daughter and tells us she loves us, I see my mother contend with the discomfort of holding pleasure and resentment at once. The same way I feel when I observe my mother with my daughter, and I see her capacity for patience and understanding of the limitations of a child, and I become sullen. Why couldn't you give that to me when I needed it most? At the same time, I'm too scorned to accept it should she offer it to me now. And her ego is too fragile to risk extending it and being met with rejection. So my mother offers what she has left of love to my daughter, and I watch from the side and convince myself that it's enough to mend our fractured past. Something seems to soften inside of you when you become a grandmother. I imagine that once you've raised your own, lived to witness them become parents, you are then somewhat relieved of the daily mundane responsibility of what it takes to keep a Black child alive. Grandmothers can simply love without abandon, without fear. Not realizing that the instructive is the other way around, as Saidiya Hartman has observed, "Care is the antidote to violence."

. . .

I can always tell when someone is raised by their grandmama. The way they speak in metaphors and dated turns of phrase. Their pace is slowed, and their intentions are not always immediately obvious. The impressions of the Black grandmother are noted everywhere, but you'll only notice if you know what you're looking for. Whether it's in the overhead of a shed or at 50 10, they were the ones who reared the children, while the young mothers labored for a thankless nation. They are the first to teach submission and discipline to keep the White folks from killing you dead. In this great American tragedy, the man so well oils his machine, that it is not he but the one who loves you most in the world, your grandmother, who teaches you how to situate your head comfortably beneath the foot of the White man. It is your grandmother who will show you which parts of yourself to bury and which to nourish. Which parts to hate and which to wield. She will teach you your inferior position not necessarily because she believes it but because she can't bear to watch you die trying to prove them otherwise.

When President Obama was elected in 2008 and he and First Lady Michelle brought Grandmother Marian Robinson to live in the White House, White Americans made noise. No explanation was necessary for Black Americans. Naturally, *Mama* was coming too. Who else could they trust to have the best interests of their daughters in a white house? It's only right that the nation would be confronted with the withstanding traditions of slavery, while the White House was home to its first Black residents that weren't butlers. Black Americans understood that Grandmother Marian would be a bedrock, for her daughter and her daughter's daughters, and she would be the mother Barack needed. When you see Grandmother Marian in photos, there is an inner stillness to her that seems as if she is guided by spirits much higher than our material world. Spirits that made the politics of the free world seem frivolous. A stillness that assured that she would not be moved by the pageantry of their new residence, but her presence alone would make it feel like home all the same. It's the same stillness I see in Betty Jean. Grandmother Marian was the one that comforted the girls and settled the fury of the First Lady when bullets pierced the windows of the formal living room when Homeland Security didn't prioritize their lives. She was there when America showed its ugly underbelly that she knew so intimately; and she sat still and unflinching beside Michelle when they called her daughter every name but God. She reminded her daughter that those people didn't have the power to define her, just as the nation never had been able to define those before them. Grandmother Marian was there to provide the girls the same groundedness that was instilled in Michelle in Chicago, the groundedness that young Barack was yearning for when he went looking for Michelle. It's a wide and persistent craving that frustrates because you can't explain what's missing. You'd need more than just words to capture exactly what it is these grandmothers provide. You'd need Florida water, you'd need the roots of one of those trees in the South that holds hundreds of years of history so heavy that their limbs nearly touch the ground before winding back up toward the sky again, you'd need thistle and stones, you'd need chunks of coiled hair with the scalp still intact, a toad's tongue and the skin of a swamp snake, you'd need roses and lilies, you'd need rainwater from a great flood and two ounces of honey with bits of the comb and a lifeless drone in the middle, you'd need to bring a witness, you'd need mugwort and elder-flower, you'd need the tail of a coon, the tooth of a gator, and the hind foot of a canecutter, the blood of that old conjurer gal that's been here before and the blackest of tourmaline set ablaze in a steel basin—and it still wouldn't be enough.

It's what Bill Withers's song "Grandma's Hands," from his 1971 album *Just as I Am,* is trying to capture. He pays homage to the fig-ure that introduced him to the power of music. With this single, he established his identity and relationship with Blackness in a way that familiarized him to his listeners. The song begins with a familiar hum, the kind that echoes generations of buried blues. The kind of hum that you might hear coming from the kitchen or the garden or the clothesline. Already, from the opening, With-ers submerges the listener in the sound associated with safety. As if to greet us with an embrace. As if he himself needed his first album to address his grandmother as a form of permission. As a kind of blessing.

"Grandma's Hands" is a meditation on grief. And also, love. Because in living a Black life, they are indivisible.

. . .

In a photo I have of Betty Jean's maternal grandmother, Rose, who raised her, she stands in a wild thicket of overgrown bushes wearing a polka-dot dress with sleeves cut at the crease of her elbow. Her hair is tied back under a scarf and her gaze narrowed by the sun. She's most likely on the grounds of the plantation in Bossier Parish where she raised my grandmother. I don't know who took the photo, but she does not smile at the viewer, her face says she's in no mood to stand still in the sun to be captured. Her hands seem to be weighing her arms down at her side. They are somewhat glowing in the black-and-white photograph, perhaps because they are more intimate with the sun than her other extremities. I am always drawn first to her hands, not her eyes, not her frame. The way her fingers curl in repose, suggesting that they are more accustomed to being in use than at ease. Her inflamed joints cast a long shadow on her spotted dress. But they still look tender. It looks like she is wearing pantyhose, so it's likely Sunday, and they had probably just walked home from Fairview Baptist Church in the summer sun. Then I imagine Grandmother Rose's hands on top of little Betty Jean's as they sat beside each other in the pew, and I wonder if she can trace her grandmother's hands from memory the way that I can trace hers.

ROSE IN ELM GROVE, LOUISIANA

. . .

Rose was born in Louisiana in 1875. In the presence of Rose, May was more of a sister to Betty Jean, as they both answered to the same authority. Rose never knew her own grandmothers because her parents had been sold away from their mothers. Rose's mother, Lilly, traveled through Louisiana in the mid-1800s by boat up the rivers, through the bayous, from towns she was too small to remember. Occasionally Lilly would speak of that boat ride she took and the pain of never seeing her father or siblings again. About the pulsing of the water beneath the basin, of how she was always unsure of where she was. She went from one plantation to the next. She may not have been able to recall the towns, but she knew the soil, she recognized the trees, and she could always read the water. And she taught Rose all that she came to know. How to read the tide, how to study the position of the sun, how to harvest, and how to sow. How to identify wild herbs and apply them to wild women to help them heal. As her name suggests, the intimacy that she had with the earth's elements was the only constant she knew. The earth does not lie or deceive. And this is why Lilly named her Rose, and why Rose would call her daughter May. These women of spring believed in the divine practice of tending the dirt even if it was tied to their labor. The earth had not betrayed them, and unlike the men who had, it offered returns. Perhaps their relationship with Louisiana's soil was the only reciprocity they reaped.

Rose never cuddled her as a child, but Betty Jean felt held in her presence, in their shotgun house on the far end of the cotton plantation in Bossier Parish. Beyond recalling fragmented memories, Rose didn't speak much, but she and Betty Jean formed an intimate bond within the folds of silence and collective labor. Betty Jean and Rose would wake before dawn, before the others, to cook breakfast for her grandfather, *Brother*, and the other grandchildren who lived there until their parents got on their feet and came back for them. Even though the land on the plantation was owned by White folks, they nurtured it as their own. Rose taught Betty Jean how to make things grow. The crops, the men. So it was from Rose that Betty Jean learned the expectations of womanhood: servitude, silent, impervious, and composed. Beside the house, they had a small patch of land where they grew yams and greens, peppers and tomatoes, watermelon and sour berries to keep for themselves. Rose also taught her how to grow flowers, not for function, just for beauty. Her White-passing grandfather hunted foxes, fowl, and coons to eat with the local White men. He'd bring home catfish from the Red Chute Bayou, from Lake Bistineau, and just behind their house at Swan Lake. Betty Jean and Rose gutted the fish and skinned the fowl. They spent every moment together until Betty Jean was of age to attend school, where she would learn to do something her grandmother could not teach her—to read.

I wonder what worlds opened for her when she first encountered stories beyond those told to her on the plantation. There were some histories that could only be learned orally. The kind told only after sundown. There are histories that everyone knows but no one speaks of in public. Like the bloody autumn of 1868. A few years after the end of the Civil War, there was a massacre in Bossier Parish. The Fourteenth Amendment had been passed allowing Blacks the right to vote as natural citizens. It is said that as Election Day neared, a White man took a shot at a Black man sitting peaceably on his porch in Shady Grove after deducing that he was a "radical republican." He missed, but some local Black freedmen restrained him and called the sheriff. They tied his hands behind his back and waited for the sheriff to arrive from Shreveport. They didn't have local law enforcement yet. The next day a mob of more than a hundred White men swarmed, killing every Black man they encountered and any Black woman who pled for the man's life.

They went into homes, they went into shops, roamed the plantation fields, and pulled pastors from churches. They shot their mothers and their wives. They dumped the bodies into Red River that ran through Elm Grove. Betty Jean always thought the river had gotten its name because of the massacre, but it was named for the red earth that held it. The Black men, many of them former Civil War soldiers, knew that if they didn't assert themselves as men, they would never know peace in Bossier. They were freedmen, but justice and liberty didn't apply to them.

The White man was mad because the Black man thought he was equal. The Homestead Act of 1862 had been expanded to include Black people in 1866. This meant that the federal government offered free land (Native American land that had been taken by the US government) to anyone who would spend at least five years cultivating it. This was initially not extended to Confederates who had betrayed their nation. This is how Rose's parents became land- and homeowners in Elm Grove. Because who knew that wild fecund land better than those who had worked it since they were children? Had watched the trees grow beside them and watched their cousins cut down from them?

Rose's father had served in the Louisiana 9th Infantry Colored troop for the Union. And the White men in Louisiana were still sore about it. So they figured they'd just kill as many of 'em as they could. Election time was always lynching time. They killed more than one hundred Black people that autumn. Men, women, babies, elders. Probably more. Quite a few Whites died too. There were bodies in fields, hanging from trees, and floating down the Red River. The heat and the blood made for an awful putrefying smell that would get in your clothes if you walked anywhere near the river. Worse were the flies that hovered as some of the bodies snagged on the riverbanks.

These were the histories that students don't learn in their lessons at school. You'll never see it in the textbooks, because the Daughters of the Confederacy would make sure of it. But the grandmothers tell their grandchildren, so they know to keep their eyes down and mouths closed when they walk down the main road. That autumn the river rose, the Klan numbers did too.

Betty Davis

THE EROTIC INTELLECTUAL

BETTY DAVIS, 1974, RONNIE SCOTT'S, LONDON

When they say she was ahead of her time, what they really mean is that everything they loved about her was everything they hated. That she had to teach them how to love her. Like moths attracted to the light so that they throw themselves up against it, only to find that they've been eclipsed by the very object of their desire. Only to then recount the encounter as a confrontation. Perhaps in some ways that is exactly what she was. However, the confrontation was with ourselves; she simply led us to the path. When a mother is at her best, she gently guides us deeper toward ourselves. Not with force but with tenderness. And when a mother loves herself, we learn to love us too.

Betty Mabry Davis's formative years were spent with her grandmother in North Carolina. A wild woman, likely born between 1895 and 1905, whose farmhouse was vibrantly adorned with lights, lurid colors, and the blues. Of Native American and African descent, she held the essence of America inside her. And in spite of all of her flaws, she is the rebellious younger sister of England.

Buella Blackwell taught her granddaughter what it meant to let the blues speak. When young Betty asked her questions, she would play a record that responded. And Betty returned to those records throughout her life in search of answers—Muddy Waters, Bessie Smith, Big Mama Thornton—each time leading to a deeper understanding of what her grandmother meant. She had blues parties in her living room and danced with every part of her body, wearing what seemed like all the jewelry she owned, attempting to embody the enormity of her insides. And encouraging others to turn themselves inside out too. Let it all fall to the floor. All that heavy. Let the blues hold it.

Before she was old enough to join her grandmother, little Betty waited daily for her to return from the fields, or other domestic work, her hands probably covered in a sticky film that told Betty how the day had gone. Her nimble fingers would roll the tobacco gum, letting it gather and build into balls before picking it from Buella's hands. The two of them would sit on the floor.

She always felt her grandmother was beside her. Not ahead or above, but beside her. When Buella put on a record, it was an invitation. Let us leave this place. A sonic transcendence. Wherever they were, no one else was.

Betty was given her mother's name, for perhaps she sought her child to be made in her likeness, only to be disappointed that she was Buella Blackwell once more. Wild, impulsive, and guided by what she saw as a reckless fragile heart. Her middle name, Gray, was given by her father. For when he sat in silent fear, fighting for a country that would put him at the front of the line only in combat, a gray finch would come to him. Return to him in his darkest moments. Offering a little hope, a little tenderness. And he knew his baby girl had that same light and perhaps she was that bird all along. He protected the bird, even against her own mother, thus she was called Betty Gray Mabry.

Betty was a child of the late-stage great displacement of Colored people. Her beloved father moved ten-year-old Betty, her brother, and big Betty north, from the land of tobacco to the factory mills of Pittsburgh. They settled near the valley of the Monongahela River. Betty collected the stories and mannerisms of the new Negroes of the urban North and brought them back with her to Reidsville where she spent her summers beside her grandmother, writing tunes, trying to make sense of it all, trying to situate herself within it on the page.

So much of Betty Davis's life is a mystery. What she gave us was plenty, and she preserved the rest. We know and don't know what happened to her when she moved to New York at seventeen to attend the Fashion Institute of Technology. We know she lived with her aunt in Harlem and made money as a model because her beauty and style translated across languages. We know she ran around Greenwich Village with Jimi Hendrix, the two feeding each other's creative curiosities in the same way that plants grow stronger when in proximity to other plants intent on rising. We know that Miles Davis became her moth and her husband, not necessarily in that order. We know she took his name because, like Tina Turner, she earned it. In fact, one could say that she helped him get comfortable in his own name. That she germinated the *cool.* Stripped away those tailored suits that never quite fit who he was but demonstrated an idea of what he was striving to be. We know Miles, just like Ike, was an up South, East St. Louis Negro, hooked on that white girl but elevated by Black ones. And despising them for it. Sabotaging them for it. Knocking them upside the head just to see them crawl. By the time Betty met Miles, it was too late to penetrate to the bone, the callouses had already formed, and nobody can make you see how beautiful you are if you refuse to look.

You have to understand that when Betty took her electricity off the page and onto the stage singing about the ways that she liked to be pleasured, Black women and White women alike were in full gowns singing about how their men didn't come home to them at night. Betty was in a bright leotard, legs so long they just wouldn't quit, tucked into thigh-high boots and spread wide open with hair defying gravity, reaching toward the gods, while singing about being the woman those men were with and how she had commanded them to her, with her *turquoise chain,* before putting them back out on the streets. She was training their men's tongues toward nerve endings. Instructing them on just how much pressure to apply if they wanted to hear her scream. Leading *him to the tip.* That he was a *bitch* when he arrived, but she was sending him home a grown man. While women were calling themselves wives and ladies, she called herself *nasty.* She was naming herself and giving her daughters permission to do the same. She commanded the stage the way she commanded the men. And after the show, while big men, like Muhammad Ali, Kareem Abdul-Jabbar, and Richard Roundtree, squirmed in anticipation of meeting the wild woman. She meditated backstage, while the residue of her heat sustained those in waiting. She was the only sober person in the Village in the 1970s. The stillness was a beckoning back of all that she had given. To get back to herself, to whom she solely belonged.

Like her grandmother, she insisted on selfhood and pleasure.

Not duty. She allowed her desires to take shape while inviting others to share in them. She was what her friend, the scholar Danielle Maggio, calls *an erotic intellectual*. The elements of desire are not merely in the revealing of flesh. She knew that it was an ensemble of elements needed to open the listener up, exactly where to press to bring the release, moving them beyond the death drive. She was a practitioner of the pleasure principle. And just like music, eroticism is organized around a set of principles, one of which primarily being owning one's body and finding freedom within it. Defying the Black woman's experience in America, as her grandmother had. Betty's grandmother journeyed to New York City from North Carolina, for the first and only time in 1974 during the dead of winter, to see Betty perform at the Bottom Line. That moment onstage, opening for the bluesman Freddie King, was a culmination of all that she had gathered on her journey. Her grandmother bore witness to the momentum she'd set in motion in her living room. Just as before, at the farm, during her performance, they transcended together. Because their relationship was largely spiritual, when Buella passed away, it was as if she had never left.

When Betty left New York, everyone thought she was coming right back. Her place was held. Frozen in time. It was her father's death that called her back to Pittsburgh. Where she and her mother were to face each other without his obstructing presence. A mother, too, can be a moth. It's hard to watch someone else fly when your wings have been clipped. And Betty Senior probably saw motherhood as the blade. She probably wondered why her husband couldn't love her the way he had loved his daughter.

Betty's mother was a nurse and read her daughter's exuberance and sensitivity as a kind of hysteria. She began to pathologize her daughter as Betty grieved her father. As she had long yearned to, but Betty was always slipping from her mother's grasp. Betty's mother saw her daughter, now without a grandmother or a father, as solely *hers*. And while she was at her lowest, perhaps she yielded to her mother's will.

Her mother believed Betty was making a mess of her life. Out there making street music with her legs and her mouth open, moaning. She took our mother Betty Davis from us. From herself. It's the mantra we've heard too many times to count from Black mamas, *I brought you here and I can take you out*. Perhaps the hardest person to save someone from is their mother. Because we often believe that the child, even when grown, does in fact *belong* to their mother, even if the water that she has brought you is scalding, even if melts away your flesh, even if you are covered in burns, *that's still your mama, and you only got one mama*.

Somewhere in Pennsylvania, Betty Davis, the mother of Grace Jones, Prince, Madonna, Beyoncé, and everyone who dared and defied, was rotting away without our knowing it. Her mother institutionalized her, and no one would see her for many years. She lived underground with people who didn't know their own names, let alone hers. She was heavily medicated, taking from her what she treasured most—herself. A gray finch without her father to fly to. Where does one go at the end of a path that leads to nowhere? The only place is inward, but there one finds so many ghosts. The ancestral ghosts that pull at you, wanting you to sing their song. Wanting you to keep building on their path. And we must.

. . .

It wasn't until her music was reissued, when her children helped her receive royalties for her music, that the gray finch was seen again in the sky. In the 2017 documentary *Betty: They Say I'm Different*, she only allowed the director to shoot her hands. The hands that she had inherited from Buella Blackwell. The hands she knew so well. And when she watched the film, she couldn't tell who was on the screen, her or her grandmother.

She didn't die alone. Her daughters found her. She had been waiting on them. And a daughter, when at her best, returns that gentle guidance to her mother as she ages, back toward herself. And a mother doesn't always give birth, she doesn't need a uterus, but she delivers us all the same. Betty Davis flouted the dominant codes and was flogged for it, only to eventually be imitated. This is what is feared most—that the wild women will corrupt the collective consciousness. American culture is moved forward by Black women who rebel. But like any child, you resent what Mother teaches you, only to ultimately replicate it.

4

AG

In the casual comedy;
He, too, has been changed in his turn,
Transformed utterly:
A terrible beauty is born.

—WILLIAM BUTLER YEATS, "EASTER, 1916"

My grandmother's life can be divided into two parts, before her grandmother's death, and after. Rose died in the spring of Betty Jean's thirteenth year. On the same day that my mother would be born a decade later. She had watched Rose descend and eventually begin to shrivel. Even a dying rose holds its beauty.

When Betty Jean thinks of that day, she remembers the smell of the sugarberry tree. All else had gone silent, the house, the garden, young Betty Jean's pulsing heart. But the smell of the shedding buds of the sugarberry tree still beckoned the mockingbirds, who built their nests, shrouded their young, and sang. They didn't sing a mourning song but songs of new life. For Betty Jean, the smell of the sugarberry tree reminds her of the promise of death.

The robins came, the butterflies too. When the persimmons ripened, she didn't bundle them in the slack of her dress and bring them to the porch as she normally would, to sit with Rose, barefoot with nothing between them but the sounds that a mouth makes when it moistens, to savor. She left them to the possums. She felt it was a kind of treason that everything around her continued to bloom in Rose's absence. What a betrayal of the earth. The earth that Rose had loved on so tenderly. She felt like the whole world around her should stop. It never did. After losing the only person who had ever given a damn about whether she lived or died, Betty Jean began to better comprehend her own insignificance. From that spring forward, Betty Jean never ate another persimmon.

It would be a time of great emergence in her life. Without being allowed a space to properly grieve, Betty Jean assumed the role as the woman of the house in Bossier Parish, where they were tenant farmers. She was responsible for all the cooking and cleaning for *Brother* and cousins, as well as her grandfather who wouldn't work much but spent his time hunting with the plantation's White owners, whom he was kin to. Being a mulatto had afforded him certain privileges that did not extend to the others. Well, except for the time ol' Mr. Hodge told her grandfather that if his son "ain't careful with his lip he was gone kill him dead." The son skipped town in the night, and no one knew where he was for years, until someone who worked on the railroad saw him up North somewhere and reported back to the family. He moved back to Bossier Parish after he retired, but all the elders had died by then and the others had moved away. Either way he lost his son, but at least ol' Mr. Hodge gave her grandfather a heads-up before he strung him up.

Betty Jean grew to despise her position in life, and on the farm, and without her grandmother beside her. This is what Rose had prepared her for. She did not envision her granddaughter having a life beyond servitude. In the short story "Girl" that was published in *The New Yorker* in 1978, Jamaica Kincaid speaks to the ways in which Black girls are raised to know duty:

this is how to hem a dress when you see the hem coming
down and so to prevent yourself from looking like the slut
I know you are so bent on becoming; this is how you iron

your father's khaki shirt so that it doesn't have a crease; this is how you iron your father's khaki pants so that they don't have a crease; this is how you grow okra.

The dreams that both Betty Jean's and Kincaid's mothers had for them did not extend beyond keeping them alive, taking care of men, keeping them satiated, and not becoming a slut along the way. The conundrum of a people only freshly set free is: How do you learn to dream beyond merely surviving when death is imminent? For Betty Jean and Kincaid, this meant that you'd have to go it alone, gathering the tools for your arsenal along the way while somehow, miraculously, keeping your dignity intact. Kincaid later published "Girl" in her short-story collection *At the Bottom of the River.* The title affirms the concept of being pinned down and stuck in a place where the sun can't quite reach you and trying to find your way out without the guidance of light, when you have yet to be taught how to swim. Kincaid, also a woman of the shoreline, born in Antigua, broke away from the undercurrents to find her way to New York City on a path wholly her own.

. . .

"Shoot. They was all just talkin. Every last one of 'em. Can't b'lieve a word come out of dey mouf. All 'cept one. Only one of 'em really did love me. The first one." *Reverend.* Betty Jean never said his name. I don't think it was because she couldn't recall it but because it would sting coming off her lips. Once you feel the frequency that love brings, you ever know its absence. Perhaps what she meant was that he was the only one whom she had ever loved. The first she chose to lie with. Once a girl is confronted with the disappointment of a love that cannot be, something splits. A rearranging. That's why they call it puppy love, not because it lacks intensity but because it's uninformed. You fall wildly, heavy, and without restraint. When you know the stakes, that's when love is a full-grown bitch.

Betty Jean became a mother at seventeen, and when *Reverend* asked her to run away with him to Mississippi, she refused. She felt she was too young to be a wife. To be possessed. For Betty Jean, such refusal would become practice. Her family members referred to her as the "Black Widow," enticing men to fall in love and have children, only to disappear and leave the man broken, withered. Many of these men went on to be preachers, as if once Betty was finished with them, only God could keep them.

It was her freedom that they desired most. If they swallowed her whole, would the residue of this resistance rest inside them? Her power was in her self-possession. While other girls her age sought to be chosen, Betty Jean was determined to define freedom on her own terms. She surrounded herself with children, by becoming the nucleus of a family of twelve. She allowed Black men to fall asleep inside of her feeling like men, but by dawn, she was gone.

When I ask her why she didn't go to Mississippi, she tells me she was too young. I wonder what dreams she had planned for herself. The dreams that would die in Mississippi but be found in Houston. Her first daughter would be born shortly after with another local older man. And then a son with a man from a neighboring farm with a sputtering lisp whom *Brother* says no one could understand but her. Doesn't all love have its own secret language?

Her sons were taken away to be raised by Betty Jean's Aunt Carrie who needed to give her husband a child that she herself could not bear. Betty Jean's mother insisted that it would be temporary, until she found her way. Aunt Carrie had an older daughter from a previous marriage to a man who divorced her after a severe illness left her with a limp. He was from a bourgeois Black family in Shreveport who refused to align their legacy with such a stain. Aunt Carrie had bet her life on a man, so when she lost her ability to have children, she believed she'd lost her womanhood and resented Betty Jean's ability to do what she wished with such ease—that is, lure men and make babies. When Aunt Carrie remarried a younger man, she feared he might leave her too, if she couldn't give him a son to carry his name. So they took Betty Jean's firstborn and gave him her husband's name. They lied and told the boy his mother had been raped. They didn't tell the boy that he was the son of a married reverend who had wanted to run away to Mississippi to raise him with his teenage mistress. He spent his lifetime believing his face was a recollection of violence and his mother gave him away because she couldn't stand to look at him. Aunt Carrie could provide Betty Jean's boys with a stable home. It was never temporary. The untethering of a mother from her child was still seen as a surmountable pain by women who grew up beside formerly enslaved people where this was standard practice. I don't think Betty Jean ever forgave her mother for this. But May was helpless to the will of her big sister. This moment only set wind to the fire growing inside of Betty Jean. It shaped her relationship with her identity and motherhood and reinforced her belief that she could trust only in herself.

Betty Jean says that every man she conceived a child with thought he owned her once she became pregnant. She couldn't teach these men how to love her, so she taught her children how to worship her. She fumbled her way through early adulthood, searching desperately for a form of belonging that she lost when Rose left. A love that endures and doesn't leave. When you experience loss at a young age, death registers as abandonment. She sometimes couldn't understand why her grandmother left her alone and what kind of God would allow it.

She built a universe around her, a tiny little galaxy of Black babies in the middle of Third Ward in Houston, Texas, unaware of the pain they would inherit by being born poor and Black in America. Perhaps to Betty Jean pain was inconsequential—it was something to be expected for a Black child. She had no delusion about the inevitability of suffering. But she had a curiosity about pleasure.

5

blackbirds

Houston calls itself the Bayou City. It is a city of asphalt on top of a vast marshland, surrounded by water, built up on water, and every year, between June and November, it is baptized by the waters. Like the shedding of the uterine lining, the city is flooded annually by hurricanes.

Time is marked by the hurricanes. When speaking to locals about the past, storm names are used to denote the years. Memories marked by the measure of the water's destruction, and so in this way, water is the ultimate ruler. The bayous and the Gulf of Mexico feed each other, swelling and relieving each other. The asphalt gets in the way of the marshland's natural absorption, wreaking havoc on the poor who are often forced to live in flood-prone areas. Those whose neighborhoods are built near the dams that will be pressured to release.

When looking at a map of Houston it seems as if the highways were built to resemble the water. As if a tear, or a stone, were dropped into the center and the loops spread outward, like ripples. The highways circle the flatlands in such a way that one could orbit the center endlessly. This is what it feels like living in Houston, an endless looping of history. Because the water won't let you forget. Its presence fills the air and the humidity clings to your skin, your hair, your throat like a threat. A warning of its imminent return. The murderous waters and winds return each year, trying desperately to cleanse us.

Once someone asked me if Houston was in the middle of Texas. To which I responded, *Do we seem like people who are landlocked? We are water people.* I had never said this before, nor spent much time considering it. I was surprised by my own conviction. But there was something in that response that still feels true when I reflect on it. The people of Houston move about like people with one foot on this side and one on the other. Like the veil between us and the ethereal is thinner. As if the water brings with it the messages of those not ready to be forgotten just yet. And I feel this to be true of all people existing alongside a menace so gorgeous. The Gulf of Mexico is mysterious and temperamental and may erupt furiously at any moment, leaving roads overturned, homes and all the histories they hold claimed by the sea, but it is so natural that most people, like my grandmother, don't even bother evacuating, she simply sweeps the water from her living room out onto the porch with a straw broom and wades through whatever remains. The sky's coloring, like a mood ring, is indicative of the water's degree of fury. When the skies glow emerald, devastation is afoot. It's not unusual to hear a local say, *I'm gone ride this one out.* Perhaps there has never been a more beautiful terror than the sea. Houston, with its winding bayous and ports, makes you feel as if you can slip out at any time. With and without your consent. The coastlines hold a significant amount of the Black population in America, the reasons are varied, but I believe it offers the illusion that one is never stuck even with no intention of ever leaving. For Black people this is an especially necessary latitude. We arrived and became one upon the nation's troubled shores. We became Black here. Our distinctions lost at sea. The coastline serves as a singular certainty for a people of unresolved origin. And to her we cling.

Starting in 1916 until about 1970, waves of Black people moved from the fields and lands they were used to in the rural South in search of stable ground in the North, West, and Midwest. A ground they could grow on, build on, and maybe even call their own. Black people in search of industry, of professions outside of field work, holding a hope that liberation was within reach, if only you could make it across the Mason-Dixon Line. The Great Migration converged with the Great Depression.

Betty Jean was born in 1933 at the height of the Depression. More than six million Black folks migrated across this imaginary boundary, dividing the South from the West and Midwestern states, free states from slave states. The Union territory from the Confederates. Some traveled as far as Canada in their pursuit of possibility. There was no guarantee, but there was a prayer that life in a Black body could exist without the daily flirtations with death.

When Betty Jean arrived in Houston, it was one of the most thriving and populated Black cities in the South. She was a part of the second wave of the Great Migration. Houston was swelling with Coonasses from Louisiana and Black folks from rural areas outside of the cities that amounted to the majority producers of cotton and sugar. The bayous and the Gulf were essential to the process of exporting to other parts of the nation. Many slavers had relocated to Texas during the Civil War, with the certainty that Texas would never, ever give up their Negroes due to their powerful economic influence.

Texas kept their slaves longer. Integrated later. And the hub of it all was just outside of Houston in the surrounding counties of Brazoria, Matagorda, and Fort Bend. The perimeter made up what was known as the sugar bowl. White Galveston residents today still shamelessly announce that they were the "Wall Street of the Southwest." Proud to be in relationship with wealth while refusing to acknowledge the suffering endured to attain it. A town whose wealth, and collapse, was regulated entirely on the backs of enslaved labor. That wealth is no longer evident, but the history of its darkness is palpable. You can see it in the clenched faces of the White folks who yearn for those golden years to return. Now Galveston feels like a sad parking lot for cruise ships. Oil drilling can be seen on the horizon, but the fruit of that economy is dispersed throughout Houston. There remains a residue of longing on Galveston Bay. The soreness about the end of slavery is still evident. The waves no longer bring commerce to the shoreline, only salt for their wounds. Galveston never recovered, but the tide winds keep the Confederate flags at attention.

. . .

Jacob Lawrence captured the alert postures of promise in his painting sequence *The Migration of the Negro* (1940–1941). Families traveled, largely by train, beyond boundaries that their families had known for generations, in pursuit of a life of dignity wherever they rooted. The tracks laid under impossible conditions on unruly land, by the hands of enslaved Black men and women who could not have known that their labor would help lead their future lineages away from the trenches of the South. Churches served as starting points for reconnecting with loved ones, for work, and for fellowship. All over America, Black people established enclaves and communities like constellations. There was always the north star, the person who dares to journey first and beckon the others hither. Moved by a collective faith. The stories told of others making it kept them in motion. New terrors lay ahead; new tools would need to be created and paired with old wisdom. Oh, but what joy to be able to move about as you please. To have autonomy of one's own limbs. The rush of unpredictability. To get up and go without permission, even without a destination.

There were migration patterns established. Mississippi to Chicago, the Carolinas to Harlem, Texas to California. Following train lines and bloodlines and rivers. Many moved to the closest city they could afford to get to. In my grandmother's case, this was Houston. In 1955, Betty Jean traveled from rural Louisiana to Houston, which despite its proximity felt like worlds away. Southeast Texas and Elm Grove, Louisiana, are similar in topography: soggy and fertile. Houston was a common landing place because of plentiful jobs and industries like the railroad, oil, and the port of Houston. For Betty Jean, it was her son that pulled her west.

When she left Bossier Parish, down by the Red River, she left her earthly connection behind. She resigned to never tending to nothing else to make it grow except *chirrens*. Not no cotton. Not no Niggas. 'Cause they don't give you nothing in return but back pain and blood. They'll cut you open and sit there and watch while you bleed. Then have the nerve to blame you for it. *Now, look what you done made me do.*

Betty Jean brought some elements of the plantation ethos with her by positioning herself as the sole authoritative figure in her house. It was, "Don't matter what you think, what did *I* say?" even if it didn't make no damn sense. Imagination was discouraged, and practicality prioritized. Betty Jean demonstrated care through discipline, often with force and manipulation. If my mother asked questions or spoke too loudly, Betty Jean would backhand her across the mouth with the swiftness of a whip, and she would feel her teeth tear into her lip. She came to associate her mother's hands with the taste of metal.

6

Third Ward

Third Ward was a Black mecca. It was a microcosm of the diversity of the Black Southern experience. When Black folks started moving in, the Jewish families along Brays Bayou, who weren't allowed to live in White neighborhoods, started moving out. But not before bombing Black cattle rancher Jack Caesar's porch in the middle of the night after he and his family moved in. Local White folks changed the name of the main road from East Broadway to Dowling Street, for Dick Dowling, an Irishman revered in Houston for his Confederate heroism after a victorious battle against the Union Army at Sabine Pass in 1863. The Sabine River delineates Texas from Louisiana and had been used to transport enslaved people, both before and after the slave trade was deemed illegal. The US Navy ships, at the battle of Sabine Pass, held crews of White Northerners, unfamiliar with the unforgiving Gulf, and at least twenty formerly enslaved Black men from the swampy area who were referred to as contraband. The road that was renamed traveled through the center of Third Ward and concluded at St. Vincent de Paul Cemetery, where Dowling's remains rest. Black people are used to White people assigning names, putting up signs, and claiming just about anything they could as their own. The issue was that White folks didn't quite know what to call themselves without owning Black people. How could they know who they were if Black people were living alongside them? How would they orient and distinguish themselves? Instead of naming themselves, they renamed streets to honor those who had risked their lives to maintain the racial order of the antebellum South and keep the Confederate legacy alive on the lips of Negroes. Just like the *N-word,* Dowling Street was repurposed to take on the meaning of Third Ward's inhabitants' choosing.

Third Ward is located just outside of downtown Houston, where many Black people—like Betty Jean—worked in service and corporate positions alike. It was one of the few areas where Black folks were allowed to open businesses. Just as was necessary in rural areas, Black people maintained their acute spatial awareness. Almost like a sixth sense, they knew where to keep away from if they wanted to remain undead. It's instinctual to know where not to go and when to leave. In Houston, boundaries were largely configured by the bayous. Third Ward, Fourth Ward, and Fifth Ward were the zones surrounding downtown that Black families were relegated to before the Civil Rights Movement.

· · ·

My mother was the first of Betty Jean's children to be born in Houston, the first three were born in Louisiana. Riverside, the local Negro hospital run by a Black medical staff, was no longer delivering babies and had been turned into a psychiatric and mental health center, so Betty Jean gave birth to my mother at Jefferson Davis, along with all the other local Black women who were no longer giving birth squatting over a basin in their living room while squeezing the hand of the midwife who delivered everybody around town and came from a long line of women who had done the same. They were in the city now; they left that country shit back in Louisiana. They were going to doctors now. Black ones. What made Third Ward singular was that there were a significant number of Black professionals who worked and lived there alongside those in poverty. The community was not necessarily divided but spatially each group knew where they were welcome. When Phylicia Rashad was asked by a White journalist if she thought

The Cosby Show was too unrealistic, she said no, because she grew up in a neighborhood where she saw Black doctors and lawyers every day. She and her sister, Debbie Allen, grew up in Third Ward and attended Jack Yates beside Betty Jean's girls. But there were layers of class in the area. My mother grew up in the same neighborhood and she only saw those doctors Rashad spoke of on television. They lived on the other side of Brays Bayou known as the Black River Oaks. They most likely wouldn't have hung out where Betty Jean lived, on blocks lined with shotgun houses, designed to resemble the rural architectural structures they'd come to the city to escape.

Betty Jean lived all around Third Ward, but always on the side of the water where the titty club was. Where the streetwalkers strolled. Where the Black Panthers gathered. In the row houses and the projects. Over near the Lark, a hole-in-the-wall where Betty Jean would fall into the throes of love late in the night only to meet it with contempt by morning. The domestics, the custodians, the service workers, and the body workers, they got off later and had different places to gather and slough off all the muck they had accumulated from working in service to White folks all day. Betty Jean didn't quite fit in with any of the social groups of the time. Yes, she was poor, but she was proud and did not feel that wealth could elevate character or make one interesting. The poor among her found her comportment to be a form of conceit and misunderstood her quiet demeanor as snootiness.

I can only recall her having one friend, Ms. Josephine. I believe Ms. Josephine was from Louisiana as well. Betty Jean didn't allow anyone but family into her home, except for Ms. Josephine. Upon first look, they appear as opposites. Ms. Josephine was outgoing while Betty Jean didn't speak to or smile at neighbors. She loved to laugh while Betty Jean found pleasure in refrain. Ms. Josephine liked to tell stories of their past and Betty Jean was content with keeping her memories tucked in. I'm not sure where they met, but she too was a wild woman. A woman who refused to be tamed.

The two of them stuck beside each other in the liminal space between the divided social classes of Third Ward.

The Black folks on the opposite side of the water went to the Eldorado Ballroom. They had their portraits taken at Teal Portrait Studio. The men married high yellow women with hair like silk with slicked-down edges. They were what the critic Margo Jefferson refers to in her book *Negroland* as "the Third Race." Morally superior to the Whites and more dignified than the common Blacks. They attended Texas Southern University, the local HBCU. Or a little farther out of town, Prairie View A&M. The only time the classes came together was in the sanctuary at Wheeler Avenue Baptist Church and on the dance floor, united only by the gospel, the blues, jazz, and zydeco, culminating in what became known as the Bayou City blues.

. . .

The title of the 1982 Black feminist anthology *All the Women Are White, All the Blacks Are Men, But Some of Us Are Brave* suggests that Black women have struggled for some time to situate themselves within the American social landscape. Betty Jean was certainly not concerned with labels. She was creating her own moral code, inventing a self that didn't fit neatly into the limitations of Blackness and femininity. Which lines would be crossed, and others not trifled with? America doesn't know what to do with a Black woman who is free. A Black woman who relies on her intuition. Moving in a moment toward what feels good to her. Moving where the tides within her pull. Defying her mother, just as my mother did, and I, too, would, branching away from the main body to forge new pathways still informed and fed by the body from which you've derived. At the time, people were looking to give away their own lives to show White folks that Black folks were their civilized contemporaries. To demonstrate to other Black folks that they weren't like the rest. In a time where everyone was looking to prove something in the urban landscape, Betty Jean chose to commit only to herself, her instincts, and her children. She knew that the consequences would be solely hers, so why not claim her life as her own? She knew that it would be her pain to carry all on her own, so why not surrender to moments that feel good along the way, even if they were fleeting? She knew nothing was promised in life to a poor Black girl but death, so she intended to live. For Betty Jean, freedom lay in her ability to choose her failures. To choose her commitments. And to choose how to live with the consequences of both. To choose to build a world around herself by using her womb as a tool to do so with complete disregard for the whispers, and sometimes all-out shouts, of judgment. To choose her problems and pleasures, choosing to not allow a man to be one of them. A no-good man wasn't a problem worth having. And why not employ her own body to create a world that satisfied her? That's what America did, used the wombs of Black women to build a new world. Used the wombs of Black women to satisfy their egos, their stocks, their legacy. Since the country's inception Black women have been a source of emotional comfort, of reliable drudgery, the sexual laborer, the physical laborer, the caretaker, and the maid. Suckling White infants whom she gave her milk to only for them to grow up and turn to her to inaugurate their masculinity, feeding off her still. The most precious and valuable tool of the empire was the womb of the Black woman. In order for America to reconcile its reality with its image of itself, it has to reckon with this history first. And it hasn't, and it can't, because it has forgotten who its mama is.

Betty Jean built her own little universe at *50 10*. She would be the sun and the moon. Each addition orbiting and reflecting her light. Supporting each other and holding each other up. Her gravity is her children and not America's ever-shifting goalposts. With her children, she could live entirely without restriction. They would love her all the same whether she had teeth in her head or coins in her pocketbook. It was within the responsibilities of motherhood that she found a place to defy and define. When no one had the courage to love a wayward woman, her children were there. She was wise enough to know the only thing waiting for you on the other side of degradation is shame. No respect has ever been gained from respectability. It is merely a taming of the shrew.

Life is always dangerous for the defiant ones. The ones used as anecdotes in stories, as evidence for reasons to stay in line. The one whose home no one allows their children to play in. Betty Jean was not interested in being a representative of her race. Or for women. When she speaks about these consequences, she responds with a shrug. "All my life people have hated me. But that ain't none of my business. My aunt hated me too. But when she was dying, I was there every day to bathe her and make sure she had something to eat. And one day she looked up at me and said, Betty Jean, I love you." They always come back around, she'd say, *Just give it some time.*

Her Aunt Carrie, the woman who had taken two of her boys and placed one of her daughters in the home of her husband's coworker, had likely intended to see her fall, and she did, was kicked a few times, but Betty Jean harnessed an inner will that allowed her to get back up. People needed to see her fail, to prove something to themselves and to prove that the social formula produced the intended sum of a life. They thought her beauty had been wasted—*all that pretty for nothing, all that good hair gone to waste*—because she didn't use it to marry well and elevate her race as was understood to be the mission of the urban Negress. Betty Jean had removed herself from the climb but not the hustle. Still, she found fleeting moments of pleasure to sustain her.

I know what it's like to work all day in service to some White structure or another, and then come home and be in service to your children, and quite literally want to disappear. Fly away. To have an insatiable hunger for something beyond the mundanity. To want to be softened and then filled up. Sometimes the yearning between your legs can seem like where the void exists. And then you go out looking for what's plentiful and free. Dick. And what you seek is seeking you right back. Flattering you.

Attentive and quick to stand in your presence. I know what Betty Jean was looking for inside that trough on the corner of Alabama Street and Sampson. And when that void is filled, only for a few moments, you can then part your lips and let out what you've been needing to release, a yell. A moan. An exhale. The sun's arrival serving as a reminder of what you must return to, just as the sun has come back to you. The void opens again, and you turn to that sweet-faced void-filler and wonder why it's just lying there, flaccid and worthless and not filling no voids. At ease. There is no disgust like leaving a void-filler lying there when you have to get up and go to work. Deep down, did she ever want the fairy tale? Just for a moment, did she ever hope to be saved?

I would always wonder how Betty Jean could enjoy anything in life while living in such extreme poverty. And then I read Audre Lorde's poem "A Litany for Survival," which begins:

For those of us who live at the shoreline
standing upon the constant edges of decision
crucial and alone
for those of us who cannot indulge
the passing dreams of choice
who love in doorways coming and going
in the hours between dawns

Where Betty Jean had come from, there were no Black people with pots for pissing and pennies for rubbing. You work, if you're lucky you can sleep, and then you wake to do it all the next day. If you wanted ecstasy, you had to seek it yourself. You had to steal it in between time and worry. This didn't change for Betty Jean when she moved to the city. She wanted to merely keep herself and her children alive and find time for ecstasy when they turned their heads away. To touch and be touched by those of her choosing. To mount a Black man and look down into his eyes and witness his clenched jaw unfurl and hear the sweet song of a baritone moan. There are a million tiny moments worth celebrating when you're in rhythm with a lover, both of you savoring in avoidance of what seriousness lies beyond the bedframe. And besides, Betty Jean understood Lorde's final line: *we were never meant to survive.* And so she lived, gloriously.

7

The Daughters

She had seven, as the book of Genesis suggests, the number of completion.

. . .

Betty Jean and her babies lived all over Third Ward before settling at *50 10* in South Park in 1970. They lived on Alabama, on Reeves and Sampson, off of Elgin and Hadley, but the only house they all resided in together, after everyone was born, was on Beulah Street. A shotgun house with a porch overlooking the dirt yard that led to the street. There were no sidewalks, everyone walked in the middle of the narrow roads that they shared with the long American-made cars. Whenever the daughters tell stories they are notated by which house they were living in at the time and which hurricane passed through while they were there. For someone to meet you in a memory, they must be oriented. Betty Jean recollects her past based on who she was pregnant with at the time. She spent most of her youth pregnant. Between the ages of seventeen and thirty-two. Her babies are her orientation. Her gravity.

I

Righthand
b. 1952

The eldest daughter was Betty Jean's right hand. They were both born on the same cotton plantation in Bossier Parish, Louisiana, eighteen years apart. *Righthand* remembers running through the parted rows of the plantation that resembled the precision of the lines between her plaits, eating watermelon on the porch with her grandfather until her stomach hurt, while her mother harvested the crop. Cotton yields in the summer. When the heat burns deepest on the peak of your spine as you hunch picking apart the bolls. When sweat beads roll off the surface of the cotton the way it does off your hair. In Third Ward, *Righthand* became the mother of the house while Betty Jean was away. Working. Fucking. Searching for a temporary tenderness. Trying to make ends meet, burning the candle at both ends until there is nothing left in the center but soot.

They were so spiritually connected that *Righthand* always predicted when Betty Jean was pregnant, but she wouldn't speak of it, she just quickened her pace, bent down a little farther, reached a little longer, and carried a little more so that her mother wouldn't strain. She didn't judge her mother, she thought she was the most beautiful woman she'd ever seen and that none of the men deserved her. She felt they used her. She blamed them for impregnating her mother. She longed to look like her mother, but never would. Perhaps not being desirable is made more painful when your mother makes men and women alike take heed.

Righthand recalls the looks that she would get from neighborhood people: "I know that's not your baby, fine as you is." She was darker skinned, coarser haired, bigger boned, and no one would let her forget this. Her mother's presence elucidated her deficiencies. The closer you stand to the sun, the longer your shadow is cast. When your mother induces suspension, making everyone in her immediate orbit acknowledge her presence, it's easy for a girl to feel invisible.

Righthand decided that instead of seeking to be desirable, she would be reliable. Duty would be her role, and she maintained it honorably. She was never allowed to be a foolish child. She simply could *not* be a child. And she didn't look like one either. She always looked grown, even as a girl, she was read as older than she was because of her stoicism, height, and frame.

Righthand knew each one of the fathers of her siblings that came after her, even when they didn't. Even though she didn't know her own father. She helped raise each one of them. She loved school and reading but there were many days when she had to take off school to help her mother tend to the children, especially when someone was sick and Betty Jean had to go to work. *Righthand* taught each of the children to read and count before preschool. Being skilled in arithmetic only meant she was burdened with calculating precisely how poor they were. Her duty was to take Betty Jean's paychecks, cash them, and pay all the debts that had accumulated between Fridays. She was the one to tell the Jewish man that they didn't have the rent money when he came knocking. She knew exactly how many cans of corn they could afford for dinner, and only occasionally she'd purchase a pound of ground beef to mix into the pot. She knew how scant each portion size should be, even though Betty Jean would often scrape hers onto *Righthand*'s plate and settle for a cigarette for supper. *Righthand* learned young that her needs' were secondary to everyone she cared for, and she carried on with this responsibility into adulthood with her relationships with boyish men.

Betty Jean cherished and protected *Righthand*, especially from my mother. *Righthand* was born four years before my mother, and for some time, it was just the four of them, Betty Jean, *Righthand*, Mama Connie, and Betty Jean's mother, May. One would assume that my mother and *Righthand* would be close, but they couldn't be more different.

"She's weak," my mother would regularly state as fact.

I knew my mother said this because *Righthand* is soft-spoken and passive. Because she wouldn't utter a disparaging word about Betty Jean, leaving my mother all alone in her fury, when she desperately needed someone to affirm her pain. Someone to look at her and say, *I'm hurting too.* Someone to whisper, *Can you believe she's pregnant again?* To say, *Ain't this some shit?* But *Righthand* was aligned with Betty Jean, they were more sisters than she and my mother would ever be.

My mother recalls *Righthand* getting the younger ones to obey her when Betty Jean was away by garnering sympathy through tears. *Righthand* remembers teaching my mother to read. My mother insists that the only thing *Righthand* ever taught her was how *not* to be. My mother was a fighter and looked down on anyone who refused to be the same. To my mother, *Righthand* was tired. *Too tired to even swat the flies from her face.* My mother's misplaced anger toward *Righthand* was because she couldn't direct it at the true object of her disappointment, her mother, about whom she felt the same. That they allowed men to use them without consequence. Mama Connie had yet to realize that there were ways to strike a blow without force.

When *Righthand* married a man nearly twice her age after high school who would leave her flesh broken open, my mother lost what little respect remained. The violent man who lived only a few doors down the street from *50 10.* He didn't allow her to speak to her family after the wedding so she would walk by slowly after work from the bus stop and wave. If her eye was blackened, she'd take the long way around, as to not frighten Betty Jean's kids, the ones she'd raised. The younger ones would run out into the yard as she passed. Crying for her to come home. It took many years before she did.

In casual conversations in the living room, Connie will bring this up, never letting her forget, *Righthand, 'member when you lived right down the street with ol' boy and he wouldn't even let you come over here? 'Member that?*

"Aht aht aht. Cut all dat out," Betty Jean will always protect her *Righthand.* To which my mother would say, *She always defends the underdog.*

II

Mama Connie
b. 1956

A daughter without a position is sure to rebel. Connie was the first of Betty Jean's children to be born in Houston and for many years she was the youngest. My mother cannot recall ever experiencing *girlhood.* Her body's response to her childhood was to forget. This isn't a conscious resolve; however, the body is always in defense of itself. In the way that white blood cells fight invasive germs, the brain restrains intrusive memories that make your body stutter. Therefore, when I speak to my mother about her childhood, she shoos me away: "Girl, I don't remember all that. I know we were poor, and my mama wouldn't stop having babies. *That* I remember." Her memories come in fragments. Mostly while we're eating or shopping for shoes. Hunger triggers the lasting pangs of food insecurity. When we say we're starving, she will tell my younger brother and me that we don't know what starving is. That we'll never understand what it means to try to sleep while lying in a bed with half a dozen groaning bellies. That we're spoiled because we've never had to walk ten miles in shoes that rub your curled toes raw. It brought my mother much pleasure to provide us with abundance to fulfill her own childhood longings.

My mother has forgotten most things about her childhood, but she clings to her anger. Especially for Betty Jean and her decision to continue giving birth to babies who were taking food off of her plate. Anger for never knowing her father, the midnight man. Anger for never being held. Never being told she was loved. Never being protected. She remembers being awakened by the shouts of her grandmother May when Betty Jean would creep back into their apartment just before dawn. The way she wished her grandmother May could do something to contain her mother. She remembers being utterly confused by all the ways a mother and daughter could be so different. The same difference she felt with her own mother and the difference I feel from her. But just beneath the surface of our interests lies a sameness. This sameness gets in the way when you're trying to hate someone. Or perhaps it's the sameness that nurtures the hate.

She can remember few childhood friends but she never forgets when someone wrongs her. She remembers her neighbor's mother didn't approve of her daughter hanging out with her. For fear that poverty was contagious. Or that poverty breeds the kind of desperation that her friend's mother didn't want her child associated with. Their neighbors had carpet in their home, they had a car and never took the bus, they had a father. My mother remembers that she would scurry home from her friend's porch when the mother pulled onto the street in her Cadillac. The feeling of being welcome nowhere really. Of never having a place where everyone was pleased with her arrival, only with her departure.

She can't recall the name of a single teacher. She can't recall her favorite foods or games. She remembers when she and her best friend Debra had a disagreement as children and *Righthand* took her friend's side and threw a mason jar at my mother's mouth to shut her up. The glass ripped open her lip, leaving a little red sea on the front porch of their house on Beulah Street. Beulah Land is supposed to be blessed with the Lord's abundance but little Connie had begun to believe God saw poverty as sin. That wealth would gain her favor. Her lip still holds the grooves of the wound the jar left behind. The blood stain remained until the next heavy rain.

My mother always remembers betrayal. She can't tell you when she learned to ride a bike, but she does recall the sound of the back of her mother's hand when it collided with her face. But that didn't sting as much as when her mother told her with frequency, "Shut up, heifer." She remembers those early moments when she began to understand the power of language. The way it could move people passionately toward anger or joy. Even as a child, she could command the attention of adults with words. In this way, she was never powerless. The more she sensed that people wanted to silence her, the louder she became. While Betty Jean and *Righthand* were bonded within the folds of silence. For my mother, it was better to be intolerable than to be invisible.

There is not a single photograph of my mother as a child. Because of her dominant presence, I have a difficult time imaging what she was like when she was small. I associate childhood with a kind of helplessness and naivete that she says she never had the pleasure of experiencing. *Righthand* says she was always competitive. A simple task like taking the garbage to the street would become a race. Removing the laundry from the line would be a jumping contest. Connie was athletic and could outperform *Righthand* at everything physical. Dancing, jumping, running. According to her sisters, she was always the fastest kid on the block. She had a quick lip, so it was only right that she outran everyone.

But *Righthand* was intelligent, and my mother is still bitter that her older sister didn't miss an opportunity to express her intellectual inferiority. Mama Connie recalls dancing around the house one afternoon as *Righthand* grew impatient helping her with her homework, as any child attempting to teach another child would be, and shouted at my mother, "You're so stupid. You're never going to be anything but a go-go dancer on Dowling." Dowling is where sex workers and strippers twirled and turned tricks under the stars. My mother can't tell me what her favorite subject was in school or what she wanted to be when she grew up. She says her only dream was to not be poor. And not work on Dowling Street. She knew she didn't want to have a million babies with a million different men. She survived by living entirely in the present. Not dwelling too much on the past or daring to dream of a future.

This is a primary violence of poverty, the limitations it places on the imagination.

III

Gone

b. 1957

Betty Jean met *Gone*'s father at the old Texas Hotel downtown. She was housekeeping and he worked in the kitchen. She stopped taking his calls and never even bothered to tell him that she was pregnant. A coworker noticed her expansion and shared the news with him. When he asked her if it was his, she didn't lie. When he asked where the child was, she simply said, *Gone*. The father, visibly flustered, asked why she had not come to him, and she asked, "And what was *you* gone do?" The only outcome she could imagine was him wasting her time, getting in the way, or pissing her off. It's hard to imagine circumstances that you've yet to witness, in this case, a man being accountable for his children with an unwed mother. She stood before him, only briefly, and as his eyes watered, she walked away. She refused to watch a grown man cry. She never saw *Gone*'s father again.

Gone was given away to a friend of Betty Jean's Aunt Carrie, May's older sister. The same aunt who had taken Betty Jean's two sons and was raising them as her own. This time, Aunt Carrie was the facilitator, giving *Gone* to some folks who weren't even kin. The man was a close friend and coworker at the roofing company where Aunt Carrie's husband worked, his wife couldn't conceive, so they took the child right off of Betty Jean's bosom. The folks said she could come visit *Gone* anytime, that the baby could stay with her occasionally, that they wouldn't keep *Gone* from knowing her mother.

Soon as they turned the corner Betty Jean knew it would be a long while before she reunited with her baby girl. She did not weep. There was simply no time for dwelling. That is a pastime of privilege. She simply locked it away in that place where all her other sorrows were piling up. That place where you think it will stay put, but like water, it always finds a way out at the lowest point. Her breasts swelled and throbbed as a reminder of what had been taken. So tender she had to sleep on her back and put banana leaf inside her brassiere for relief. She swears that the milk leaked for far longer than any other pregnancy. Her body doing what her mind could not—brooding.

She didn't want to give her up, but she yielded to no one except her mother. The mother has absolute power. Betty Jean gave away three of her children simply because her mother said it shall be so. And maybe this is why Betty Jean continued to have more. Seeking comfort to conceal the throbbing. To make up for those lost. To exercise her power through the womb.

Many years later, Betty Jean would take two of *Gone*'s daughters away from the harm of their home. When I asked my grandmother why *Gone* allowed her to take her children, she simply replied, *What was she gone do?* There was no higher authority, except God.

The older couple could afford to give *Gone* a room to call her own in Sunnyside, with a television, a telephone, and a closet full of clothes that weren't hand-me-downs. Just as it had been in the plantation South, her family was selected, and she was left to endure whatever may come.

Gone was told by the older couple that Betty Jean was her cousin. Everyone played along. She would see the woman she called cousin Betty at Aunt Carrie's house sometimes and she was especially attentive to little *Gone*. She loved her cousin because she always seemed curious about her, noticing if her hair had grown, noticing mosquito bites turned scabs on her legs. *Gone* wore the small seashell necklace her cousin gave to her every day. One day when she was nine years old and sitting on the old cool-cup-lady's porch who lived next door to her, she asked *Gone* where she had gotten her pretty little necklace. *Gone* proudly told the cool-cup-lady that her cousin Betty had given it to her. The cool-cup-lady replied, "I wonder when they gone tell you that's your mama. Not your cousin."

The day *Gone* legally became an adult, without prior notice, she moved in with Betty Jean and her siblings at *50 10*. At that point it would have been Betty Jean and six of her younger children living there. Everyone knows that if they don't have nowhere else to go, they can turn up to *50 10*. Mr. and Mrs. who had adopted *Gone* told her if she left, she couldn't take nothing but the clothes on her back. And that's what she showed up with. Betty Jean didn't ask no questions, but she knew something musta not been right over there if she came running on her birthday. Betty Jean hugged *Gone* tight. Tight enough so that *Gone* could feel her say she was sorry. Sorry for letting them take her and sorry for what she'd suffered through. Tight enough to let her know she never had to leave again if she didn't want to. Tight enough to let her know that this is what we are built for, to endure. All *Gone*'s siblings simply moved over and made space for her in the room they shared at *50 10*.

IV

Artemis

b. 1961

Shortly after *Gone* was born, Betty Jean met an intellectual man at the local hole-in-the-wall. Low ceilings, low lights, with chestnut-paneled walls. The Lark was where one went after the respectable Negroes had all gone home for the evening. When everything else closed, the Lark was beginning to simmer. Where the nine-to-five men with tailored pants, but no cuff links, whose days were spent bent over a broom, a machine, a White man's garden could be found beside the women who had spent the day on their knees cleaning. Where they came to stand up and stretch out and shake off.

The Lark slouched between Alabama and Sampson Street.

There was no sign out front, but it was filled with brown, ground-dwelling songbirds. Where the bluesmen turned up after their paying gigs to experiment and locate inspiration within the lips of full-mouthed women. Because who knew the blues better than these women? And if you hit the right note, to raise the temperature in the room, then they might tell you all about it.

Maybe they met on the dance floor. Or perhaps Betty Jean stood alone at the bar, a cigarette in one hand and a sweating can of Coca-Cola in the other. She didn't drink much and would point out alcoholics on the street to her children to show them what they shouldn't be. She told them addiction was in their blood, because her daddy was a drunk. But I suspect they wanted to know more about their own daddies than hers. She told them, *Well I know mine and it ain't done me a bit a good.*

Artemis's daddy was from the other side of the bayou, Riverside Terrace, where the Black bourgeoisie lived, but he made his way across the room to Betty Jean. He was a professor of musicology at Texas Southern University. Naturally, any music man would find Betty Jean alluring. The swaying of both her hips and her voice are a ballad.

He fell in love with her that night and never stopped loving her. He begged her to marry him. And she considered it. But before she could even begin to envision what their life would be like, where they would live, what their weekends in Galveston would be like, his mother called to inform Betty Jean that he was promised to someone else. Promised as expectation or a degree of measurement signifying excellence? She told Betty Jean that her son would not wed someone who wasn't college-educated and that she had been misinformed. Betty Jean threw up her hands and stepped back, but her rising belly held two expectations.

The professor married the other woman. The woman from the other side of the bayou. The ceremony was hurried, the consummation was fruitful. The mother had saved her son from the hoodoo of the backwoods Louisiana girl. She'd advised him for years to never let those Louisiana girls cook you no gumbo or spaghetti, because they put drops of their blood in it, to cast their spells. He tried for years to see Betty Jean on the side, but she refused. He never met *Artemis* and *Apollo*. And he died young of a broken heart.

. . .

It felt like the twins were summoned after the storm. Betty Jean, May, *Righthand,* and five-year-old Connie were inside of that little one-room guesthouse behind Ms. Curtis's big house on Alabama Street. Betty Jean could barely reach past her belly to board up the windows and the wind kept whipping the nails from her hands as she struggled to bend down to retrieve them. She and May moved the furniture to the middle of the house and huddled in the bed they all shared. Hurricane Carla was a category 4 storm when it made landfall in September 1961. Carla was the first live broadcast of a hurricane, and the world beyond the coast witnessed the rage of the Gulf waters. And just as the waters receded, Betty Jean's broke. The twins were born in the wake of the storm.

Artemis came first into the world, perhaps making sure it was safe for her brother to enter before beckoning him forth. She would forever protect him. May helped her daughter bring the twins home from the hospital. *Righthand* was there to greet them, as she was responsible for little Connie, who was no doubt disappointed by the discovery of two babies instead of one. If Betty Jean knew that there would be twins, she wouldn't have informed little Connie. Children were expected to adjust, they were not consulted or even informed of the changes to come. For years *Apollo* would speak only to *Artemis* and no one else. When he eventually spoke to others, everyone looked to her for a translation and this was the beginning of her understanding of the importance of being tied to men. She was the eldest of the second wave of Betty Jean's children and despised each new arrival just as Connie had.

. . .

Once the twins were toddlers, Betty Jean was pregnant for about five consecutive years. *Artemis* sank deeper into literature for her escape as the years passed and grew especially attached to Greek mythology. She stole a copy of *The Iliad* from the library because she tired of renewing her loan. She would lock the door to the bathroom and sit inside the empty tub for privacy as she drowned out all the noise. The kids playing in the street in the day, the whirring of police choppers surveilling overhead, the screams of fiends in the night. In the bathtub, with Homer, she couldn't hear the knocking of the others pleading to be let in.

Artemis's mouth was even more reckless toward her mother than her older sister Connie's. I think Connie respected her fearlessness but saw her younger sister as uninformed and self-destructive. Cruel for cruelty's sake. For Connie, destruction itself was never the goal, her speaking out of turn was always a part of a tactic, sometimes to triangulate, sometimes to intimidate, but never just for thrills. This is what made *Artemis* dangerous and her younger siblings feared her wrath. *Artemis* defied in ways that Connie never would. *Artemis* was more intellectual and appreciated that integration brought her closer to White folks. *She's so strange, she loves being around White folks,* her sisters would say. She'd leave the house for days, staying out with friends and sleeping over at their houses. When she came home, Betty Jean met her with a leather belt wrapped around her fist, the buckle dangling at its end. And *Artemis* could endure like no other, never crying out for mercy. Betty Jean stopped whipping her after an episode where she exhausted herself to the point of nearly passing out. *Artemis* stared stoically into her mother's eyes with raised brows until she had finished. Her own kind of conquering of the Titan. What can one do with an unruly child except hand her over to God. No one else wanted her.

Artemis took her frustrations out on her siblings but wouldn't allow anyone else to trifle with them. Once, while in a joust with a girl in the bathroom at Jones High School, she announced that should there ever be another disagreement with her younger sister, *Come see Artemis.* She was the impenetrable sister known for her grandeur and dramatic performance. When *Artemis* made her victorious announcement, she didn't realize there was a girl hiding in the bathroom stall. The girl approached *Artemis* with hesitation and introduced herself: *I am your sister.* Their father had died years earlier of complications of the heart, but she had heard of her twin siblings before his death, and she invited the twins to visit the home of her paternal grandmother, the one who had made the call to Betty Jean. *Artemis* told the stranger that she had enough sisters to call her own and did not seek more.

She was the type of woman who preferred men. She didn't have any male figures to look up to growing up, so she created fictions. This is how we children of unsettled environments sustain ourselves, by disassociating into fantasy. Once *Apollo* no longer needed her, she would seek other men to support. A warrior in search of love who found herself married to men who would easily take her life. She married three times and each husband was worse off than the one before. She took each one of their surnames and still uses them interchangeably, depending on what mood she wants to embody. Her last husband was a member of the Aryan Circle, and he pushed love to its limits by testing his wife's loyalty. *What's the point of being with a White man if he gone stay locked up? She may as well be with a brother,* my mother said, shaking her head in disappointment. Meaning, this is a White man who could extend none of his White privilege to her sister so what exactly was the reasoning behind her choice? It was a power move of a different order than my mother's. *Artemis* needed to be needed by someone who socially occupied a higher position. Even if he was a lowlife, he was White and male.

My mother called him *Jailbird* and kept a clipping from the *Houston Chronicle* on top of our refrigerator that she pulled out as a prop as she told one of her favorite stories to visitors. The article explained how *Artemis*'s car had been the getaway vehicle in the racially motivated murder of a seventeen-year-old *boy.* That *Artemis* was a witness in the defense of her boyfriend and his brother, who had matching swastika tattoos. Her car had been identified by the honor-roll sticker on its bumper that her daughter had earned in elementary school. Her boyfriend had been driving, his

brother riding shotgun. Her boyfriend said it had all been a misunderstanding.

This is how the "misunderstanding" happened . . .

It was the boy's summer between high school and college, and
he'd saved up from a summer job to buy a cash car. The boy and
his kid brother borrowed his father's pickup to go view the car.
After viewing it, he departed to pick up a cashier's check. But he
never made it home. As the boy pulled out of the parking lot, no
doubt excited to purchase his first car, he cut off a small sedan
with an honor-roll bumper sticker. *Jailbird* was driving that sedan.
Enraged by this, he circled the car to intimidate the boy, following
him for miles until *Jailbird*'s brother rolled his window down and
aimed his 9 mm at the driver's side of the pickup and the bullet
went straight through the boy's head, past his kid brother in the
passenger seat, and out the passenger-side window. It happened
so fast that the truck kept driving straight for a while before veer-
ing off the road and into an apartment building. *Jailbird* sped
away. Betty Jean and the sisters found it peculiar that *Artemis* had
left her car backed into the yard at *50 10* for some time, they knew
she was up to no good, but no one asked.

The boy was somebody's baby. He died in his kid brother's
arms in the pickup on a summer day in Houston in 1999. The
parents lost both of their sons that day, in different ways.

The Aryan brothers were only caught months later because *Jailbird* boasted to friends about killing some Nigger. Naturally, all
of their friends were criminals, and one of them offered the Harris County Sheriff's Office information in exchange for a lesser
sentencing on a petty possession crime. The informant wore a
disguise during his testimony for fear of the Aryan gang's retali-
ation. The trigger man received a life sentence. *Jailbird* got thirty-
five years. *Artemis* married him while he was in prison. She drove
to visit her husband on the weekends with her baby girl from her
previous marriage, the one who had earned the honor-roll sticker,
beside her. Since birth, since pulling *Apollo* forth after her, *Artemis* needed to be needed to feel alive. Her own daughter helped

raise *Jailbird*'s nephew. Every time I saw my cousin she had that blond baby on her hip and we all squinched our faces in confusion when she brought him to *50 10*. *Didn't his uncle kill that Black boy before he could even start college?* we'd ask in a half-joking way. Betty Jean would say, *Well the baby didn't pull the trigger. Leave him 'lone.* Aren't Black people always grouped together as responsible for one another's actions? Why do White men get to be the lone wolf? But I would never talk back to my grandmother this way. *Artemis*'s daughter didn't put that blond baby down until she became a wife herself and had twins of her own with a man who she tried to cool in his fits of rage, after he shook the newborns for crying and shook her too for consoling them before he was tended to. *Artemis*'s youngest daughter learned her place in the world while sitting beside her mother on those drives each weekend. And the ripples spread endlessly across the surface of the water until something obstructs the proliferation.

V

Red
b. 1963

They called her *Red Devil.* They even made up songs about her. *Red Devil, Red Devil na na na.* She was high yellow with fine slick red hair. On wash day, which was every Saturday, while her sisters were getting their hair combed, pressed, and braided, Betty Jean told her, *Get back, and go put some water and grease on them edges.* Said she had good hair and didn't need nothing done to hers. *Red* yearned for those moments when she could have her mother's undivided attention. She wanted to lean her head forward over the kitchen sink and feel her mother press her hands into her scalp. To sit between her mother's thighs for a short while. This may be why she became a hairdresser. To share those intimate intervals with Black women and make them feel beautiful. Each week Betty Jean came to her salon and tilted her head back over the basin while *Red* gave her what she had always wished for, a few moments alone. Just the two of them. It's easy to think that if you provide to others what you've always wanted from them, they will then be able to give it back to you. That maybe they just need an example of how to do it, and once you give them that *feel good* that you desire, it will become instinctual for them. That you can in fact teach people how to love you. This was *Red*'s attempt to demonstrate the affection she craved. Anyone who has ever tried to convince someone to love them has failed. Betty Jean and *Red* spoke care in foreign languages. Each expression communicated to the other went unheard. Betty Jean couldn't see that *Red* tried all she could to please her mother in hopes of getting her attention. Cleaning and tending to the house before her mother had to say a word, hoping her mother might notice and ask, *Who done this?* So that *Red* could say, *Me, Mama. It was me. Red* couldn't see that Betty Jean could only show care by being there. By not leaving as her father had. Everything else was inessential.

Red always thought that if her father could just see her, he would love her. She thought that if she got one shot at it, she could charm him. She describes herself as a daddy's girl who never had a father. Betty Jean told *Red* her father would park outside their home for hours watching his baby girl play in the dirt with her sisters and brother. Drinking from a bottle tucked inside a brown paper bag trying to decide if she was his, trying to work up the courage to say so himself. Sometimes he would creep by slowly on his way home from working at the ship channel. Sometimes he would park in the empty lot across the street where a house had burned down but its charred remnants remained.

Until one day he got out of the car, approached the small beige house sitting on cinder blocks, and looked down at the girls playing in the dirt, but as he drew nearer, he saw what he couldn't see in the distance, she had clustered rashes around her nose, elbows, and knees. *Red* had impetigo. He didn't get any closer before turning away and denouncing her, *That ain't none of my child.* He was never seen in the empty lot after that. I imagine Betty Jean shared this painful truth because she wanted to release her daughter from the fantasy of his return and put devastation in its place. To help her daughter who was quick to cry and quicker to please to understand that she needed *some* anger to survive. *Red* reserved her anger for her mother, though, especially when she called her heifer. *Red*'s response was to pick up the white pages phone book and threaten her mother, "I'm calling my daddy." Searching for the name of a man she never knew. Betty Jean snatched the phone book and slung it against the wall. *How you want somebody who don't want you?* Betty Jean knew what it was like to wait for a drunk father who was never coming, so she couldn't sit by watching her baby girl carrying around this phantom man.

Sometimes our mothers tell themselves they are extinguishing our dreams to shield us from the burns of disappointment. But we become ruins all the same.

· · ·

Red always felt slower than the others. She hated class; she would walk to her elementary school and sit outside on the railroad tracks until dismissal, then walk home with the others. While raising multiple children as a single mother in poverty, Betty Jean depended on a kind of sameness between them all. Distinctions were inconveniences. Every child was raised as if they had the same intellectual capacities and determination. If you fell behind, it was assumed that you weren't disciplined enough. *You up there runnin' your mouth at that schoolhouse instead of paying attention to the teacher.* There's simply no time and no resources for a diagnosis of a child's mental capacities. The children were thought of as purely physical beings, their emotional and intellectual needs were not considered. And as a result of feeling she was dumber than all her sisters, *Red* dropped out of high school to attend the local beauty college. She still resents Betty Jean for allowing her to do so, instead of helping her find the resources to keep up in high school. Later in life *Red* found out that she was dyslexic. This discovery provided mild relief in understanding why school was painful, but even more so reminded her of the levels of neglect she'd experienced as a girl.

What she lacked in intellect she made up for in charisma and style. Each of Betty Jean's girls plays a role and is careful not to tip into someone else's lane. *Righthand* was dependable, *Artemis* was the warrior, my mother, although ever chic, was the courageous one who went out to find resources and bring them back to the tribe. And my mother may have thought her little sister was overstepping a bit, if *Red* sensed this she didn't recoil. When it came to fashion, *Red* says my mother was her idol. She was much younger so my mother was an adult experimenting with looks when she visited *50 10* and her little sister admired her commitment to beauty and ability to command the room with an elegant authority. *Red* took notes and went to the streets to try it out in her own way. She was building her own community outside of the family and was criticized for it. Betty Jean taught them that they were each other's friends and not to trust anyone but family, and most of the girls held true to this. But when *Red* struggled to find camaraderie at home, it was her friends who watered her.

The best dancer, the sharpest dresser, and there was no skater at the rink more fly. She could hold center stage at the salon with a story that would leave everyone folded over howling, begging her to stop or else they might burst at the seams. Begging her to keep going because nowhere else could they experience this euphoria. She was the storyteller. The beautician that you looked forward to seeing every Saturday but knew you were going to be there all day because she was going to set down the curling iron and step from behind the chair to talk with her hands, impersonate with precision, and reenact full-on scenes so that you felt that you were at the theater. A one-woman show. When you walked out, your spirit was lifted and the hair was laid. Put into the world what ye have yet to receive and sit content with the promise of the next lifetime.

VI

Daddy's Girl
b. 1964

She remembers her sisters being jealous of her. *Everybody else had that Louisiana hair. I was the ugly duckling. But I knew my daddy. I was always a daddy's girl.* I imagine that by this time Betty Jean was growing weary. *Daddy's Girl* was her eighth birth and *Red* was barely a year old, so she considered settling down with a taxi driver that the other girls called *Cabbie.* He would sometimes offer to drive Betty Jean and *Righthand* home from the washateria on the corner of Ennis and Elgin. *Righthand* was skeptical of him from the start but didn't dare tell her mother so. They had known him from around the way. Nobody knows where he came from, but he was always creeping around Third Ward. Seemed like he never had any customers in the back of his cab. He tried for years to get Betty Jean's attention, until she finally let him in. It was the first time Betty Jean had a man around to rub her feet while she was pregnant. Take her to work and pick her up from *both* of her jobs. But he was a jealous man. Suspicious that she was slipping off to see other men. For reasons that were not entirely clear, she allowed him to live with them. After all, she was getting older, and I'm sure it wasn't as easy to carry a child to term at thirty-two as it had been at twenty-two. And not having to take the bus into downtown every day for work didn't hurt either. He had made himself indispensable, or so he thought.

When *Daddy's Girl* was born in the early summer of 1964, he slept with her on his chest every night. He doted on her endlessly. Betty Jean smiled a bit more but found all that kissing on the child to be excessive. The other kids watched and yearned to be held in the same way. He refused them. He kept his girl's belongings separate and didn't want *Red* to share bottles with his baby girl. In his eyes, she was better than the rest because she was *his*. And if their own daddies left them, they couldn't be worth much.

In Third Ward, Betty Jean was pregnant by *Cabbie* again before *Daddy's Girl* was even two; except this time, they fought throughout the entire pregnancy. When Betty Jean's next daughter was born, *Cabbie* said she wasn't his. To which Betty Jean didn't assuage his doubts: *Well then, if she ain't none of yours then the other one ain't neitha.* She stripped away what made him whole in this world, his masculinity. While he was away from home Betty Jean found another place to rent, and when he returned, they were gone. Betty Jean loved a departure. Some people have trouble with exiting, they linger near the door, threatening but anxiously or, perhaps, hopelessly waiting to be lured back. Not Betty Jean. She won't even tell you, and you'll never really know because she keeps her purse on her shoulder at all times. Betty Jean could leave like no other. No one knows the freedom of mobility like Black folks. And she exercised this frequently.

Mine, is how she'd lay claim after her victory. Betty Jean saw her babies as a kind of creation. Something she and God had gotten together and agreed upon.

Mama Connie, who had never laid eyes on her own father, not even a photograph, played along most of the time. Once when she saw *Cabbie* standing outside the corner store, she yelled from the sidewalk, popping her hip out to shelf her hand, *I bet you don't know where we stay at!* In exchange for telling him where they lived, she required compensation. Even as a girl, my mother's loyalty was always to herself. He offered a piece of bubble gum, they settled on two. She knew there would be an ass-whooping waiting on her when she returned, so she shoved both pieces in her mouth at once and took the long way home.

Mama Connie reported back to *Daddy's Girl*. "I just saw your daddy outside." *Daddy's Girl* sat at the window near the front door every day waiting for him to come get her. And after Connie told him where they lived, he did. He had moved in with another woman by then. He would come by to pick up *Daddy's Girl*, and not his younger daughter, let alone any of the other children in the house. *Red* would beg for him to take her along, desperate for a father even if it wasn't her own. "Only *that* one." Pointing into the house as if selecting live seafood from a tank or ripened fruit from a pile. *Daddy's Girl* would step forward with great pride, happy to be carried away from the rest. These visits went on for a time, until *Daddy's Girl* came home crying with her caramel skin looking more like cherrywood. His new girlfriend had made her sit out on the porch all day in the sun until *Cabbie* got home from work. Said she was dirty like her mama and didn't need to be inside. *Cabbie* blackened her eye in response. Only making her despise the child more. It seemed that the bond between father and girl was disrupting both of their homes equally. It is likely that his wife envied *Daddy's Girl* for the same reasons that her sisters envied her, because they wanted to know what it felt like to be loved by a man without being desired.

Betty Jean didn't allow *Daddy's Girl* to visit her father's home again. But she still waited for him by the door. Looking out the window each day for him to come save her. And he never did.

Daddy's Girl had none of the privileges of *not* being the youngest and none of the benefits of being the youngest. Her position left her often spoken over or deemed frivolous. She never quite found her place in the world, at *50 10* and beyond its walls. She shape-shifted to whatever man she was with and never had a problem finding them. Chasing the ghost of her father. He was gone before she started school and her memory betrays her by not allowing her to recall his face, so she conjures him. She would ask her older sisters, because they knew it well, to tell her again how he looked. She won't allow herself to resent her mother for not encouraging her relationship with her father. But I can tell in the way she clenches her jaw as she recounts this loss to me that she's holding it there, between her teeth.

Mama did the best she could and we always had food on the table and a roof over our heads. Being fed, but not necessarily nourished, was the criterion for care. *Daddy's Girl* holds this same grace for her father, who never came back for her. Who wasn't there to protect her when Betty Jean's boyfriend *Mr. Pepper* would kiss her long and deep with his tongue caressing hers when she arrived home from elementary school and Betty Jean was still at work. *Daddy's Girl* never told Betty Jean, because she thought her mother might kill him. At six years old she understood the consequences of her voice and the limits of justice. It was because of this man that Betty Jean was able to purchase *50 10.* They bought the home together with his veteran's mortgage loan benefits; no money down and a low interest rate. He was a truck driver for Dr Pepper and brought home a steady paycheck and cases of Diet Dr Pepper each week. At her tender age, *Daddy's Girl* knew that Betty Jean could not afford the home alone, on just her janitor's income. She knew how precarious their housing circumstances had been before finally settling at *50 10.* She knew that since *Mr. Pepper* came around they didn't have to share chips anymore, they each got their own bag, or that they weren't just taking bologna sandwiches to school, or that for the first time there were leftovers from dinner. So she opened her mouth, closed her eyes, and clenched her fists when *Mr. Pepper* beckoned her. She sacrificed herself for *50 10,* for her mother.

It wasn't too long before *Mr. Pepper* was gone, because he slapped *Artemis,* no doubt because her sharp tongue had bruised his ego, and she called Connie to report the incident. My mother, still in high school, apparently threatened him with a knife to his throat. *Lemme tell you one goddam thing, these are my sisters,* she said, wielding the butcher knife around the living room of *50 10* while the others watched the spectacle, *and you bet not lay a hand on nan nother one or I'll slit your throat. Hear me?* Somehow, my mother was always at the center of these stories from their childhood. Somehow, Connie always had the courage to speak out, when everything in the world tried to silence her. She knew quite young what many of them came to understand later, that no one was coming to save them. That Black women had to save each other. When Betty Jean returned to *50 10* after working her second job, she told him exactly where to go.

Betty Jean had met *Mr. Pepper* in Third Ward; he was a deacon at the church next door to them when they lived on Beulah Street. He had gotten to Betty Jean by suggesting that Mama Connie and *Righthand* join the youth choir. He watched their comings and goings for months before asking Betty Jean if her girls had been saved. This man who was calling himself holy took Connie and *Righthand* to the waters and baptized them, to wash away adolescent sins. Since he couldn't cleanse himself of his own.

As *Daddy's Girl* predicted, after his departure from *50 10*, their lights were cut off regularly. And she never told her mother, or anyone, what he'd done to her. She wasn't the only daughter he had abused, they each suffered in solitude, to protect not him but the home. Everybody paid for that house. When we gather at *50 10*, we are greeted with the whispers of the past. We just keep building new walls.

VII

The Baby
b. 1969

No one thought the youngest girl would be carried to term because of the miscarriage Betty Jean suffered only a few months prior. *Cabbie* was giving her hell. *Righthand* remembers Betty Jean being hospitalized after she passed out due to stress. For the first time in all her pregnancies, she was placed on bedrest. Only *Righthand* knew that she was prescribed antidepressants. Nobody else knew that this man had somehow gotten to what she protected most, her heart. And from those flames *The Baby* was born.

The Baby is the slightest. Betty Jean and all the others are five foot eight with size ten feet. Allowing for them to share clothes and shoes throughout their lives. But with *The Baby*, they'd have to take the hem out and remove the toilet paper stuffed into the toes of the shoes after she'd been in them.

Cabbie denied *The Baby*, so she refused him right back. And eventually, she accepted Christ as her father. He was a spirit just like her sisters' fathers, but he wouldn't betray or refuse her. We all need something to believe in, and her chosen father was just as unlikely to knock on her door as her sisters'. So years later, as her belly grew in our guest room, my baby brother Shannon asked, *Who is she pregnant by, Jesus?*

My mother infantilized her baby sister. She was working as a dental assistant and while she lived in the guest room my mother encouraged *The Baby* to look further ahead, to become a hygienist or go to dental school, but she recoiled defensively. Being righteous means content is a practice in gratitude. Being pious often means that one becomes closely acquainted with shame.

Betty Jean's first and last girls possess her temperament. Mysterious and quiet until ignited, and immovable, even in the face of sensibility, once they've made up their minds. Perhaps that's why they are Betty Jean's irrefutable favorites. *The Baby*'s laugh sets her apart from the rest. Distinct, brazen, and easily aroused. It is her most endearing characteristic, as she is otherwise cold. She can look into your eyes and still feel many worlds away, making her difficult to understand or get close to. This distance allows for a self-containment that means she is reliant on no one for her satisfaction. But it also means that her own daughters are unable to reach certain parts of her. In shielding herself from life's thorns, she misses out on the sweet parts too. As a family, as a nation, of resilient women, emotional castration is a reflexive measure. Disavowing us of the ability to receive and allow in what we need most of all, *love*.

· · ·

While Betty Jean was a woman committed to difference, her seven daughters were raised in a time when sameness was expected for acceptance. Each of her daughters married and had children of their own but no more than four. *The Baby* was the last to marry and is the only one who remains so. Though seldom acknowledged, they all went to sleep with the same fears that I had, of *ending up like your mother.* They each saw their mother in different ways. Some held fast to delusion and disregarded their sisters' bitterness, while others openly expressed their hurt as a result of their mother's choices.

Her daughters learned something that Betty Jean couldn't have imagined in their home in Third Ward. They learned to know shame. Back in Elm Grove, there was no shame in being poor, partially because they were still orienting themselves around how to be free, and partially because they were all mostly from enslaved families turned sharecropping families. The shame of poverty was not hers to bear, it was her country's.

Betty Jean didn't accept handouts. She refused welfare and food stamps. She said she had gone down to the social services building once and the White folks started asking her questions about the fathers of her children. This was back when the government would give you a bag full of powdered cheese, powdered eggs, canned meat, and corn syrup to raise a family on. Betty Jean left that office and told herself she'd never go back. That bag wasn't worth the trouble. And even though they didn't have enough, when Betty Jean saw the parents of the family down the block strung out on drugs, she would send one of her daughters down to the other end of Beulah Street to pick up their kids so they would have something on their stomachs before school. Where Betty Jean had come from in Louisiana, you don't walk past somebody's baby when they're hungry. Even today, when we pass unhoused people on the road, my mother lets down her window to pass some cash, and as we pull away, she says, *That's somebody's baby.*

All the kids on the block wanted to play at *50 10,* because any home with a gaggle of children is going to bring about the most inventive play. The grandest hide-and-seek. The most enduring game of tag. The yard was always filled with objects that they would build worlds with. Joy lived in their home right beside suffering, and throughout their lives, the girls have always had one another in moments of darkness and of triumph, they are never alone in the world. Black people have always found ways to love through the most impossible circumstances.

Later in life, my grandmother learned to know pleasure. Betty Jean's pleasure looks like sitting in her chair at 50 10 submerged in the sounds of her children and grandchildren and great-grandchildren and great-great-grandson all about her. She's retired, her body is at ease in knowing her children are alive and not in prison. In belief that she'd earned her right to rest. Sure, she had stolen moments of fleeting ecstasy with her lovers in her youth. But the pleasure came not from the act but from the consequence. Everything she's ever cherished in life was brought forth through her womb. On the other side of struggle, she found pleasure in surviving to tell the story, shamelessly.

The Bayou City is saturated with rainwater that comes nearly as certain as the sun and drained through systems that slurp up the collected waters before dumping them into the Gulf. They keep thinking they can sweep it away. The excess, the futile, the cumbersome. During hurricane season, the Gulf throws it right back. But with more force and more fury, and full of heat.

Conforming

CONNIE

////////////

Her power is to open what is shut;
to shut what is open.

—OVID

8

1956

My relationship with my mother is like my mother's relationship with water. There is probably nowhere else my mother would rather be than held by the water. But she doesn't know how to swim. So the very thing that comforts her also terrifies her. It is one of life's cruelties, to love most what you fear most.

Everything that brought me discomfort as a child was met with narratives about my mother surviving on next to nothing growing up in Third Ward. If I complained, she told me and Shannon that she was *taking us for a little ride*. She'd drive across town from our home in the suburbs to Third Ward. Sometimes during the day, and sometimes at night, for dramatic impact. She'd point to an empty lot on Beulah Street where one of the houses she'd grown up in had been. She'd stop in front, look to us in the backseat of her Mercedes-Benz through the rearview mirror, and ask us, *Do you know what it's like to go to bed hungry?* She'd tell us we'd never *not* had what we needed. And we'd cry because our fear of her was greater than anything beyond the windows. I feared she might open the door and tell us to get out. That she'd abandon us there to see how we fared. One time when I was about seven and my brother about five, she left us at the grocery store because we'd run off to play in the toy aisle after she'd told us time and again to stay close to her. She'd taught us to page her on the intercom whenever we were separated. My brother and I were notorious for making a swift turn onto the toy aisle while my mother shopped, assuming we were behind her. Only on this day, when the manager paged her—"Connie, please come to the customer service desk"—she didn't show up. I don't know how long we sat there crying before she walked in the front door of the store and saw us on the floor cradling each other. She was furious because we'd made a scene. In the car, I noticed that there were no groceries, but the last time I'd seen her the basket was full. I asked her what happened to the groceries, and she ignored me. But when we got home, the groceries were on the counter in our kitchen. When I said, *I can't believe you left us,* her response was, *I bet you won't ever run off again.* And ever since then, I always thought that if I stepped out of bounds, she would leave me. Today when we all talk about it, we laugh so hard it hurts. But it wasn't funny when I was at a store in Manhattan with Shannon, and I stepped out to take a call and he came out sobbing because he said he hates being left in shops. He was thirty and I was thirty-two.

So when she took us on those long drives to Third Ward, I knew she was capable of leaving us. *Next time you think about getting upset over something you can't have, you better think about this.* She wanted our reference for gratitude to be her own, but how could we relate? We did not in fact know what it meant to be hungry. Or to sleep in a home without windowpanes. Or to have our electricity cut off. We were just children doing what children do, being helpless and endlessly needy. Recently, my mother asked each of her adult children if they ever felt safe in our home, and independently, we each told her *no. But I gave y'all everything.* And what she means is, she bought us everything. But she never gave us herself. Not even a portion of her. She gave us affection, tucked us into bed at night, and told us she loved us, everything Betty Jean hadn't given her. But she shielded us from her heart. I think she gave us all she had to give, all she had left, the parts that hadn't been severed.

· · ·

In order to understand my mother, I have to understand that she was born into a country on fire. In 1956, the year she was born, there was the Montgomery bus boycott over segregation, which mobilized a generation of Black revolutionaries and catalyzed the Civil Rights Movement. When Rosa Parks refused to get up, the majority of Alabama's bus clientele, Black domestic workers, Black women, refused with her. President Eisenhower's administration came to perceive Black activists as terrorists, and Black unity and liberation as a threat to White supremacy, and they regulated it. An undercurrent of fear gave rise to the enforcement of the integration laws, which the government presented as progress. In reality, it tore apart Black communities and led to the streamlining of the Black dollar from the local general store to the larger White-owned markets, but not the other way around. Black businesses collapsed, and White industries rose. This wasn't necessarily the case for Betty Jean because her household received groceries from the local market on loan until payday, so the shopping was kept localized. But community bartering and consideration of circumstances was what was lost when the local markets went dark.

The *Brown v. Board of Education* Supreme Court ruling in 1954 wouldn't be fully enforced in the Houston Independent School District until 1980. Local government ensured that these things take time, with gradual change, or else risk inciting riots. Just as with the end of slavery, which General Granger announced to Black folks in Galveston, Texas, two years after the enforcement of President Lincoln's Emancipation Proclamation of 1863. For nine hundred days, Black people labored under the merciless Texas sun for Texas White folks, unaware that they had been legally freed. Even so, Juneteenth is not what it proclaims to be. The Galveston area plantation owners made an agreement with the Union soldiers that allowed them to keep their slaves for one final crop of cotton. The final harvest. Harvest season is in August, the hottest month of the year, sometimes reaching 120 degrees. The previous season had yielded the highest-grossing cotton the country had ever seen, and the year of Juneteenth promised to be of even greater value. You know, no sense letting all that good cotton go to waste. But the Blacks were expendable, especially if they were calling themselves free. The Union Army agreed, but General Granger had already promised the enslaved that they were free. When they tried to exercise their freedom, the Union Army enforced their confinement to the crop. Guarding the train tracks and ports. These men they had fought alongside in the Civil War were willing to take their lives if they tried to leave that money on the table. Even if you gathered all the Whites in the region, they couldn't pick all that cotton in the August sun and come out alive. This context helps one understand the conception of a viciousness against a people with such significance that, without them, an entire industry collapses.

Black folks took to the water. Traversing the marshlands from Galveston and Brazoria along Buffalo Bayou to Houston. Hiding in trees, sleeping in swamps, and sometimes the homes of abolitionist Quakers along the way. The route was dense with tangled thickets that grow near waterways to prevent flooding. If the mosquitoes didn't eat you alive, the gators would. Makeshift rafts were constructed and left along the banks for others to use at their risk. Going into Houston meant moving against the current. But once you arrive, if you arrive, the bayou leads directly to its center. And those that drowned would find their resting place in the waters, flowing into the Gulf of Mexico, which feeds into the Atlantic, and maybe their souls found their way back to the shores of their native lands. But for those who stay, willing to die en route to freedom, they practiced ways to fix their mouths to call Houston home. Buffalo Bayou leads to the end of Emancipation Trail depositing the journeymen at Freedmen's Town.

I try to imagine climbing out of the water, soaked in the residue of what you've been through, making your way to the church to find your mother and your grandmother and your daughter whom you'd been sold away from years ago. Looking into the faces of other Black people to see if you can find them there. That dimple, that scar, that mole, these fragments you've kept to identify your heart. Hoping they were there, in the Black mecca. Houston had one of the largest populations of Black people due to the numerous plantations in the surrounding counties that made up the Sugar Bowl. And many more migrated from Louisiana and other regions for work. A mother never forgets her child's face, no matter what lines and divots of endurance are etched. I would recognize my daughter by the birthmark on her right leg, the same one I have, the two moles on her right shoulder, placed exactly in the same spot as mine, one flat and the other one raised, dangling as if it might fall away, but it never does. Even if she were grown and old, I would probably see a constellation of freckles gathering along her neck and cheekbones, same as my grandmother, my mother, and me. Once we have children, the women in my family develop these tiny speckles that build like galaxies across our faces as a notation of motherhood. I would never stop searching. And I am sure that I would probably find her living somewhere near water.

In the deliberate design of Houston, the bayous serve as natural safety pools to regulate flooding, and urban design uses its banks to contain Black people and slow their spreading. But even the bayous can change direction. Houston is built atop an aquifer, so when the water doesn't find its way through the bayous, it rises up from the earth, from beneath the city, through the mud and the sediment, and once it meets the sun, the journey has rendered it artesian. An ingenious insistence.

. . .

By the time Betty Jean gave birth to Connie she had settled herself and her two daughters in Third Ward. Betty Jean asked the doctor to tie her tubes, since America's ruinous birth control trials on the women of Puerto Rico hadn't been completed just yet. The White doctor decided that she was too young. Third Ward was all she knew. Never traveling too far outside of the fold between Brays Bayou and Buffalo Bayou. A majority of the city's Black people resided inside the delta-shaped area spanning from Interstate 45 southward toward Brays Bayou just outside of downtown where many of them worked, and east from Almeda Road to the railroad tracks that sealed the area. The Negroes were kept at a contained distance, but not beyond reach. In Third Ward children were told to be inside by the time the streetlights came on or else they may get picked up by some of the White men in white lab coats and taken to the medical center for experiments. Third Ward is adjacent to the renowned Texas Medical Center. Many Black children went missing and it was known around the neighborhood that they were being abducted for the advancement of medical research. Even within the urban landscape, Negroes are never not in service to the nation. Must American innovation always come at the expense of the Black body? Years later, in her book *Medical Apartheid,* Harriet Washington proved that these were not merely urban myths.

For quite some time Connie was the youngest child. The second daughter to Betty Jean. Ever curious, she flirted with the boundaries Betty Jean put in place, the ones reinforced by her older sister *Righthand.* She came into the world beautiful and running her mouth; she learned to speak earlier than any of Betty Jean's other children. Always occupying the center or else disrupting from the margins. Her grandmother May told her she's just like her father. Charismatic and hilarious. Connie asked May to tell her the stories of her father that her mother refused her. "Oh, he was black black black," her grandmother said. "Blue black. But he was always clean clean clean. Sharp! Only Nigga I know wear white from head to toe and don't get nothin on 'em." Connie, too, had an eye for fashion and design. She sketched and sewed her own clothes. It became her space for self-expression and distinction. Whereas her mother and *Righthand* would throw on just about anything. While they were simply making themselves decent, Connie wanted to dazzle. To be seen. To stand out in any way that brought attention to herself. She could do everything well. Dance, run, sing, sew. But she did nothing exceptionally. Perhaps she could have, had anyone taken an interest in the girl. She lost interest easily. Trying new ways to find her way to the center, even if, or perhaps especially when, it meant breaking hearts.

. . .

The twins, *Artemis* and *Apollo,* came along when Connie was five years old. Taking up space. Crying as babies do. While *Righthand* sometimes stayed home from school to help Betty Jean with the twins, Connie rejected her mother's requests to help with any subsequent babies. In these years of endless gestation, Connie became acquainted with rage and held fast to resentment. Betty Jean couldn't understand her exuberance and need for constant attention, which had always come so easily to a reticent Betty Jean. She needed her daughter to fall in line with the rest, but she was a defiant child. Colorism contributed to why Connie couldn't imitate her mother's manner.

Connie saw nothing of herself in her mother. They were incompatible. As a girl she couldn't comprehend what she saw in her mother as complacency. Blamed Betty Jean for her father's absence. Over time, the yearning she had for her father faded into refusal. No longer allowing herself to think about if he had her tiny but mighty ears. Her long narrow fingers and wide stubby toes. No more. She resigned, *If he doesn't think of me, why should I think of him?* But he always lingered there on the edge of memory. A phantom upon whom she could project her fantasies. A blank canvas. Maybe he was a businessman who made millions in gold in California and one day he would come to claim his heir. She had to have inherited her ambition from someplace. Maybe he was a model in magazines, and she would see him one day and know right away that it was her father. Tall, dark, and impossibly thin with a bright smile like her own. As long as he wasn't there, she could have her ghost. He could be anything. And since

Betty Jean's children had different fathers, it was something, perhaps the only thing, she could hold as her own. My mother would never allow herself to say it, but she never stopped searching for her father. Looking for him in the face of every man she ever met.

thirteen

Maybe this age is cursed for girls in my family. Or maybe all girls. When Betty Jean was thirteen her grandmother Rose died. When I turned thirteen my father left home. When my daughter was thirteen her father disappeared. For my mother, she was thirteen when she first encountered the culture of Whiteness.

When Connie was thirteen, Betty Jean purchased *50 10* with the man she was living with on Beulah Street, *Mr. Pepper*. The man was a deacon at the small church next door and had deviant thoughts that arose as he watched Betty Jean's girls playing in the yard unattended. Betty Jean came home one day to their shotgun home with an uncharacteristic buoyancy. She announced that they were moving into their own home and they wouldn't need to move from place to place any longer. When Betty Jean and the deacon and the eight children journeyed fifteen minutes south, down Scott Street across Brays Bayou, past Loop 610, they arrived in South Park to a single-story yellow house with a lush green lawn shaded by two grand live oak trees with a tall gas lamp that flickered in the middle of the yard in the evenings. The yellow was soft and warm like a freshly laid egg from a young hen. South Park was a post–World War II middle-class White suburb of mostly veterans and their wives who kept their yards pristine as a concealer for the mayhem of tending to men intimate with death. The streets are commemorations for war generals. South

Park was already a grief grounds when Betty Jean moved in; who knows what those walls held before her family arrived. *50 10* is on a street named after the commander of the Flying Tigers squadron, known for the shark face painted on their fighter jets that attacked Japan after Pearl Harbor. The entire block was White then, but after Betty Jean and her eight children moved in, it would only be a few years before they were all gone, except that one old lady too tired to join the flock in flight.

My mother didn't want to leave Ryan Middle School in Third Ward to attend Hartman in South Park. Segregation had been slowly spreading across the city. Black students in Third Ward had been forced to break their ties to friends, teachers, and the communities that watched over them, while their mothers and grandmothers worked, to attend White schools in other neighborhoods. Never the other way around. The best Black teachers were placed in White schools. As Black families and networks splintered, such "progress" in Texas only shored up segregation. When Black children trickled in, White people relocated beyond the city limits, outside the reach of public transportation and proximity to government-funded housing. A most peculiar migration of birds.

In South Park, my mother was the only of her siblings in middle school, and therefore she was a lone Black spot in the class photograph of White faces. As a child of the midnight man, Connie began to recognize herself as *other* in ways that she never had in Third Ward. The contrast of her darkness in proximity to the paleness of her classmates and teachers became a place of fascination. Blackness is not the absence of light but rather the complete absorption of it. It creates mystery, as all that exists inside its depths is largely unseen. A mystery that titillates fantasies for White fear. But perhaps what they fear most is being absorbed by the immensity of Blackness. Enveloped in a darkness as profound and infinite as the galaxy in which we dwell. But in the darkness of Connie's trembling, yet stoic, face *her* fear was misjudged as anger.

She absorbed the influences of her environment, mimicking her White peers in speech and demeanor. She learned to hate herself, her skin, her nose, and the cadence of her speech. Her hair got straighter; her posture more erect. She withheld her breath from her nose to increase her pitch. Besides literature and arithmetic, her most lasting curriculum would be the mastery of imitation. Integration's achievement was in reshaping the American urban landscape by learning Negroes how to live in proximity to their Anglo countrymen by prioritizing their comfort while disregarding their own. Connie found that she could disrupt the depth of her Blackness when she smiled without blinking while holding her breath, to put her White peers at as ease. Priming her for affirmative action, which aided in solidifying her position in America's middle class. So that she may achieve what she'd craved most—exceptionalism. To stand out in some way that identified her as an individual both within her household and beyond.

Connie's pursuit of the privileges afforded by Whiteness only deepened her resentment for Betty Jean and the poverty of her childhood in Third Ward, which superseded all memories of any love or joy that had filled her shotgun house. Or perhaps that love had never existed, at least not in the ways that she yearned for. Is there a greater psychic oppression than learning to imitate the cultural norms of a people who see you as less than human and then going home to hate yourself and your mother for not aligning with those imposed ideals? Feeling yourself so hopelessly far from the center, not realizing that you are your center? Betty Jean had left Elm Grove, Louisiana, to afford her children a chance for a life beyond the cotton fields, but no one could have predicted the price of admission.

As a teenager, shame was becoming too heavy to bear. My mother's experience with integration helped her calculate social equations. She understood that to be successful you had to be able to speak the primary language of our homeland—Whiteness. White-speak is the reason my mother raised me in a predominantly White suburban neighborhood, so that I could speak with fluency what she spent her life rehearsing, and what better way to conceal that past than through the mouth of your child. Where Betty Jean had no interest, Connie's tongue stiffened, and the gulf between them widened. White-speak is not just a language, it's an understanding of pauses, small talk that lives above the surface, its passive aggression and getting comfortable with tasting the blood as you grind your tongue between your teeth without breaking eye contact. It's laughing in a register that doesn't reach beneath your upper respiratory tract. It's refraining from using your hands and projecting but not shouting. It's only nuclear family and not extended. It's a lot but not too much. It's boisterous and subtle. It's keeping quiet and not reacting while Mr. Charlie touches your thigh under the table and Mrs. Ann notices and politely excuses herself for the ladies' room. It's quid pro quo not blackmail. It's "Sure, no problem, Tom," when in fact there is a very big problem, Tom.

But at thirteen my mother couldn't get her tongue to do what she wanted, more still she'd never be lighter skinned. At thirteen, her place in the social hierarchy of America was revealed to her, and she saw no way up. She understood that she didn't just come from the bottom, she *was* the bottom. Discouraged and flattened further by the integrated classroom, Connie dropped out in middle school. Connie walked to the bus stop as if she were going to school each morning but stopped short of the door. School had been her escape and now she sat at home while her siblings were in school and her mother away at work. She had never been home alone, there was always someone. When the school called *50 10* to report her absence, she took the calls as Betty Jean. It was not the first time she'd mimicked her mother's voice to get out of trouble. In her hopelessness, her mouth became even more unbearable for Betty Jean, but Connie had nothing to lose or look forward to, so she took the beatings and absorbed the impact, strengthening her endurance with every blow. By this time, Betty Jean had given birth to all eleven children, eight of them living at home and sharing one room, the girls had one bed and the boys had one bed. It would be weeks before a letter reached home notifying Betty Jean of Connie's absence. But she couldn't miss work, with all those mouths to feed, to make sure little Connie was getting on the bus, and there was no threat persuasive enough to force her to return to school and sit beside White students who made her feel like less than nothing.

May, who still lived on Beulah Street in Third Ward, took off work one day to go and speak with her granddaughter. And my mother can still recite her words to this day. Out of both love and fear she said, *Look here, you ol' Nigga gal, that's my daughter you disrespecting, and when you hurt her, you hurt me.* Only in that moment did it become clear to little Connie that her mother was someone's daughter. That her mother was the only daughter of the only person who she felt loved her. That May loved her because of Betty Jean, not in spite of her. She had perceived her grandmother's judgment of her daughter's choices to mean that she, too, hated Betty Jean. But of course, to children, there is only love and hate. It is only as we grow that we learn about the in-between parts, and we spend our lives in search of ways to name them.

Ultimately, May took Connie to live with her, in hopes of saving her. Both Betty Jean and May saw something worth salvaging in the midnight girl.

At the time, May was living with her son, *Brother,* in a fourplex on the other end of Beulah Street from where Betty Jean had lived. May was married once upon a time, but they divorced after he too succumbed to Betty Jean's beauty. He'd tried to repress his urge to invite his wife's daughter to bed, but he couldn't control it any more than a man can restrain a sneeze in spring. He knew it was wrong, but when confronted, all he could muster was, *I'm a man, May.* As my mother says, *A man, is a man, is a man is a man.* May left him and lived with Betty Jean until she was found passed out between the bed and the window of the White folks' house that she tended to. They were executives at Red Cross and often gave May clothes and food to take to the swelling home. May was upset that morning because Betty Jean stayed out all night with somebody's son, while May was home keeping the kids. When the sun rose and Betty Jean still wasn't home, May grew distressed in deciding between getting to work on time or leaving the small children home alone. That morning May shouted while Betty Jean stood still. Seemingly without regret. Before the sun reached its peak, May had passed out, and at the White folks' house, no less. That's when *Brother* brought May to live with him. The only dependable man that May ever knew was the one she had birthed. He never married, had one daughter with a sex worker from The Lark, and played house with other men's wives. But he went to work, provided for his daughter, and took care of his mama; he was known as *a good man.*

Brother worked in the copy room at Xerox downtown. He went to work in suits while his sister Betty Jean wore uniforms and hairnets. But he had been able to graduate high school, while she was forced to drop out. He disapproved of his sister's life-style choices, and as a result spoke sparingly to my mother while she lived with him. He spoke only to issue commands and repri-mands. He had decided quite early on, as many others had, that because of the circumstances in which little Connie was born, my mother's life would never amount to much and therefore wasn't worthy of care. As if doting on a Black child were such a nui-sance you need not invest if a return isn't promised. And nothing is promised in Black life, not even life itself. To "give" love isn't accurate, the practice is actually one of self-preservation. To love is to restore oneself, like the regeneration of cells in the body, and so it is also an act of self-love to love on somebody. The choice to withhold is a slow slitting of the wrist. In refusal of this needful verity, we discover more ways to die.

· · ·

Every night for five years little Connie slept alongside May and shared parts of herself that had been buried so deep, they were unseen, even to her. In that small sacred space, she was turned inside out. No one asked little Connie how she felt. Her interiority.

It was there, lying next to her grandmother, that Connie learned how to dream. This is the power of love, even when provided a mere morsel, it breaks you wide open, allowing a little light in. Her grandmother saved her life. Or rather, told her she had one to live. And later, when May was dying with dementia, Connie brought her to live in our home. I would stand outside the French doors of the study that became May's bedroom and watch them. My mother brought in a medical bed, hired a nurse to be with May while she was at work, and purchased a new television so she could watch her stories. She sang to settle her while she pressed warm water into her skin each night with a sponge, carefully lifting her swollen limbs to moisturize them with lotions and oils. I met a version of my mother that I had never encountered. She was tender and gentle and endlessly patient. Each night Mama Connie curled up into the hospital bed beside her grandmother, whispering memories into her ear that May had forgotten. Reminding her that she had lived a life. A simple but no less glorious one. They laughed without shame. Without covering their mouths to muffle the sounds. It was as if they were both girls again. Or girls that they had never been allowed to be. My mother never loved nor cared for anyone the way she cared for her grandmother in her final days. She never allowed anyone to love her the way May loved her. Not even her children. In that bed, between them, was a sacred tethering that transcended realms.

Her grandmother was the first person to tell her that she was loved, not for anything in particular that she had done. Not conditionally. Just for being. The bedroom they shared on Beulah Street, when she was thirteen years old, was the first place Connie had ever felt safe, where she learned to release the breath she held in her chest. Just one room, and it wasn't even her own, where she could begin imagining a life beyond the preoccupation of surviving the day. But just beyond the bedroom door was the threat to all that she had come to hold dear. Upon moving in, *Brother* told her she had until graduation day to stay with them, and after that she would need to find another place to live. As a girl, there was not much room for thinking of the future, the consideration of immediate threats were prioritized. A survival instinct that she never learned to dismantle. This threat loomed. Little Connie didn't want much, just to be a wife, a mother, to escape the uncertainty of poverty, and most of all, above all else, *power.* Everywhere she has ever been, it was clear that she wasn't welcome, not to say that this didn't bother her, but she learned how to endure. Like scar tissue, the sensation is there upon contact, but it ceases to register in the brain as pain.

10

Bobby & Connie

CONNIE AND BOBBY AT PROM AND AS NEWLYWEDS.
THEN LATER, CONNIE IN HOUSTON AND BOBBY IN ALASKA.

Even though Connie lived in Third Ward on Beulah Street with May, zoning laws didn't allow her to attend Jack Yates High School, which was only a few blocks away. She was forced to attend school where her legal guardian resided, thus she had to take two city buses to school each morning. And so the stars aligned. It was at Jones High School in South Park that Connie met the fair-skinned young man from a middle-class family who became my father. South Park was tipping toward a Black majority in the few years since she moved in with May and *Brother*. In the boys' basketball locker room, this light-skinned fella heard that Connie was saving herself for marriage. She felt the preservation of her chastity was the only leverage within her control; it also was a way to distinguish herself from her mother. Connie's boyfriend at the time, a boy called *Bear*, for his big brown burly frame, bragged about how he would be the one to convince her to allow him *inside*. *Lightskin* saw this as a challenge. After finding out where Connie lived in Third Ward, he shows up on Beulah Street, and just as Connie and her grandmother May descended the stairs of their apartment, there he was. Squinting up at them, standing beside his brand-new car, with the sun shining on his face, he smiled. He asked the midnight girl to go out with him. He introduced himself as Bobby but May called him *Sunshine*.

His family was entrepreneurial and had what appeared to be everything that Connie wanted: a home that they owned, cars, and a garden full of roses. He had three brothers and a room of his own, while she shared a bed with her grandmother. His clothes were tailored, while she made hers on the sewing machine May had given her. She rode the bus and could walk seventeen miles without complaint. He wooed her when he pulled up, starched down, in his white 1974 Monte Carlo they called Ghost. The two were rarely seen apart. And everyone seemed to sing their names together as one—*Bobby-n-Connie*.

At eighteen, and saving herself for marriage, Connie refused to go back to her mother's house, so she married *Sunshine* and gave birth to his son *Junior* within a year. Unlike her mother at that age, she turned to a man for salvation. *Sunshine* was my mother's way out, a gateway toward White ideals and fair-skinned children who she wouldn't allow to suffer as she had. They'd have to find new ways to suffer. *Sunshine* was fickle and unreliable, but he made up for what he lacked in dependability with quick-witted charisma. He could hold his own in any room, while Connie was just glad to get in the door. She was a quick study. Connie and Bobby could captivate any audience to will their way into wherever they wanted to be. Bobby says Connie is the one true love of his life, and even though I believe the same is true for my mother, her pride won't allow her to utter the words. When I asked Connie why she married Bobby, she said it was her only way out. When I asked Bobby, he said they both wanted the same thing and began rubbing his fingers together, prosperity at any cost. Not unlike Betty Jean, Connie saw men as tools, disposing of them when they were no longer of value. She wanted to prove her mother wrong. Hoping that she could one day say to her, *Not all men, Mama.*

Bobby says he remembers being in bed beside my mother in an apartment they rented on Broadway and watching her belly rise and fall in her sleep. As the belly grew so did his anxiety. He knew he needed to make money, and he knew how to hit licks, but he wanted clean money, consistent money, so he could stay out of jail. Shortly after their nuptials, while Connie was still pregnant, Bobby took a job working offshore for an oil company headquartered in Houston but drilling off the coast of Alaska. Beside Americans and Russians alike, he worked three months in the Arctic and one month off. It was during this time that he met masculine men with feminine names and would give his only daughter a Russian name years later. He began reading Russian novels and writing home to Connie suggesting literature and food to try. He wrote to her about the northern lights and the midnight sun. He begged her to come. Connie never wrote back and never read those novels, and certainly never went to Alaska. She became threatened by the man he was becoming while away from her. She still held those insecurities her older sister, *Right-hand*, presented her with when she told her she wasn't one of the smart sisters. Neither of my parents even considered attending university, but they were both clever. Bobby is guided by curiosity, Connie, by suspicion. Nevertheless, they were both seekers.

He returned home infrequently, but they met in Los Angeles as a middle ground. Attended Lakers games back when Jerry West was the coach. Back when the game had the elegance of Kareem levitating toward the goal, players could wear gold chains on the court, and Kermit Washington could break Rudy T's jaw and still have a job. It was a time of not-so-subtle Black visibility. The restaurants that Bobby discovered as his culinary interests expanded included white tablecloths. Connie frowned and refused to try the food that she couldn't pronounce. She felt he was losing his way in Alaska, or rather, losing her way. These are the complications with striving, there is an attempt toward a fictional concept of becoming *better*, but along the journey of idealized ascendance, it often only intensifies self-hate. Bobby grew frustrated with her for not allowing him to explore without criticism. He played with his tone and accent a bit, switched up the style, trying on new ways of being. She thought, how could he love these beige places and still love her at the same time? She feared she would be left behind if he grew too quickly. He already had a head start on her, which she both admired and resented. But a phrase that she often recites is, *If you stick around long enough, the shit will flip.*

· · ·

What Bobby and Connie had in common was that they were both the golden children of their respective families. The ones that got out and stayed up. Bobby had come from a middle-class family plagued by mental health disorders that were exacerbated by addiction. After the war ended, many soldiers came home hooked on heroin, and his older brother's friends had all been drafted so he got caught up in the rapture. Another of his brothers followed suit. And the youngest one was too cute to stay out of trouble. At one point early in my parents' marriage, Bobby was the only one of his brothers not in prison. He bailed out his brothers, put money on their books, paid for collect calls, raised their children beside his own, played Santa for them, soothed his mother as she wept and promised her that he would never go to prison. He was the second of four boys, and the lightest-skinned one too. He wasn't exceptional, but he was more palatable. Less likely to be read as suspicious. He did drugs, sold drugs, and all the other things his brothers were doing in the '70s. Well, except for the youngest son, who was notably the most handsome, who pursued White women as lovers and used them to knock on the doors of homes in River Oaks, Houston's wealthiest neighborhood. The White folks would see a White girl through the peephole and open the door without hesitation. Meanwhile, my uncle was around back robbing them blind. There were a few murders involved. No one really talks about that, though. He has been in prison since I was born. I only know his face from the high-school graduation photo of him that hung on my paternal grandparents' living-room wall, beside one of my great-grandmother with long braids as white as cotton resting heavy on either side of her head and a portrait of Martin Luther King Jr. The photo suspended my uncle in time, preserving him. When I asked my grandmother, "Who is that?," she always said, "He's a *bad* man."

My father was cunning and there is no doubt that his fair skin is partially what kept him out of prison. His father was also a hustler and entrepreneur, but his main gig was being the personal driver for the CEO and founder of Delta Airlines, whom he'd met in Bryan, Texas, where his people were from. His father's mother with the white braids was a hustler too. She was Native American and Black and was the first Negro woman to open a bar in Freedmen's Town. She was also the first to open a restaurant in Bryan. My father came from a long line of entrepreneurs who'd skirt the lines of legality in pursuit of stability. And due to the hurdles put in place to keep Black folks out, this is often the only way.

Bobby was no different. And Connie clung to him, absorbing. She is the type of person you only need to teach once, a master of mimicry. Her taste has been shaped by the palatability of White folks. By her desire for couth and acceptance. But she can't really tell you who *she* is. When asked what she likes, what her dreams are, she turns to the shadows of her suffering: *I always just wanted to survive.*

They shared an unshakable will and the gift of discernment. But they both bore their siblings' burdens on their backs. Both the second in line so they didn't feel the pressures of being the eldest, not in the middle, but also without the reckless selfishness that being the youngest brings.

As Connie learned new ways of life, she felt beholden to report back to *50 10* to share her discoveries. One of her first jobs was at the post office downtown, where the women came to work dressed to the nines before changing into their uniforms. My mother learned about designer clothing and dental insurance. She brought items back to *50 10* and took her sisters and her mother to their first dental appointments. Betty Jean had lost her front teeth; the babies stripped them. Cracked, chipped, and then clean out from the gums. Mama Connie bought her mother new teeth. She was ashamed to see her mother smile in public, but Betty Jean had none and didn't even bother to cover her mouth. Connie knew how to smell shame and exploit it with her sisters. She was also considerate and quick to share everything she knew. There takes a certain level of understanding to be able to exploit others. She paid for abortions and birth control pills, she helped hide cars in our garage so they weren't repo'd. She tried to talk her sisters out of marrying broke and broken men.

This understanding of familial obligation was what kept Bobby and Connie together for so long. They became a kind of hero duo. They understood that success meant nothing if everyone else is still struggling.

In 1982, on one of their trips to Los Angeles, during one of Bobby's offshore breaks, Connie landed at LAX and *Sunshine* was missing. He had gotten drunk, or high, or crossfaded at a party the night before and missed his flight to LA. Connie depended on her husband when they traveled because she had no experience, and he had been traveling since boyhood to visit family that had migrated North. Vulnerability made her angry. Connie's courage is tested when she is in foreign places. When you have lived among people with nothing to lose, you see the depths to which humans are forced to sink to survive, which made her suspicious of everyone and cautious of journeying into new places alone. She found a pay phone and called Betty Jean at *50 10*. Anytime anyone is in trouble they can call *50 10*. Someone is always home, and the number hasn't changed in forty years. The precarity of everyone's lives in the family meant that no one lived anywhere for very long, but *50 10* is headquarters. All of her kids, and grandkids, and even the men who had been married into the family call *50 10* in an emergency. If you have one phone call, one quarter, you call *50 10*. Betty Jean gave Connie the phone number of her cousin Shell who had migrated to LA from Elm Grove. It didn't matter that Shell had never met Connie, or that she hadn't seen Betty Jean since their days harvesting cotton beside each other, she picked Connie up from LAX.

Gone had been living in LA for a few years and had cut all communication with the family back in Houston, so Connie had no way to contact her. *Gone* had left Houston with some man she went to church with growing up in Sunnyside. She had two baby girls in tow, from two other men. The first baby was made with a man *Gone* met at a club in Houston called Change of Pace. The second was a railroad man Connie had introduced her to.

"I told her to marry that man, 'cause he had good benefits and a pension, and she went and got knocked up," Connie said with thinly veiled disappointment.

"I told her I would pay for the abortion, and she started saying something about the Lord. I told her Jesus wasn't gone put food in them kids' mouths."

Every story my mother recounts about her siblings includes

her as a central character trying to save them from themselves. Desperately hoping someone will come and save her right back.

Gone's second girl was fathered by a married man who was separated from his wife and cheating on *Gone* with his cousin. When his cousin found out *Gone* was pregnant, she shot him dead at the Fourth of July cookout. Come to find out the cousin was pregnant too. Their children were born one month apart. My mother often says of her sister, "If it wasn't for bad luck, she wouldn't have no luck at all." *Gone* went to church for guidance and found a man from her past. He was *the preacher's son*. She had grown up across the street from him, so in some ways it was a return to the darkness of her girlhood. Her adoptive parents had both died and she inherited the house she'd grown up in, but *the preacher's son* convinced her to sell it. Told her that they'd move west, buy a house near the beach, and be a family with her two girls. *The preacher's son* promised to marry her once they moved to LA. They moved into a rental, a duplex. He said it would only be temporary. The other unit was occupied by the preacher's wife, who was on the run from the church—and her husband—to start a new life with her girlfriend. Nothing was quite like what he said it would be when they arrived.

When *Gone* moved to LA, Shell helped her get settled and even kept the girls a few times while *Gone* looked for work. Then one day the line was disconnected. No one could get in contact with *Gone*. There was growing concern back home at *50 10*.

So, while she was in LA, Connie asked Shell if she knew where *Gone* was living. Shell lowered her eyes and nodded. So much communication between Black women lies between the words. My mother asked Shell to take her to her sister.

Gone lived in a small unremarkable building that was falling apart on the outside. It was the middle of the day and the blinds were shut. Shell waited in the car. My mother knocked and knocked, no one answered. She kept knocking still. She saw the blinds rattle.

"I see you!" my mother shouted. "Open up this door."

This is typically how Mama Connie pushes past her siblings'

boundaries. In her heart, she has good intentions, she simply believes that she knows what's best for them. And they yield to her.

Gone cracked the door, a slice of light shone down her face. My mother pushed the door open enough to slide in and hug her sister, who stood like stone in her embrace.

"Whatchu doing here, Connie?"

Her younger sister had the kind of terror in her eyes that my mother remembers from visiting her at the home of the family who had adopted her. Swollen sullen eyes that said she had put something between herself and the world. Eyes that said there were secrets to be kept. Mama Connie is the woman who shows up and uses her power to expose and ignite. My mother has never been afraid of the flames, as long as she's doing the inciting.

"Well, hello to you too." Connie could sense that something wasn't right in the house but didn't want to show it, so she smiled brighter and widened her eyes, elevated her octave.

Looking back over her shoulder, *Gone* whispered, "Whatchu doing here?"

The preacher's son sauntered out in loungewear. My mother embraced him. Letting him know that she recognized his power and surrendering her own. Connie's ability to read a room is uncanny. "Meek with sneaky eyes," she later described him to me. "You know what I'm talking about. The type to throw a rock and hide the hand." My mother knew *the preacher's son* from Houston. "He wasn't shit then and he ain't shit now." She was disappointed by her sister's lack of judgment and didn't refrain from communicating this. She was resigned to the fact that *Gone* was just like Betty Jean. But she wasn't. *Gone* was never in pursuit of power like Betty Jean and Mama Connie. She was in pursuit of love, even if it came at the end of a lash. Mama Connie never pursued anything without quantifiable benefits. My mother could never see herself in her mother. But I saw their wills as parallel.

Ever perceptive, my mother used her charm to disarm *the preacher's son*. She was determined to find out what was going on with her sister, but more important, her nieces. She saw her sister as a lost cause, "but the babies," she'd say, "they didn't ask to be brought into this world, they deserve a shot at life." This was her way of providing for young girls in our family what she had always hoped someone would have provided for her. Just a chance.

Connie directed her attention to *the preacher's son*. She complimented him. She asked about his mother. She made him feel like a man while her sister stood looking at her feet. After carefully and woefully communicating her circumstances, my mother asked to stay the night. Only then were *Gone*'s girls allowed to come from the back where the bedrooms were. The girls ran to my mother, one on each leg. My mother reserves her deepest affection for children and animals, the only creatures she knows to be true.

When she tells me this story, my mother can never quite recall what was in the home, only what wasn't. All the things that make a house a home were absent. There was no table to gather around. The type of place where they stood over the kitchen sink to eat. There were no photographs as evidence of past lives. A small sunken-in sofa too tiny to hold them all at once was paired with TV trays beside it. She only remembers the place being an array of objects that looked scavenged. There were no children's toys on the floor or laughter in the air. Only the hot dry musk of bodies barely hanging on.

While my mother half listened to his bullshit about how he was looking for work and how California was superior to Texas, she observed her sister and her nieces. The girls were around five and seven years old, but they moved like older children. Like she and her siblings had. They took care of themselves mostly and were quiet, careful, and jumpy. The younger one had a gash on her face. When my mother touched it gently, the girls both looked to him. The older one spoke up to say her sister had fallen while they were playing. *Gone* carried a Bible through the house and recited scriptures without context. She talked about Jesus and how she wasn't worthy of his grace.

My mother asked to use the phone, the man pulled a cordless from the pocket of his pants. She called my father in Alaska, shared the address, and, through their own coded language, alerted him that there was some shit going down at her sister's house. If she spoke in a high-pitched tone with only positivity to share, this was a signal to my father that something was off-key and she couldn't speak openly, but that he should get to LA as fast as he could. She had no fear of *the preacher's son* for she was certain that he was a coward. "Oh, I wasn't bit more bothered 'bout him. They know who to mess with. And it ain't never been me. 'Cause I'll tell it." While many of her sisters found solace in silence, my mother learned early that her power was in speaking out, and loudly. Once while visiting a neighbor, who was also Betty Jean's first cousin, my mother was pushed down on the couch and straddled. He laughed and told her to undress. She screamed for help and didn't stop, even after he tried to hush her. He relented and pushed her out of the house telling her he was only playing with her all along. She told him that she was telling everybody. And she did. He never bothered her again. Years later, when my mother was grown, he was imprisoned for impregnating his adolescent niece. To which my mother shook her head and said, *I told y'all he wasn't right.* Instinctually, she understood that the loud are less likely to be preyed upon. She couldn't imagine that there were mothers who would muffle the screams of their daughters.

When my mother asked *the preacher's son* if she and *Gone* could walk and get pizza for the girls for dinner, this was Connie's way of getting her sister alone. Before they could clear the corner my mother interrogated her sister.

"The hell going on over here?"

Gone looked over her shoulder before responding, "Connie, all I can say is that Jesus provides."

"Girl . . . cut the Bible bullshit."

"I know the Lord brought you here." *Gone* went on quoting scripture with her Bible tucked to her chest as they walked. My mother kept trying to get through to her, but she could see that there was a vacancy. "There was nobody home."

After having dinner my mother helped prepare the girls for

bed. She ran them a warm bath with bubbles using kitchen dish soap. She sat on the floor beside the tub as they splashed. It was there, in the water, once the suds started to settle, that the tiny wounded back of the younger sister was revealed. Covered in intersecting welts. Some scabbed, some so ripe. Her body was a map of all they had endured.

My mother slept between the two girls that night in the bed they shared. She held the younger one and wept silently under the moonlight. When she asked the older girl if the man she lived with was nice to her, she told my mother of the things *he* always did to her. *He,* the man who stayed home with the girls each day when *Gone* went off to work. In a faint whisper, she told my mother that *the preacher's wife,* who lived next door with her girlfriend, had instructed the eldest girl not to speak to anyone about what was going on in their home. *What happens in your house stays in your house.*

My mother was upset to find my father outside the next day in a two-seater convertible to pick her up. She usually loved the flashy, but not during a crisis. My mother is at her best during a crisis. It's where she's most comfortable. When the stakes are high, her strategy is unparalleled. If my life was on the line and I had one phone call, I would call her every time. At the hotel room, Bobby held his wife while she cried and shared what she'd discovered. Then she cleared the tears and they quickly devised a plan. A few hours later, knowing her sister would be away at work, my mother drove back to the duplex. *The preacher's son* opened the door in a bathrobe with nothing underneath. He slowly caressed the coils on his exposed chest as he greeted her. I think perhaps in another life, my mother could have been an actor. She smiled through her disgust, and asked *the preacher's son* if she could take the girls for ice cream. He hesitated. My mother kept smiling and rambling to the girls about how much fun they were going to have. He stuttered. Then, betraying his judgment, he agreed. With her hands on her knees, my mother gave her greatest performance, "Who wants to go get ice cream? I'll race you to the car."

My father was waiting at the street corner, pacing and smoking a cigarette. "Uncle Bobby," they screamed in unison when they spotted him. They drove directly to LAX, four deep in a two-seater, with the girls wearing mismatched shoes and the clothes they had slept in. My mother told the girls they were going to get ice cream at Granny's house. My father dropped them at LAX and he stayed back. At the airport my mother stopped at the same pay phone she had used to call Betty Jean when she arrived in LA.

"Mama, I got 'em."

All the sisters were waiting for them when they arrived at *50 10*. They embraced the girls, braided their hair, and greased their scalps. A bed was placed in the middle of the living room for them to sleep on comfortably. The women never asked the girls what they had been through, but with hot plates and warm baths, they told them that they were safe.

There were many different conversations happening at once. The living room where they gathered was a symphony of sounds with an undercurrent of subdued grief. When the phone rang, the room fell silent. If they were all there, they knew there was only one person who could be calling.

Betty Jean answered in her slow drawl.

"Connie got my kids?"

"They here," Betty Jean confirmed.

"I knew the Lord sent Connie to save my girls. Praise Jesus. Praise Jesus. Praise Jesus," *Gone* chanted before she was cut off by her mother.

"You just sat there and let that man hurt these babies?" Betty Jean never saying more than she must. Incapable of performing the way Connie can. And she doesn't repeat herself.

Gone was silent.

It was weeks before *Gone* showed up at *50 10* with a swollen eye trying to take the girls back to LA. Betty Jean told *Gone* that *he was going to have to come on over here and get 'em himself. And I got something for him when he get here.*

The women at *50 10* decided that the girls would stay there and go to school at Bastian Elementary in South Park. Betty Jean's girls came daily, making sure they were fed and clothed and protected. Betty Jean was still working as a janitor at the police station downtown, where she was beloved by the city's first Black police chief, Lee P. Brown. Like my grandmother, he had come from a sharecropping family in the South. Prior to Houston, he was the public safety commissioner in Atlanta where he led the investigation of the Atlanta child murders case where twenty-eight Black boys were abducted and murdered between 1979 and 1981. Two years of Black boys and a few girls disappearing, and one man was convicted, but only for a few of the murders. Brown was aware of how politics get in the way of justice for Black children. He knew the police culture of clandestine vengeance.

Betty Jean kept a framed photo of Brown in the living room of *50 10*, on which he had written, "Ms. Betty, you are one of a kind. I am thankful for your friendship." Betty Jean barely said two words most of the time, but was never invisible, because her pride took up space in a way that made the weak uncomfortable but empowered the brave. Working with Brown at the police station was the first time that Betty Jean was in proximity to a powerful Black political figure. And perhaps she wanted to make up for all the ways that she couldn't protect her girls in the past. But in some ways it was already too late, the cycle had begun and was gaining momentum.

Not long after they'd arrived in Houston, Betty Jean confided in Brown about the abuse the girls endured, but the Houston police had no jurisdiction in California. However, after a series of interrogations with the older girl, they soon discovered that the abuse had begun in Texas, before they relocated to LA. A warrant was drafted for *the preacher's son*'s arrest and extradition to Houston. But there was no justice, *Gone* dropped the charges, as their legal guardian, stating that she just wanted her girls to move on and stop having to relive the past through testimony. She figured that the girls were young enough to let the memories dissolve into their bodies. That maybe at five and seven there was still hope for them to forget. Even at their smallest, Black girls are seen as a dumping ground. A place to exorcise sexual fantasy without consequence, a practice as old as the nation itself.

Without the girls, *Gone* was of no use to *the preacher's son*. She came back to *50 10* and it was never spoken about again, at least not collectively. Betty Jean didn't allow *Gone* to be alone with her daughters for years. *Gone* went to live with *Righthand*. And like any wound left untreated, the infection spreads. I wasn't born yet, but upon arrival, I just fell into the fold.

· · ·

These kinds of stories kept my parents together. Stories of how great they were as partners. Like superheroes, the saviors of their families. Most of the time it involved a man fighting one of the sisters and my father would be called, and he'd show up with one of his guns that he kept under the mattress, under the seat of his car, or in the drawer of his desk. Or if one of his brothers had stolen another family member's belongings and pawned it, my father hunted down the item while my mother rode shotgun. When the FBI was looking for my father's brother, my parents may or may not have driven him to the country to lay low. They had bail money, abortion money, they knew attorneys and police officers, big men, bad men, and mechanics who could put a transmission in your car in the front of the shop and heal your chronic pain with acupuncture in the back. My mother played the bad cop. Her tongue was so swift and sharp that sometimes it takes a moment to realize you're bleeding. She was born with perfectly straight white teeth, but even with her wide-mouthed smile, she was terrifying, but the light behind her wide eyes beckons you closer. Long and lean with the same smooth skin color all over. My father was the good cop, the one with the jokes and end-less chatter. Speaking at such a pace that you don't have much time to process or disengage from his compliments, charm, and pseudo-compassion. He had a way of being approachable but was the type of cool that you can only have when people believe you keep the heater on you at all times. The embodiment of Tupac's "I ain't a killer but don't push me." They had grown up together and were rhythmically in sync. Down like two flat tires. Keeper of each other's secrets. Sometimes my father says my mother was skittish, he'd have to talk her into doing things that weren't always necessarily legal. She didn't need much convincing, if it involved helping her family or capital gain. They were both street smart and knew how to read and dissect a situation without saying a word to each other. However, they did not think that anyone else could read them in the same way. And most couldn't. Connie and Bobby gloated about this to their children. They fought furiously in the car on the way to a family function, but once inside they'd be laughing and feeding each other. I remember seeing my mother whisper to him in the middle of a party through clenched teeth, "Get your filthy hand off me." And then I'd see my father kiss her and they'd laugh. This was confusing to me as a child. I remember wishing they could keep the act going when we got home. But on the car ride home, they returned to shouting and shaming. In the middle of bickering, they would turn to the backseat and tell us, *You see how we did that? Nobody knew we were upset with each other, that's how you gotta do it. Don't let people know your business.* But the people were our family members, and my parents were always in their business. Occasionally they found such pleasure in their performance that they forgot to fight on the way home. Sometimes they had pretended so well, that their love for each other was reignited and I would put my ear to the door of their bedroom to listen in on their passion. It reminds me of a time when I was speaking about my depression to one of my professors, a fellow melancholy Black woman writer, who said that sometimes you can just fake laugh and it works the same muscles.

When my parents fought, it usually began with my mother asking a question my father didn't want to answer. He was, and still is, the type of man who seems like he is hiding something behind his smile. And even if you know he's lying, there is something sedative about the way he looks into you, as if in that moment, you have every part of him. His eyes settle on yours with a curiosity void of judgment. Like he can see what others will walk right past without notice. The beauty that he acknowledges in you is the beauty you love most about yourself, the beauty seldom seen. What others criticize, he compliments as quirky and singular. When you speak to him, somehow you seem more clever, more funny, more free. He's entirely present and there is nowhere else he'd rather be. This is what I adored about him most as a girl, his attentiveness. And even though he wasn't around as much as my mother, his intense regard for me in those moments was more intimate than most of the time I spent with my mother, because she was always having to perform many tasks at once. I imagine that this is why my mother loved him as a sixteen-year-old girl. Because his heedful gaze reminded her of the way that her grandmother prioritized her. But once my father is out of your sight, he's gone. He's not the kind of man that can be contained, you must let him go and only hope that he returns to you. He doesn't seem to linger too much on what he left behind. One can't help but assume that wherever he's flown away to, he is making some other woman feel like she is all that matters to him in the world.

· · ·

Shortly after my mother returned home with the girls from LA, my parents divorced. My father came back home less and less. My mother says he was living with another woman in Alaska, and she's probably right, he'll never admit it, but she knows that man better than her own hand. He was young and making more money than he had ever seen, and he stopped sending it home to my mother. The ultimate betrayal. For my mother, infidelity could be tolerated, but giving money to another woman and not sending it home to your wife and your son was unforgivable. In the mid-'70s into the early '80s my father decided to stay in Anchorage on his days off work and spend them dancing, doing cocaine and women, and abandoning the family he had committed to back home. He had gone from being his mother's son to being my mother's husband without being forced to grow up. He was a man-child never held accountable for his actions, for he knew that he was my poor Black mother's only way out, so he thought she'd never leave him. Or perhaps he assumed what Betty Jean had predicted, *When you get pregnant they think they own you.* But he had miscalculated my mother's ability to persist without him. Sometimes a baby can awaken a version of a woman that was previously latent. By the time he came home to Houston, *Junior* was already calling some other man Daddy.

Mama Connie was forced to move to *50 10* temporarily. She didn't have time to grieve her husband, she had a son to raise. Unresolved anger can be useful. But this time she wouldn't wait on a man to save her, she got a job working at the post office downtown, only a few blocks from where her mother worked as a janitor at the police department. Like Betty Jean, she came to understand that a man is no place to build a home. But she still needed to figure out how to raise one.

Iberia Hampton

IBERIA AND FRED HAMPTON, 1957

Iberia always said her youngest son talked too much. She feared what might happen to Fred when she sent him South to visit his grandparents in Haynesville, Louisiana. Whenever they were down in Claiborne Parish, her son asked why they had to follow the signs that said *Colored* but back home in Chicago the signs didn't exist. She tried to tell him the signs were there all the same. How does one explain to a child the fatuous rules of America as lacking in logic but also to follow them as if life depends on it, but at the same time, that your life is worth fighting for?

Iberia witnessed what happened to little *Bobo* when he went to stay with his kin down in Money, Mississippi, that summer of 1955. Iberia always said he also talked too much. Where she came from, there were consequences for running your mouth. *Bobo* and Mamie lived next door to the Hamptons in Chicago, the men of their respective households worked at the corn-processing plant and Iberia would sometimes babysit the rambunctious boy who was always getting into something or other. *Bobo* was hard-headed, but sweet as pie. Child might say anything, just like her youngest son. He was older than Iberia's boys. Both her son and *Bobo* had lisps, so that's probably why that White woman down in Mississippi fabulated that the child was whistling at her. No boy deserves to be mangled, dragged, and dumped in the Tallahatchie River. Too many rivers in this nation have held our dead.

Iberia didn't attend *Bobo*'s funeral. "I wanted to remember him as the active and saucy kid I babysat." She believed in preserving legacy for a life lived, not for the ways that a Black boy can be killed. And she didn't look at that issue of *Jet*. But she told the story of Emmett Till to Fred and his brother, so they understood the consequences of those signs she knew so well in Louisiana.

Iberia and her husband, Francis, grew up in a town about an hour north of Elm Grove, tending the same land that their great-grandparents had worked as enslaved laborers. Where they were raised to be intimate with the earth. Claim it as their own. Know how to shield the crop from the night creepers, and how to eradicate the soil of invasives. They knew precisely how brutal the summer would be by how soon the forsythia bloomed. They felt that land was more their home than anywhere else. As if they had blossomed from it themselves.

Iberia was the eldest of Eli and Lizzie White's four children. She was as powerful as her name, which feels like a universe all its own. Or that of a great nation. It's possible that she may have been named after the European peninsula, but more probable that her name is in commemoration of Iberia Parish, the soggy region of southeastern Louisiana where the Spanish and French settled along the Gulf Coast. When she migrated to Chicago with her husband, the Northerners called out to the South whenever they addressed her.

Iberia's heart will ever be in Claiborne Parish, but she wanted her children to have a chance at a life and education that she didn't. As a child, she was forced to walk five miles each Sunday to stay with her aunt in town because Black kids weren't provided school buses. On Fridays she walked the five miles back home with her siblings, and the bus driver would pass and intentionally splash them with mud and the kids would spew hate from the windows.

After Iberia birthed all three of their children at Cook County Hospital, she stayed home to take care of them until her youngest, Fred, was school-age. When the time came, she went to work with her husband at the corn-processing plant. That's when the family moved to the suburb of Maywood, just west of the city. Iberia was the union steward at the corn plant that employed mostly Black folks who had migrated to the North. During a five-month strike, Iberia cooked meals for 1,700 employees every day at the union hall. Over those few months, she demonstrated to her children that no individual is more important than the collective.

Fred studied her closely. When he wasn't playing football or his saxophone, he was somewhere talking, reading, or listening to orators like Malcolm X and Martin Luther King Jr. to reproduce their cadence. As a curious teenager, he wondered why each morning at school he was made to pledge allegiance to a nation that had made no promises to him. He made comparisons between his experiences in Chicago and the ones his grandparents told him about during his summers and Easters in Haynesville and began to recognize the patterns.

Iberia believed her youngest son would be a lawyer someday.

After being teased in school for having a *watermelon head,* he learned how to use words as a defense. Iberia taught him that sometimes, you have to teach the people to unlearn the ignorance they inherited. She encouraged him when he spoke up insisting that his high school allow Black girls to be on the homecoming court. And thought it was valuable when he decided to join the youth chapter of the NAACP. But when Fred gathered an interracial group of his peers to march to Maywood city hall demanding the construction of a desegregated swimming pool at the recreation center, she grew concerned. Water has always been a site of great contention in the country. The pools, the fountains, the shorelines. Maywood refused in fear of increasing racial tensions of a newly integrated suburb. Fred was arrested for disturbing the peace, his own was never promised. That's when the FBI added him to their list of disruptive Negroes.

Iberia encouraged her son's audacious commitment to justice, she just didn't want him to be center stage. She reminded him of his intentions of attending law school, but he felt the people needed him on the ground, he said he would go back to college later. She knew from back home that the White folks will make an example out of the loudest of the group. After the murder of Martin Luther King Jr., Iberia's intuition was validated, but it was too late, something had shifted inside her son. Fred left the NAACP and joined the Black Panther Party.

Iberia felt it coming: *He spoke too much truth for them to let him live.*

The last voice that Fred Hampton heard that night, before he was murdered, was the first voice he'd ever known. The voice that told him not to make himself too visible. But also taught him that his community was worth protecting. In the darkest and most silent hours of the night, when she was sure that her thoughts could be heard by no one but God, Iberia wondered if she had been to blame. Should she have not talked to him plainly about race in America so frequently, should she have stayed in Louisiana, should she have insisted he be brought home to Maywood that night as planned? Maybe she could have protected him if he was close to her. That she could have shielded her boy on that bitter December morning. Iberia had felt it in her bones that something was off that night. She was up late, restlessly looking out at the snow falling gracefully, but far too soon.

Fred dozed off during his phone call with Iberia that night. A few hours later, around four in the morning on December 4, 1969, J. Edgar Hoover and COINTELPRO organized a military-level assassination of her son. To some he died a martyr, to others he died a terrorist, to many he was the chairman, but to Iberia, he was still her boy. Fred's bedroom at their family home in Maywood was still just as he'd left it before moving to West Monroe Street only a few months prior.

Iberia was at work inspecting bottle caps when she was informed of Fred's assassination by her eldest, her daughter Dee Dee. She had been bracing herself, but there is no way to prepare for burying your son. He had only just joined the Black Panther Party a year earlier. She didn't necessarily agree with certain elements of the party, particularly the conspicuous attire. But she supported their Free Breakfast for Children Program, which provided hot meals for kids before school. The Panthers consulted nutritionists, collected donations from local food merchants, and depended on members and volunteers to prepare the food, Iberia being one of them. Hoover saw the program as an act of communism, only for the federal government to imitate the program a few years after neutralizing Fred.

Iberia walked out of the corn plant slow and sullen toward the car where Francis was awaiting her. They sat for a while in silence, before Francis drove them home. When a close friend came to check on her later that day, Iberia was sweeping the floors, her face as still as stone, while Francis's eyes were filled with tears. For years, he would tear up anytime Fred's murder was brought up. Iberia believed Francis "wasn't tough enough" to handle their son's murder.

I wonder if Iberia and Mamie Till ever sat down together after

Fred was killed. What they would have said to each other. Perhaps there are no words for this kind of grief. Iberia and Mamie both left the South to settle into homes where they believed they would watch their boys grow into men and fathers. Chicago was a destination for those with hope. Chairman Fred said Black people aren't free anywhere, no matter how far they travel. *The suburbs can't protect you.* Iberia and Mamie both used Raynor and Sons Funeral Home, but they buried their sons in different ways. They both had open caskets. Fred's bullet wounds to his head were covered with makeup and his body embalmed. Till's body was half gone and bloated from floating overnight in the river. The smell of his decay met the mourners at the door. Iberia buried her son in Louisiana, beside his grandfather, just outside the church where Iberia and Francis met. Placing him back where he had come from. Mamie brought her boy North to be buried. Till is memorialized in Mississippi where he died. A statue was erected in Maywood and that pool was eventually built and named after Fred Hampton. *I didn't want the place where Fred was killed named after him . . .* Iberia wanted Fred to be commemorated where he had lived, while others wanted to memorialize the street where he had died. *Who would wanna walk around a street and see a house that their son was murdered in, and the street that he was killed on—you don't have no feelings for me.* There is a long history of not having feelings for Black mothers. Iberia has been largely erased from Fred's legacy. As the Black mothers of America tend to be. Her strength is misread as indifference. But where do people think Fred came from?

Revolutionaries are not born, they are created. All that he learned from Iberia was in opposition to everything he was taught in America. From Iberia, he was educated to believe that he was beautiful, and he had every right to be here. In America, he was a nuisance, and, as Galeano deduced, his life wasn't worth more than the slugs he was riddled with. It was in this tension, between the immense love of his first country and the false promises of his homeland, that the chairman was shaped.

Iberia's care for her son was transmutable. It permeated his speeches that energized young Black people to believe their lives were worth more than nothing. Love in its highest form extends through and beyond its intended recipient. It's everlasting and infinite and cannot be destroyed. You can feel it in the earth and radiating from the trees at Bethel Cemetery in Louisiana where Iberia spent every Mother's Day after Fred was killed until she herself was buried there beside him. Fred loved his people because *he* was loved. There is nothing more revolutionary than love.

Imitation of Life

I'll never forget the emerald green carpet, routinely shampooed. Before bed, my mother sat in the middle of the sinkhole in the sofa and beckoned me over with the slap of a wide-tooth comb on her round brown thighs. The carpet left prints on my backside as I sat between her legs, directly in front of the television set, which was usually turned down too low for me to hear over her gossiping into the cordless phone. Her legs pinched my shoulders together as she traced the comb down the center of my scalp, beginning directly above the bridge of my nose, for symmetry. If I squirmed, she'd sting me with the comb. *Hold still.* The womanly smell between her legs as I leaned my temples against her warm skin, the supple strength of her thighs, the cool blue grease she worked into my relaxed hair before plaiting it. We weren't allowed to watch television often, and my mother was strict about R-rated films, but we built our Fridays around TGIF television: *Boy Meets World, Step by Step, Family Matters.* My mother loved dark-skinned Aunt Viv on *Fresh Prince of Bel-Air* because she had gone from rags to riches, Philly to Beverly Hills. These are my most vivid memories of home, when the TV was on and she would disappear into a trance, briefly released from obligations.

By 1959, more than 85 percent of American metropolitan households had televisions. Betty Jean's aunt Eloise in Louisiana purchased her a television in the late '50s. Where my mother's memory splinters, American popular culture helps me fill in frames of her life. Bringing clarity to the ways that a young impressionable Black girl began to see herself projected back through television and magazines. My mother speaks often about the unforgettable moment when she saw Michael Jackson and his brothers commanding the center of the American lexicon, and subsequently, the collective pain of watching him transform into a White woman. Only to live long enough to later witness White women reconstructing their bodies to resemble the physicality of Black women.

Stick around long enough and the shit will flip.

I consider Connie seeing Diahann Carroll on TV as Julia and how she idealized her. She looked like the type of woman that never sweat. Not too loud and just funny enough. Gorgeous and permed. Except she wasn't married, and for my mother, marriage is the ultimate demonstration of both commitment and respect, never mind love. But Julia was a widow. Maybe that's even better. The social status without the worry. In 1968 when *Julia* premiered, my mother was twelve and living on Beulah Street in Third Ward with her mother, *Mr. Pepper,* and seven other children sharing one bed. She had never met a woman like Julia, a Black White woman. A woman who was unmistakably Black, but lived in every other respect, from voice to acceptance, the lifestyle of a White woman. The show was released after the Civil Rights Act was passed and the creator of the show, Hal Kanter, later admitted that the role was written for a White woman but the studios felt pressure to "give the Negroes something" so they would stop all that marching, rioting, fighting for equality. Let the Black women settle a brewing nation. While also setting the standards of expectation for young Black viewers like my mother. She would have to become a Julia if she was to reach the pinnacle of American existence.

Television always served as a barometer for my mother's dreams. Like many other American families, it was where we were able to escape collectively and call it intimacy. Where Mama Connie could project herself into a narrative and work toward making it her own. If she sees it once, she can store it, try it on, adjust it to her size. My mother didn't watch TV necessarily for retreat but rather for notes on advancement. A blueprint of what could be done and where the limits lie—so she could push past them. Her own experiences were never reflected. Hollywood has yet to conceive of a character like Betty Jean and her daughter Connie.

When Connie was growing up, the Mammy figure was on the decline, but Hollywood clung to her desperately. The Black maid was the desexualized and comely companion to the glamorous White feminine mystique. The Mammy, ever the beloved American figure; so much so that the United Daughters of the Confederacy fought to erect a Mammy monument for all the Negresses who had dutifully raised them and their children. The wife of a disgraced pharmaceutical giant once told her Black worker that she only hires Black single mothers. "There is no one more loyal than a Black single mother." Surely something of generational family lore. I share this only to say that historically, and presently, the Mammy is missed. The monument prototype was of an Aunt Jemima–type figure dressed in a long dress, hair tied back under a kerchief, not in pursuit of beauty, only duty, while White babies and toddlers crawl all about her. Her own are out of the frame. Somewhere with their grandmothers, or perhaps sold away for having Mister's face. A plaque in the middle reads, MAMMY. Black women lobbied Congress to vote against it, but the narrative persists.

In one of my mother's favorite films, Blackness was merely a prop when Annie (Juanita Moore) played the doting live-in domestic in *Imitation of Life* (1959). Annie helps her mistress Lora (Lana Turner) appear beautiful, feminine, White. Blackness was constructed as a narrative device to define Whiteness in the American project and in the film. Much of Annie's interiority is left to the imagination. The Negress provides differentiation. There is an alluring, almost erotic intimacy between Whiteness and Blackness. Beauty cannot be measured unless the injured character is beside her. The essayist Elaine Scarry says that injury is the most accurate opposite of beauty. When someone is unattractive, my mother sometimes says, *Lord, she looks hurt.* Not just ugly, but weakened. Is Annie not an injured woman? Meaning bruised, suffered, abused? My mother resisted aligning herself with the hurt domestic. And I admire her determination to give herself a name of her own choosing. Regardless of her circumstances, my mother never saw herself as a victim, since to do so would be a surrendering of all agency.

Annie, the Mammy, wasn't allowed any depth in *Imitation of Life* because she didn't have hold of her narrative, she went where others took her, she arrived no place on her own. Even in death, her daughter Sarah Jane had put her there. Round-faced and docile, her character has no details except that she is a Black mother. She's not alluring or bearing sexual prowess of any sort. And if it is so that White men bear no attraction to Black women, then where did poor old Annie Johnson's mulatto baby girl come from? The coconut tree?

So, who does my mother aspire to be in this adaptation of Fannie Hurst's 1933 novel? My mother was young when she first encountered *Imitation of Life,* no more than ten, but she already knew she could never be White, so she surely did not aspire to be the glamorous blonde that is Lora. This film made such an impression on my mother that in a rare moment at Blockbuster she selected the VHS for me, insisting that I see it. I was around the same age as she in her initial encounter, and she saw it as a kind of rite of passage. I wonder if she was attempting to preempt any shame that I may carry about her Blackness. As we watched that night she wept intensely, as she only could while watching films, because she could impose herself on the characters, crawl inside of them, and feel their suffering without having to acknowledge her own. Empathy was more acceptable than vulnerability.

My mother saw herself in Miss Sarah Jane. The tragic mulatto girl who wanted so desperately to be White, to be accepted, that she hated her mother for who she made her. The same way that my mother blamed Betty Jean for making her poor. For establishing her social status without her consent. She could relate to Sarah Jane because she didn't ask to be brought into the world under such cruel circumstances. How dare she? It's not expressed explicitly in the film, but Sarah Jane's father is unknown, and perhaps Annie the Mammy is to blame for his absence. Isn't Betty Jean the reason my mother never had a chance to know her father? Connie weeps for Sarah Jane because she knows that a pain with no one else to blame, but the one who gave you life, is a violence with no name.

· · ·

Me imagining my mother as *Jet* Beauty of the Week:

CONNIE IN HOUSTON

Jet Magazine

If your mail is late, it's because all the mail carriers at the Houston post office can't stop looking at Connie. When she's not at her desk, she enjoys shopping at the Galleria, dancing at The Change of Pace and long walks along Galveston beach. She grew up in Third Ward, has a high school diploma and plans on becoming very rich one day.

. . .

The post office, where my mother worked for three years after her divorce from my father in the 1970s, was a fashion show. No one came to work in their uniform, they came dressed to be seen and to be chosen. The men drove their long cars with the diamond in the back and a sunroof top. And the women strutted past so fly, looking only from the corners of their eyes. My mother took notes from women with names like Paula, Shirley, Diane, Barbara, Deborah, Claudette, and Marie. She had looked to *Jet* and *Ebony* to understand how to put pieces together. Few were the women in *Jet* with skin as Black as my mother's. Dark-skinned women on television were few. When my mother saw women who looked like her, they were all sex and no grace. They were the loud friend with no depth or character development. Usually fat. Usually in the ghetto, content and happy to serve others, easily recognized as destitute. So naturally my mother would reject the dark-skinned women, seeing beauty only in the fair. But she still looked in the mirror and repeated the newly famed mantra, *Black is beautiful,* with hopes of one day believing it.

She had style and a keen visual intelligence, but she had always made her own clothes. Now that she was making a reasonable salary at the post office, she could buy designer clothes like the ones the ladies wore to work every day. She'd seen women like this in magazines, but never so close that she could reach out and touch them. These women's nails and shoes were polished, and they had standing weekly beauty-shop appointments. Their appearance was a priority, unlike the women of my mother's family. She felt she had found some people like her, strivers. You know how many lives were saved by the post office?

During this time my mother was closest to *Red*. *Red* worked in one of the first Black-owned salons in Houston. Mama Connie went to *Red*'s salon and pointed out the short, permed cut she'd seen in one of the hair magazines. Since she divorced, she had been spending her nights dating all kinds of men. Club promoters, realtors, mailmen, engineers, and even one of her eldest brother's colleagues at Enron. An entire generation of Black men of my mother's age were drafted during the Vietnam War and sent back as deeply disturbed veterans weeping into the breasts of women ill-equipped to understand what it's like to go to sleep to the sounds of screaming children in your head. But they try still. The men talk endlessly about Agent Orange. Some of them have track marks in their arms and it's too humid in the city to keep them covered. They stay out late to delay the nightmares, and my mother and *Red* are right there beside them, both of their sons sleeping peacefully at *50 10* with Betty Jean.

My mother was a young woman dating during the 1970s, porn's golden era. Earth, Wind and Fire and Gerald Levert still called it lovemaking, but there was an understanding that being a freak was not just encouraged, it was expected. There was a sexual revolution taking shape as Desiree West was having sex with White men on camera aligned with the rise of sex work in urban environments. The development of the whore and the pimp duo. The cops followed as well. Getting blown as they dangled freedom above the ladies' heads, history loops, but now Black women were in on the gains. There was a tension between exploitation and self-sufficiency and it was a delicate one. They weren't just Nigga gals no more, they were sistas, ladies, queens, ma'ams, hoes, foxy and fine. America was struggling to control the narrative of what these women were, but they certainly weren't Mammies. The story was slipping from their grasp. The Welfare Queen was a desperate gasp. The story of Black women was fraying and my mother enjoyed being able to play with who she wanted to be.

My mother met a mailman who asked her to quit the post office and just be his wife. A man who made his money the clean way and paid his taxes on time. The kind of man who had good credit, loved his mama, and didn't care what he wore on his back. As long as his woman was happy, he was happy. This man who *Junior* was calling Daddy while his was away on the Arctic sea. She obliged as it was what she thought she'd always wanted. With nothing to do but shop, do aerobics videos, and keep things tidy in their home while her man was at work and her son was at school. She started to break out in hives. She lost her appetite. She was bored. Her body was rejecting a life of leisure. She didn't know how to not hustle and motherhood wasn't all that interesting to her. She didn't particularly like cooking and she didn't really know how to let a man love her. She didn't know how to allow anyone to love her.

She wanted that old thing back. That old, familiar, complicated thing.

won't you celebrate with me
what i have shaped into
a kind of life? i had no model.

. . .

. . . come celebrate
with me that everyday
something has tried to kill me
and has failed.

—LUCILLE CLIFTON,
"WON'T YOU CELEBRATE WITH ME"

Pfeiffer Drive

My mother sometimes bends her head back to the sky before tenderly saying aloud, *Look at me, Mama. Look what we did.*

Never questioning her presence. Comforted and kept alive by the thought of being loved from above by her grandmother, the most high. As if it were just the two of them there. Never turning to me to explain. Never really sharing that joy with me. As if I couldn't comprehend what had been overcome because I had not been born the daughter of Betty Jean. Even when she attempted to tell me, I couldn't fully comprehend what her childhood was like. You had to be there. You had to breathe it and feel it up against your skin. Like if you try to describe to someone the anatomy of a punch. The impact so substantial and dizzying, all one can relay is the pain and evidence of the bruise. The aftereffects more lasting than the swiftness of the action. As a result, Connie's parenting style relied heavily on lessons on how to elude and fortify. There were no instructions on healing. And without this element in place, she would become the fist.

Little Black girl from Third Ward. Can you believe it, Mama?

. . .

Eleven years after my parents divorced, they remarried. Like many of us, my mother has a conflicting desire to be understood while concealing all that she is. On some level, I think she felt my father understood something that she didn't need to explain, which was one of the reasons she loved him. This time around they didn't just go to the courthouse; they had a ceremony and my brother *Junior* was the ring bearer. My mother wore a white satin fish-tailed dress with lace trim that she'd borrowed from her friend Diane, from the post office, along with white satin pumps and white sheer pantyhose. *Junior* and my father wore matching tux-edos and bow ties. Only *Red* was asked to be a part of the wedding party, but all of my mother's sisters were present. In a portrait I have, *Gone* stands out in monochromatic red, *Righthand* is in prints beside her, *Daddy's Girl* smiles youthfully beside my mother who is in the center. *Red* beams proudly in pink, the bridesmaid's color. *Artemis,* effortlessly striking, wears a casual collared white dress with a yellow belt and *The Baby* is on the end, shorter than all the rest, in stripes. A rare image of all seven of Betty Jean's girls. They look beautiful and it's almost chilling that they don't look like what they've been through. Betty Jean and May both carried pink lilies to match the bride's bouquet. My paternal grandmother decided to come at the last minute, having chosen not to attend the celebration of their first union. She always said my parents were *just two people with a misunderstanding.* She didn't support the first marriage nor the second, but she never held that against me. *Brother* gave my mother away, not because they had become close; he was the only man she knew who would actually show up. Even the groom was questionable.

My parents yearned for a daughter and my mother was deter-mined that all her children share the same last name, even if she knew the man behind the name was not reliable.

Within a year of their wedding, I was born on a wet spring night in Houston. My mother nearly died in childbirth. She had been in prolonged labor and was neglected by the medical staff. I went into distress from the pressure and the umbilical cord curled around my neck. My mother sat waiting for someone to check on her. Eventually a nurse stopped in and realized my mother's uterus had ruptured. And my mother was lying still and quiet.

Artemis was working in the hospital as a CNA and says everyone was speaking about my mother in the nurses' lounge, only for her to go to maternity and see that it was her older sister. Others came to witness the woman made of steel who lay silently waiting while the doctor and nurses erratically tried to stop the bleeding. She was suffering but didn't scream or cry out in the pain because she *didn't want to be a problem for anyone.* She nearly died to avoid being an inconvenience to the White medical professionals. My arrival was less a delivery and more a detonation. From then on, *Artemis* vowed to attend her sisters' births as an advocate. To pull their babies safely to this side, just as she had *Apollo.*

. . .

I have a photo of my father in protective surgical gear as he held newborn me in the operating room while my mother rested after a blood transfusion. My father named me after a surrealist Russian novelist he'd read while living in Alaska. *A School for Fools* by Sasha Sokolov. In the novel, So-and-so suffers from a dissociative disorder that he feels he inherited from his grandmother and the reader follows along through the subconscious of his divided selves. It's a modern take on the Narcissus myth, the man who fell in love with his reflection in the river. One of the Russians that my father worked beside had left a copy on the shared bookshelf at one of the stations on the coast in Lonely, Alaska. My father says that when you work on the water, it feels like you all exist as one people, without rank. The water is the great neutralizer. Detached from the social pressures of the world, he recalls walking across the border into Russia to pick up items from a shop near their station. When you're out on the water for months, innate human behaviors emerge, and you're forced to confront what made you think you were anything more than just a man. He said that it's only when they returned to the shores that they became Americans and Russians. On the water, they were just men. He speaks of Alaska today as if these were his best years. The years that didn't include his wife and children. Nor his mother and brothers. A place where he was inaccessible to everyone but himself. Now, every time he calls my name, he is calling out to that cherished past. I like the idea of being a part of this past that he remembers fondly because he doesn't carry the same regard for his time at home with us on Pfeiffer Drive. Perhaps I am the river reflecting back his prior self. He stands still, living only in his head with his memories, while I move, steady and slow, to stay alive.

He was never the same when he came back from Alaska. I was born just after he returned, and from an early age I could sense the absence of something that I desperately wanted to fill for him. Like when you find a seashell in the sand, still carrying the sound of the ocean within it, gorgeous in its intricacies, but you can't help but recognize that it's cradling the ghosts of its previous inhabitant. My father returned to Houston as a cenotaph. He'd only come home because he'd slipped on the deck of the ship, misaligning a vertebra in his spine that required surgical correction and, more devastating, disqualifying him from offshore work. After the surgery, the cold caused his spine to tighten, immobilizing him. He lost a bit of his dignity. His aspirations wavered. Over time, he gradually lost interest in the appearance of Black exceptionalism. He stopped getting dressed, wore T-shirts and jeans. He had wanted to open a restaurant in Houston, but my mother and his parents discouraged it as frivolous and not lucrative. Instead he opened a car wash and called it Midnight Sun. Alaska ever in his heart. Most of his employees were young people in need of their first job, Hispanic men without documentation, addicts, or men recently released from jail. The sons and nephews of people he knew that he hired to help them get back on track. His first car wash was in Montrose, and his clientele was predominantly young gay White male professionals. His downtown location was more corporate suits, high-profile drug dealers, local entertainers, and a number of car dealerships. At some point, I believe he stopped seeing himself as one of the stars and realized he was now the help. Even if he did own the business.

He sank into a visible and prolonged depressed state. My mother says, "He forgot who he was and started acting like the crack-heads." He wouldn't sing his blues, but he listened to them on his record player. He had a vast record collection. I grew up in an Isley Brothers house, an Isaac Hayes house, a Frankie Beverly and Maze house. I loved the music, and now every time I hear Ron Isley's voice melt into the track, I think of my father. I adored him. I thought he was the most beautiful man. He felt like a redemption in my life, but he was rarely around. I cherished the sporadic moments we shared. He went to work early and stayed late. I can't imagine there was much work to settle at the car wash after dark, so he was probably spending time seeking the thrills that broken men believe will make them feel whole. I would sometimes see glimmers of the man he once was. When he was stepping out. He followed fashion trends in *GQ* until he no longer bothered with the subscription. I sat on the counter in my parents' bathroom and watched him shave, even though I hated the smell of Magic shaving powder. His head first, then everything on his face but his mustache. He'd ask for my opinion on what to wear and once he was dressed, he would turn up the music, extend his hand, and ask me to dance with him in the living room, *Put your feet on top of mine.*

A few years after me, Shannon was born. We were raised along the same bayou as our mother, but about an hour across town from Third Ward in a White suburb folded between Harris and Fort Bend counties near the headwaters of Brays Bayou. Just beyond the sharp bend in the bayou, almost like it was pointing at us, sat our modest white brick home. Our neighborhood was a triangular-shaped unincorporated area between Alief, Mission Bend, and Clodine, but which one we lived in remains unclear. Though not entirely accurate, I've always said we lived in Alief. Our home was built on flood-prone prairie land originally settled by an array of Anglo immigrants who grew rice and cotton. Before them, the area was home to the Akokisa tribe who traveled by water across the region. When my parents purchased the house in the '80s there was a construction boom and population influx in the area with the arrival of corporations like Shell Oil and Halliburton taking root. My mother's motivations were stability and security, so she settled her family closer to the origin of the body of water she knew so well.

We were the only Black family on our cul-de-sac but over the years there was a slow increase of Black and brown people. Each year Shannon and I followed my mother into the principal's office on the first day of elementary school while she asked if any Black teachers had been hired yet. Each year there was a polite *no*. It was six years before there was another Black girl in my class. Each year there were a few more until nearly all the Whites were gone. My mother's concern was rising as she noticed more Black students in middle school. She wanted Black educators for me, not necessarily Black peers. Our neighborhood was just beyond Alief's boundary, which is one of the most diverse neighborhoods in Texas. So I attended elementary school with people who lived near me, but by middle school I had friends who lived farther away and were from South America, Nigeria, Mexico, and Vietnam because our zoning had expanded beyond our little triangle. Alief randomly sorted students to attend one of two high schools that were connected by an annex. Which meant we went to school with children from a range of different socioeconomic backgrounds within Alief and who didn't necessarily reside near us. If I wanted to hang out with a friend, my mother asked me if they lived in an apartment complex or a house. The former was a no. The latter would lead to the follow-up question: *Do they own the house?* How could I know that? I just lied. She treated my friends that rented their house just like her neighbors had treated her, as if poverty is contagious. All human malevolence is muscle memory.

We lived in a single-story house that felt large to me then. Through the foyer with its black-and-white-checked tile, my bedroom sat to the left and the kitchen, which connected to the garage, to the right. Past the foyer was a high-beamed open-concept area where the living and dining rooms were held together by the wide white brick fireplace, where my father and I tended fires together in winter. It was important to my mother that we ate together as a family, usually at the breakfast nook in the kitchen, and shared stories about our day. My parents' primary suite took up most of the right side of the house and me and my brothers' rooms were on the left side. When my father was home, he was gardening, as he had with his mother as a boy, and he planted a raised flower bed with a sago palm that he nurtured tenderly. In the backyard there was a Jacuzzi where I hid turtles I'd taken from the bayou and kept as pets until my parents found them and made me return them. Soda cans riddled with BB-gun pellet holes lined the fence, and there was a large pecan tree that I remember sitting under with Betty Jean on her rare visits. She taught me how to crack the stubborn shell with the lower palm of my hands. She didn't believe in using the nutcracker my parents used. She showed me how to tell the rotten and the young from the ripe. We sat for what felt like hours under the tree. I gathered the smooth brown orbs from the grass, and she shelled until our bellies were full and our gums held the residue of the nuts' white flesh.

Though my mother spent a lifetime trying to forget her childhood, the water holds memory, and I think she felt its comfort. Perhaps the proximity of the bayou wouldn't let her release the past. Her greatest fear was becoming her mother, having children that she couldn't feed with men who couldn't support her. She wanted a house on a cul-de-sac, foreign vehicles, the American life she had seen on television and worked tirelessly to attain. She taught us how to swim almost as soon as we learned to walk because she loved the water but she never learned to traverse it. She made sure our teeth were perfectly aligned with braces, took us to the dentist and every other doctor her insurance allowed for. She held us each day and told us she loved us as her mother never had. She tried in every way she knew how to do things differently. But naturally, she still came to be more like her mother than she ever realized. Those old wounds can't be resolved through what you give your children. She needed to tend the little girl in her. Because only a confrontation can change the direction of the waters. She didn't want to feel the pain of recalling her past, she had already lived it once, no use suffering through it again.

. . .

By raising my brothers and I in a White suburb, it was like we were first-generation native speakers in the only homeland we all have. Just as my mother spoke the language of the Black urban experience and her mother the language of the old plantation South. The tools my parents provided us for survival didn't always apply to our suburban environment. And the guidance we actually needed, they weren't equipped to give, like how to love your Blackness when every friend you have insists on questioning your difference, not with curiosity but with contempt. Instead, we had sparring matches in our living room so that we knew how to fight in case we were jumped or robbed. They taught us that if one of us is in a fight, we are all in a fight. They taught us how to love, and how to hate ourselves too. One day when I was eight or ten, my mother told me to thank her for marrying my father, the closest she could get to White without being with a White man. I knew what she meant; if my lips were fuller, skin darker, or nose more substantial, I would be less beautiful. It would be more difficult for me to move through the world if I were less palatable. I should be grateful for the way she meticulously sculpted me. Molding me in the image of her fantasies. Shannon, who shares my mother's midnight skin, was in the backseat beside me when she told me this, and I couldn't help but wonder what he felt in that moment. I never asked, but I can imagine he felt less lovable. I grieved for what they didn't allow us to do in our home—to love ourselves wholly. But how could they? When my father self-abandoned, leaving his soul in Alaska, providing me and my brothers with only some faint semblance of what he once was. When my mother was still emotionally in that shotgun house on Beulah Street waiting for someone to tuck her in and tell her she's safe. They never came. They are never coming.

She made it clear to everyone that where we lived was her house, her universe, and that we were to orbit her on command. *I'm the only one who slams the doors in this house,* she'd say. *Don't you dare raise your voice long as you staying under my roof,* she'd say. *You ain't got no room, all these rooms are mine.* My mother believed in the impact of dramatic effect and went to great lengths to demonstrate that she'd stop at nothing in pursuit of superiority by way of fear, especially if it induced shame. Once when I slammed my bedroom door in frustration, she was on my heels with a power drill. After all, she is goddess of the hinge. My door was carried away to the garage along with my sense of selfhood. I retreated further and further into myself. I spent many nights in my closet reading and writing poetry. Trying to bend words into shapes on the page that resembled what lay inside me so that I could make sense of why I was ever born and convince myself of reasons to stay alive. This infuriated my mother, because as I found ways to disappear within our chaotic home, she had less access to me. I am told that from a very young age, when my mother came searching for me, I was usually found somewhere tucked away, behind the curtains, or under a bed with a book, successfully unable to hear her hollers.

In my mother's home, we each had our own room and there was always a spare. For all my mother's aspirations to leave her past behind, she still believed in helping her blood by sharing her space with them. We hosted nearly all of the holiday gatherings on Pfeiffer Drive. Connie was at her fullest when she surrounded herself with those who clung to her for survival. My mother's contentment resides not only in her independence but also in others' dependency on her. The extra bedrooms were always occupied by those in need of a place. She wanted to see them rise, as long as they didn't attempt to eclipse her, lest she be rendered useless. The religious auntie who was pregnant and unwed; the cousin whose father never could, and whose mother never would, love him; my schoolmate whose mother's weekend trips turned into weeks-long binges; the kinfolks, the coworkers, the aggrieved. She took in everyone, a queering of the Hollywood home life that she mimicked. A duty I was taught to continue, of putting all above self. This is where she felt her value rested. In her ability to build worlds from lack. To provide water from an empty well. The very value of her existence was also what led to her deterioration. Sacrifice and womanhood inextricable. And my father can take like no other. His gratitude is fulsome, but his memory is short. He forgets that he just had his water, that perhaps my mother is thirsty. My mother says she doesn't need much. Boasting about how she can survive on so little. My father accepts her share and she resents him for it. It won't be long before my mother is asking me to give my water to my brothers, the boys need more, she says. They are weak, she says. They cannot endure all that we can.

Touchstone

She did things the right way. Once she became a mother and wife, all prior life vanished. Her origins were never disclosed. Perhaps the South, a strangled drawl sometimes slipped out. From time to time, she spoke Mexican Spanish, not Boricua, not Dominican, so she probably migrated to the North with her people from Texas, landed in Harlem, but never burdened her children with this trail of tears. None of that mattered when she became the doctor's wife. She's now made of stone, a monument standing without texture at 10 Stigwood Avenue in Brooklyn Heights. She was born there, conceived by a man titillating the Black yearning for a portrayal of American normativity. *Make me over / I wanna be made over.*

All prior sins washed away because she did things *the right way.* Like when Serena Williams yelled at that umpire during her match at the US Open in 2018. She smashed her racket in exasperation and shouted, "I have never cheated in my life! I have a daughter!" And she wasn't a cheater, she's a champion, but she thought she might somehow be relieved of suspicion once she became a mother, *the right way.* However, she was without one of the necessary qualifiers. The only Black woman to ever achieve this status is Clair Huxtable.

The Black Madonna for baby boomers looking to make a home that didn't look like their grandmother's because Reagan and

Moynihan said they were doing it wrong. In 1965, one year after the passing of the Civil Rights Act, when he was the assistant secretary of labor, Moynihan decided to investigate the modern-day issues with those synonymous with labor, the Negroes of America, he didn't point to racial injustice, discrimination, the penal system, unequal education, environmental injustice, or hundreds of years of slavery; he wrote a ninety-page report on how the matriarchal nature of the Black family structure is responsible for the struggles of Black people. Moynihan said your mama and your granny, your beloveds, were in fact the reason you were poor and living in urban chaos, not the structural failures of the nation.

Clair was the remedy and the diorama. She could help dispel all those myths White America created over the years: the Mammy, the Sapphire, the Welfare Queen. Her household didn't allow cousins sleeping over or summers down South. Clair's home was a nuclear *Leave It to Beaver*–esque family. Their kids had unrestricted access to a refrigerator certain to satiate. Dazzled by her pitch-perfect directives. She is feminine and forbidding without losing grace or being read as angry. Her wrap was always fixed just so, never coiled at the roots, with an effortless elegance. Her children were well mannered, but she didn't birth them. She was never pregnant. Never physically marked by the vulgarity of pleasure. She may very well be a virgin. The immortalized one placed on the top shelf of the étagère. The problem with being shaped gorgeously in stone is that it doesn't have malleability.

Clair provided aesthetic frameworks of Black opulence for the upwardly mobile in need of a blueprint their parents couldn't provide. She was a glimpse at what a color-blind future might look like if you follow suit. She promised progress and hope, but never calculated the costs. Contort yourself into the molds of White American ideals and forget what those very ideals had done to your ancestors. The cost of the ticket is your soul. She set an impossible precedent. Strivers needed a goalpost and *The Cosby Show* provided. America's mom couldn't provide practical protocol for the boomers on how to talk to their children about police or what to do if you're offered a crack pipe, or how to hold your hands if a Korean shop owner thinks you're stealing orange juice, or how to plead for your life if you get a flat tire on the roadside and a White man approaches you with a gun because he doesn't quite like the look of a Nigga in a coupe. For eight years, Clair served as a post-racial middle-class standard. Even Marge Simpson had more political range when she captivated the Thursday night syndication spot. It was impossible for Clair and Cliff to sustain their position in America's living room suggesting that we were beyond race as Americans sat on the sofa watching the television set that Sunday afternoon on March 3, 1991.

The Rodney King footage marked the beginning of a shift toward reality television and O. J. Simpson's televised murder trial offered a kind of redemption. This was the commencement of the eroding of the veneer. Both rendered Black life as spectacle, while actively unraveling the myth of the Cosbys. The myth Orenthal James Simpson believed when he declared, *I'm not Black, I'm O. J.* Television was shifting from a source of hypnotic deception to a place to bear witness to what Black America knew to be true but tried desperately to ignore while they were keeping up with the Cosbys. Delusion can be so comforting. Hell, you almost have to live in its embrace just to get out of bed in the morning. To believe the American lore that all it takes is determination and bootstraps and doing it *the right way.* The delusion is imperative. Maybe Frank Wilderson is right, there is no post-Blackness before the apocalypse.

Railroads

My mother was constantly focused on what stories were being communicated through posture while working out how to meticulously curate her own, and ours. How one carried oneself. She may not remember a name, but she can spot someone by the way they walk. Her attentiveness to visual detail is keen. As kids, when we were shopping for shoes or clothes, we would try on the garment and my mother would inspect Shannon and I before saying, *Now let me see you walk.* Shoulders back, chin up. *You walking slue-footed. Turn those toes in,* she'd tell my brother. I was told to lengthen my stride, to glide. *Walk like you got somewhere to be,* she'd tell him, *you look lazy. I hate a tired-ass walk.* She told me I needed to find the rhythm. *Every man I've ever had told me my walk was what got 'em.* Twist a little bit. *Pick up that shoulder,* she'd tell him. She had self-corrected her own feet that veered outward. She was pleased with all the ways that she was self-made, that she never accepted what she was dealt in life. That she alone changed her circumstances. She believed a walk told a story.

Her ability to read a walk provided her with an opportunity that changed her life in 1977. Before I was born, she had taken Betty Jean shopping for new clothes at Gulfgate Mall when she saw a familiar gait.

"Mama, don't that look like *Cabbie* over there?"

"Naw," Betty Jean says looking elsewhere.

"I know that crooked-ass walk."

Cabbie had always high-stepped with his lead leg and dragged the other. He walked with tight hips and tense strides. Perhaps from all those years driving. He walked like a man in slight persistent pain, but holding too much pride to say so.

"Cabbie!"

It was the father of Betty Jean's youngest girls, *Daddy's Girl* and *The Baby.* He was smitten and visibly excited to see Betty Jean. She refused his cordiality, clasped her hands together, and softly muttered *Hello* and *Just fine.* My mother remembers him well, since she was old enough to have witnessed his arrival and departure. He didn't inquire about his daughters. He boasted about a job he had as a railroad man, surely to impress Betty Jean, or perhaps to inspire envy or regret in her. He induced neither in Betty Jean, but my mother has a way of making people feel as if they are ten feet tall when it serves her, and in that moment, he could use a few inches. *Cabbie* had a salaried union position with benefits, a railroad pension, and a 401(k). Said he'd seen the job in the paper. The Southern Pacific Railroad had been sending Blacks and women to the Job Corps for training before being hired. The federal government paid a significant portion of the railroad salaries for newly hired women and people of color to encourage diversity. *Cabbie* rambled on for as long as he could to my mother while never taking his eyes off Betty Jean.

Back at *50 10,* there was always a *Houston Chronicle* lying around. Betty Jean always makes time to read the paper. In the classifieds it read "No Experience Needed." There was a typing requirement and a ninety-day probation period for all positions. My mother informed her sisters about the opportunity, but says they were mostly uninterested. Only *Gone* and my mother responded to the classified ad and went to the Southern Pacific Railroad offices downtown to apply.

My mother had no typing experience, beyond the required high-school curriculum, but she was always elevated under pressure, if the stakes were high enough. In her case, poverty had conditioned this muscle. One mistake can impact you and your family's lives significantly, which is why my mother was unwavering with disciplinary actions. Freedom is expensive. It costs a lot to make mistakes. In poverty you have to learn from what your mama is telling you because you can't afford risk. The stakes are always high. The room for human error is low. More still, poverty is mostly reactionary. Life can feel like it's happening to you, creating a pressurized environment that conditions you to be adaptable at a moment's notice. Interestingly, even though I have never experienced poverty firsthand, I replicate my mother's practices with my own daughter. I can sense her anxieties about making a mistake, breaking a glass, losing a key, or misplacing a water bottle. And in her tension, I ask myself, is that glass worth more than your daughter's peace of mind? And can't you just replace it? My daughter says to me, *I'm only a kid, I'm going to lose things.* She grounds me. Aren't there enough pressures on a teenager? Who cares if she loses a key? But because my mother grew up in a home that was burglarized frequently, she gave us sermons about how our neighbors may find the key and break in to rob us while we're away. She had conspiracies on the duplication of the lost key. *Now everybody and they mama got a key to our house.* Which confused me because my White friends on our street didn't even lock their doors.

When they arrived at the Southern Pacific Railroad Gone was a secretary and could type three times as fast as my mother. They were both single mothers seeking security. They had both lived in and out of *50 10* when life drew blood. One of them believed anything was possible and the other felt their chances were unlikely. Only Connie got the job. She failed her typing test, but ever audacious, she asked the Black lady in HR to give her another chance, and was allowed to go into a separate office to practice on the typewriter. She passed the test, and the Black HR lady submitted her highest score.

When my mother was hired by the Southern Pacific Railroad she was twenty-three and there were still "Colored Only" foun-

tains and bathrooms. It was the late '70s so this had long been
banned. But Texas is known to cling relentlessly to injustice. Her
employers did everything they could to deter her from staying on
past her probationary period, but all she could see was *Cabbie* in
the mall grinning, his hands full of shopping bags.

Hazing ensued over the next ninety days.

On her first day of work, she assumed that she would be at a
desk, but she was told that the Coons worked outside. For her
to understand a position in the office, they said, she needed to
work the tracks first. This practice was not a new one, it was a
way to keep the good ol' boy system in place and deter Blacks and
women from infiltrating the railroad and occupying prime positions. Connie was assigned to the night shift, just as Betty Jean
had been, and so she too left her son with his grandmother while
she worked twelve hours through the night. My mother's new
colleagues drove her down dark roads and dropped her off alone
in the middle of a deserted entanglement of tracks and empty
railcars without proper equipment; it didn't matter to them that
my mother was still afraid of the dark.

The railroads, one of America's greatest industrial develop-
ments, stitched the states and territories together so that they
might become one nation. They are the thread that binds. And
Black people are the needle. This history between Black people
and the railroad is a long and winding one. Railroad construction began in the early nineteenth century, and by 1861 enslaved
people had constructed most of the 8,784 miles of rail tracks in
the South. Slavery ended in 1865. The demand for enslaved people
to lay the tracks increased so that there was a dramatic increase in
the price of slaves during this time. The demand for cotton was
unprecedented, and the railways provided a means of transport-
ing goods beyond the limitations of the waters and riverways.
Enslaved people brought the industrial age to life in the South.
Before emancipation, enslaved people were leased out to railroad
companies to construct rail lines across the undeveloped terrain
of the early empire. The enslaved were taken from their plantation

homes to temporary campsites to lay tracks, build trestles across swamps and waterways, chop wood, dig up the earth for road-beds. Southern Texas and Louisiana are marshlands that I have trouble simply walking through leisurely in the summer; I can't imagine constructing tracks in those thickets with the threat of wildlife and the oppression of the sun. It was so dangerous that slavers insured the enslaved laborers that they loaned out and railroads were responsible for medical expenses when laborers became ill due to the work conditions. The railroads sought out enslaved laborers locally so that they may be more acclimated to the topography of the regions in hopes that they wouldn't become ill, particularly with malaria. Some railroad companies even purchased their own slave labor so that they could work year-round because rented slaves meant that plantation owners wanted their laborers back for harvest season.

The enslaved worked beside paid Irishmen, who had a high turnover due to the working conditions. Most of the enslaved laborers were boys and men, but there were women and girls as well. Women who cooked for the men and were also relegated to chopping wood for trestles, shoveling to clear paths, and helping to carry loads. There were no distinctions made as to where the women slept, so one can imagine the sexual violence that ensued. Back then, as now, Black women were masculinized, and it was assumed that they had a high tolerance for pain.

My mother was terrified her first night on the tracks, not only of what unknown awaited her in the darkness but of the White men as well. She cried only after they left her in the pitch-black surrounded by towering iron train cars and the sounds of the night. Just because a person doesn't scream, it doesn't mean that they are not hurting, it could mean that they have no more breath to give.

My mother worked for eight years as a clerk in the office after clearing the probationary period. By the time I was born she had been promoted to marketing and sales, where she had regular business hours with weekends off. As a child, I visited her office often. She had a small cubicle among a sea of others. She had an extension that I would call her on frequently just to say hello or ask her to help me control Shannon, or she would call me at home after school to remind me to take the chicken out of the freezer. There were a few other Black women working on her floor in marketing, and one Black man, *Cabbie*. I don't recall ever meeting him. She spoke to him every day at work. He never asked her about his daughters but would occasionally ask, *How your mama doing?* One evening at *50 10* my mother asked *Daddy's Girl* if she wanted to see her father and she nodded, afraid to speak aloud the affirmative as to not upset or invite a response from Betty Jean. My mother picked her sister up on her lunch break and brought her to her office. As they got off the elevator *Daddy's Girl* scanned the room to see if she could recognize him. My mother simply threw her hand in a direction and said, *There go your daddy right there,* and kept walking to her desk. She didn't help facilitate and didn't hover. But she did strain to watch the awkward exchange from her cubicle. *Cabbie* was polite, in the way one may speak to a coworker as you wait for the coffee pot to finish percolating. *Daddy's Girl* was shy and probably hoping her father would take her in his arms the way he had when she was a girl or apologize or offer to make up for lost time. She probably held her breath through most of it. Nevertheless, he never gave her what she had been waiting for at the door for all those years.

Eventually my mother eclipsed *Cabbie* in rank. The company was merging with the Union Pacific Railroad, and to keep her job, she needed to move to a different city. Her position no longer existed in Texas. Only field and managerial positions remained in Houston, everything else was going to Missouri and Colorado. She had never lived outside of Houston, but losing her job was far more terrifying. By this time, I was ten years old. It was the middle of the school year, I was in fifth grade, and suddenly we were driving to St. Louis to live in a middle-class Black neighborhood called Florissant. I may have cried the entire way. My father didn't join us. He stayed in Houston as there was a promise that we wouldn't be gone for long. My mother predicted that if she demonstrated her commitment to the company by moving to Missouri, the company would reward her in return. While in St. Louis she made connections and continued bidding on managerial positions back in Texas.

Our time in St. Louis was impactful for me as it was my first time living in a neighborhood that was predominantly Black, but what made it different from Third Ward was that it was entirely middle class. I began sneaking out to go to the mall with my friends while my mother worked night shifts. I wanted desperately to be accepted by my new Black friends and I would do just about anything, even if it meant betraying my mother and myself. I went to school in one outfit and came home in another that I had hidden in my backpack, something I knew my mother would never allow me to wear. A short skirt, a halter top. I learned how to double Dutch, and do the splits, got my first boyfriend and invited friends over while my mom was working and had my first kiss on the patio in the backyard. I mean, he pushed me against the house and pressed his lips to mine and never asked if I wanted to, but it still made my heart flutter all the same. To be desired for the ways that my hips spread and the burgeoning of my backside was intoxicating. Although I've never really felt like I fit in anywhere, it felt good to come so close.

I screamed in the bathroom when I saw the blood. I knew what menstruation was, but to be greeted with a small pool of red in your yellow panties that had the word *Wednesday* above a little daisy is startling. I yelled to my mother that I was bleeding, and she became upset. She yelled as if I had done something wrong. Betty Jean had never told her what to do when she started bleeding, but *Righthand* was there to guide her, and all the girls in her house shared pads and when they ran out, they constructed makeshift mounds from toilet paper.

After her angst settled, my mother took me shopping to find which pads worked best for me. I remember feeling ashamed to carry the boxes to the checkout line. I still don't understand her anger that evening when I called for her in the bathroom. But I suspect that it wasn't actually anger, it was fear. Maybe she wasn't ready to have another potential problem to consider, me getting pregnant. Shortly after that, she shipped me back to my father in Texas in the middle of my sixth-grade year. I was eleven. That little pool of blood in my panties that had *Wednesday* and a little flower on them had changed everything.

When my mother returned to Houston about six months later, she was a manager, which meant that she was no longer working in cubicles and answering phones. She was now supervising the train yards with White men who came to work in pickup trucks, pistols in full view and tobacco tucked into their bottom lip. Men who wore cowboy boots and Wranglers and had reddened, leathered necks. There were no more office politics, it was railroad culture, which was established back when the original tracks were laid. Everything changed for her because none of the rules she had become accustomed to applied. My mother always says, *Every time White folks tell you what it takes to get ahead, as soon as you arrive, they move the goalpost.* She was making significantly more money and had officers' benefits, but we barely saw her.

I was in middle school; I needed someone close to me. My father was there, but he wasn't there. I still adored him, but he was merely a physical presence. I couldn't confide in him because I was invested in impressing him, and my inner world was not honorable. Only now, as a single mother, can I see that my mother must have felt so deeply alone and overwhelmed. My father wasn't supportive emotionally or practically. And even though I couldn't understand her experiences fully, I did feel the weight of responsibility to provide her some relief by cleaning the house incessantly, helping with Shannon, and staying out of her way.

She worked inside of a trailer that sat on gravel in the middle of a train yard with what felt like endless winding and intersecting tracks that looked indistinguishable to me, but somehow, she could tell them apart. Trains coming, going, and idling. She managed the crews operating the trains regulated by strict FRA rules on the number of hours teams were allowed to work. Naturally, those White men didn't want a Black woman telling them where to be. Every simple task became a negotiation, a haggle, or an all-out fight. And the Black men weren't any better, they didn't want a Negress telling them when to pull the train out of the yard. She had the authority to test any train in the region, at any time, with a red-light signal that she kept in the trunk of her car. Whenever we were stopped at a crossing for a passing train, she would turn down the radio and verbally evaluate the train's crew. Tell us the name of each type of train car and what they held. She told us which neighborhoods trains were allowed to blow their whistle in and how they were to remain silent when passing through wealthy White neighborhoods. She knew which managers over-saw which tracks and criticized their choice of train-car order. She made the same joke each time, that she should stop the train just to piss off the crew. She loved the idea that she could and wanted her kids to know that should she choose to, she could bring two hundred tons of steel to a halt. At least at home, with her children, her power could be actualized. The respect she felt she deserved was our job to avow. The recognition never realized, became our responsibility to ratify. At home, her power was never questioned, for me, it was palpable. But her need to assert it was never satiated.

In the early managerial days, when she walked into work, she wasn't acknowledged. She smiled and said good morning. She brought doughnuts from Shipley's. But her colleagues never greeted her. The crews and other managers talked among them-selves. She was invisible. Worse than any name she was ever called, being erased every day felt the most demeaning. The crews that she managed often stalled to drag out time until they could no longer work due to the federal regulations. These regulations were put in place after railroad unions were formed due to the fatal working conditions that began during slavery. It was dan-gerous work. Workers could be crushed between railcars, fall and lose extremities, cause derailments due to fatigue, die in an explosion, and this doesn't include the lasting health conditions from exposure to hazardous chemicals. Even after slavery ended, Chinese immigrant laborers were recruited to work in the railroad industry because White Americans refused to sustain the working conditions that enslaved laborers were subjected to. The railroad is still a dangerous environment today, but with many more ordinances. My mother studied the FRA regulations because she knew her subordinates were watching and waiting for her to slip up so that she could be reported. White railroaders would openly threaten her, letting her know her days were numbered before she was back at a clerk's desk, answering phones. That affirmative action was over. Being called a Nigger bitch was a regular occurrence. But really it was those insidious daily passive-aggressive violences that cut deepest. The *N-word* is dismissible. But passive-aggressive behavior induces paranoia. Like when you get a splinter, the larger more obtuse punctures are no less painful, but they are more manageable. It's those tiny slithers that hurt most. They're more difficult to see and therefore more challenging to extract. And when you think you've gotten it, you still feel the lingering discomfort. And you question, did I get it? So you dig deeper into yourself to be sure nothing remains. Perhaps it's gone, perhaps it's a phantom. The sensation lingers long after the invasion.

I am certain that there is much that my mother never shared with me. Things that she endured to provide a stable home for her family. My mother said she never let them see her cry. *Never.* She persevered, received promotions, got passed over for many of them, but every once in a while, they knew to throw her a bone to avoid a discrimination lawsuit, and she went on to become the first Black woman to occupy nearly every managerial position she held. The firsts always suffer most. They must fight for what they have already earned and be content when the young White boy with no experience, but who has just graduated from college, is given the position you bid on. They are confronted by the limited imaginations of the White people who have never lived in proximity to Black women but feel resolute in the stories they've been told. The firsts must hear all the White folks tell them that they are their first. Even when they look you in the face and tell you that you're beautiful, it is speckled with the idea that they never thought they would utter those words, which is to say, beautiful for a Negress. If you're articulate they tell you that you're not like the other Blacks, you're different. Instead of thinking that maybe, just maybe, they had it wrong all along. Although these moments were insulting, my mother long held the desire to be exceptionalized. To stand out in some way as a superior Black, to be selected as special, not like the rest, which is what she had always wanted from her mother. She longed to be identified as singular in some way. So even though it stung, she enjoyed being recognized at all. But it is dangerous to become dependent on the iron fist for your validation.

It exhausted her, the work, the yearning, the resentment. My mother would come home limp. Her body nearly lifeless. I know she thought of us as she endured the tireless terrors of the railroad. Thinking of the mouths she had to feed, thinking of what she was running away from and toward. She'd return home to us depleted. She was a fighter like no one I've ever encountered, but she always told us, *You have to pick your battles, boo.* Sometimes it takes weeks to get over the wounds of biting one's tongue. You're left with the lingering taste of metal as a reminder of all you've swallowed. Then you're tormented with the rehearsal of what you should have said, reproaching yourself for not being quick enough with your retort, but satisfied with being equipped for the next encounter, which is sure to come. This, too, is a form of battle.

If her children asked her for anything when she got home, anything whatsoever, Mama Connie's refusal usually began with, *Now you know I been up at that job with them White folks all day . . .* And that would be enough for us to know to get somewhere and sit down. The impact of White aggressions follows you home and shapes the way you parent. On a cellular level, it's consuming, leaving space for very little else. Love is the redemption, but even that requires that you pull from an empty well. Thirty-seven years of service to a company that often reminded her that she was an affirmative-action hire. That her promotions were quota-based. The civil rights policies that came to be in my mother's generation didn't come easy. She needed to prove her right to hold every position, to them and to herself, while many of her colleagues' families had worked for the railroad for generations and were legacy hires. It could very well be that my mother's family had too, but we'll never know.

There was one coworker who I remember particularly well, Diego. I recall sitting beside the bathtub listening to my mother tell me about her day at work and despising the man who delivered my mother home to me each day in such a sour state. He also stood out because he was Mexican and I assumed that minorities would be supportive of one another, but it seems that even in the absence of Whiteness, its forces are still active. The fear that there can only be one diversity hire, so a minority will see the only other minority in the room as a threat, instead of the pool of White men. My mother was the only woman in her department, which covered train operations of a particular train yard. This included organizing which types of trains are coming and what materials they are carrying. Rocks, chemicals, vehicles. Certain trains cannot go on certain tracks through certain areas, and trains require specific types of crews to operate them. And the crews must be provided transportation via limo (van) to and from their worksites. My mother and Diego managed this yard along with a White man. She worked 11:00 a.m. to 11:00 p.m., and he took over from 11:00 p.m. to 11:00 a.m., and then they'd have the middleman as a swinger and they'd switch shifts after a while. But every time she got to work Diego complained and insulted her work practices. He reported her to the White men above them. He was not a woman, and he was not Black, and therefore he felt socially superior. He felt he'd earned his right to be there, and she was merely a quota hire. She had more seniority than him, but he had a college degree. I feel many non-Black minorities and women often forget that they also benefit from the civil rights laws which Black people put their lives on the line for. He thought he was one of the good ol' boys, but they prefer for their minorities to know their place, and Connie knew the game well. There was a promotion on the horizon for which both my mother and Diego applied, and he was sure that he would get the position on merit. Connie knew it wasn't a merit game. It was a game of if you could make the White men feel comfortable around you. None of them got to where they were on merit. Connie received the promotion and Diego was fired shortly after. It was one distraction out of the way, but others took his place. The railroad is highly competitive and organized around an order put in place hundreds of years ago. Just like the rights of way cleared by enslaved Black people, the grooves of history remain engrained.

A few years ago, my mother and I were shopping in a resale consignment shop in the Heights, the upper-class Houston neighborhood where she lives now, and she asked the man behind the counter for a price without looking at his face.

He said, *Connie?*

She looked confused, *Yes?*

It's me, Diego.

I was nearby but I moved to see his face. My mother had forgotten him, and I was still holding a grudge. Because of him micromanaging my mother and reporting minor infractions, she had to be earlier to work, more alert, and double-checking and second-guessing herself. Which meant hell for me at home.

Diego?

There was silence as he awaited her recollection that never came. She had erased him.

Diego . . . from Lloyd Yard.

Oh my, Diego, she said smiling with great pleasure. *Yes. Hi. How are you doing?*

I'm good, what are you doing over here?

I live over here.

You live over here? He had to confirm that he was hearing right. *Wow. This is a nice neighborhood.*

Yes, I've lived here since I retired from the railroad.

Retiring from the railroad was a flex because they provide unprecedented benefits, especially for managers, and their spouses also receive their own individual railroad retirement funds. This was put in place to support the wives of railroad men who sacrificed by keeping the family while their husbands were away most of the time. They had not considered that there would be Black women like my mother working at the railroad when they created these norms. Everywhere she went, she had not been what they had imagined.

She went on to tell Diego that she'd never been in the shop because she doesn't particularly like secondhand items, but her daughter had dragged her in. She only obliged because her daughter was visiting from New York City. She's in grad school at an Ivy League school up there. She told him everything that he wouldn't expect to hear from the high-school-educated Black woman who he had looked down on back then. He visibly gagged. We couldn't get both feet out the door before she grabbed my arm, tilted her head down to me, and raised her brows, *Sa, what I tell ya? Stick around long enough and the shit will flip.* We folded over in laughter. It felt like some sort of victory for all the hell he'd put us both through. But it wasn't really, because it proves the narrative that there is only room for one exceptional minority.

The railroad wasn't just representative of a pathway to security for my mother; it served as a representation of Black freedom. On any given day during the Great Migration, you would see crowds of Black people at the train stations in the South. They weren't just there to catch trains; they were there to see folks off. Those that they knew and those that they didn't. It was inspiring to see people leaving, disappearing into the unknown, even if it wasn't yet your turn, it provided hope that one day it could be you. The Colored cars were run-down and untended so there were women at the station selling plates of hot food for passengers who would be traveling for days, often stopping at stations along the way that didn't allow Black people to use the bathrooms, let alone eat, so they took to the woods to mind their business and packed enough food to get them where they were going. There were ministers there to pray for a safe journey and whatever they might be met with on the other side. And as the train pulled out, there was sorrow and jubilation as they waved them away until the train was out of sight. For a people whose mobility was taken, locomotion provided a means for independence and escape. Just as it does now for migrants taking *the beast* toward America's southern borders. Once my mother came home devastated after a train car on the yard she was managing was found to have a migrant family dead inside. She slept for hours to escape what she'd witnessed, but her dreams tortured her. It was known that migrants would ride on top of and inside train cars, but this particular train car didn't have proper ventilation, so the family suffocated. It was one of the cars you get into through the top and it empties out through the bottom, but there was no way to climb out once inside. Hopper cars meant to carry loose unpalletized materials like grains, fertilizers, coal, not people. There was a mother and her children inside, and I think my mother saw herself in that mother. A woman who would stop at nothing, even if it cost her life, to secure a safer environment for her children. And in witnessing the depths of the despair that would make you climb into a dark train car, it made her fear what would happen if she were to lose her job. This was a constant fear that my mother spoke of during my childhood. I couldn't understand it as a girl, but as a mother, as a single mother, I now see what was at stake. What it means to have no one else to depend on financially to ensure your children are fed and well. In these reflections I feel ashamed of my needs as a girl and the resentments I carry now as a result of this neglect. I couldn't have my mother because she was at work giving the railroad all she had to give. It is a nearly impossible task to balance: playing the White folks' game at work to stay on board, being the financial provider for your children, and somehow within that trying to keep yourself alive. I can understand why my emotional needs were tertiary in this equation. And still, as a child, I needed her. I needed more than a house, and food and clothes, I needed emotional caretaking. She simply could *not* provide this. Where on earth was she going to pull that water from? She couldn't even provide it for herself. There was no time to grieve and be angry, so she repressed it. Just as her mother had. And she probably thought: *Oh well, I don't have it as bad as my mother did cleaning the floors of the jail cells.* And Betty Jean probably thought: *I can't complain, at least I'm not picking cotton.* And here I am, feeling ungrateful, in my New York City loft crying to my therapist over Zoom about what my mother couldn't give me and how she still can't, because she'd have to open up sixty-eight years of grief and anger to heal the wounds that would make her stop hurting me.

The questions I've always asked myself, since I was a girl, are, *Do I have the right to feel this way? Have I earned the right to be sad? Have I suffered enough to call this pain my own?* I work for myself writing from an office overlooking the Hudson that I've painted pink and call *The Writers Womb.* I am able to pick my daughter up from school every day, cook dinner for her each night, and read to her before bed. A privilege no one in my family before me has had. They were working nights for White families, White companies. But then I tell myself that everything they did was so that I could have the time to feel all that they couldn't. The grief I carry is not all my own. It's theirs too. Generations of repressed grief and anger and traumas and sadness which no one before me ever had the privilege to fully feel. So it was passed to me. This is actually the freedom they were fighting for. The freedom to live fully in their own bodies. Generations of learning that our bodies are our own to claim. And I benefit from their sacrifices, the times they went against what they believed in just to keep their job, the blood in their mouths and stones in their bodies, but that also means I have inherited the duty to feel it all. And it's oh so heavy.

My mother has always believed that if you work hard, you can earn your right to freedom. To a more leisurely life not dictated by your physical and emotional exertion. Freedom is often not considered a birthright to people born from a lineage of exploited laborers. The railroad was a path toward the liberation my mother imagined just as it had represented this for many Black people in America. It was the great savior horse that delivered so many from the South to the North. It was how many escaped slavery. After building the tracks, enslaved laborers would hitch rides north atop the train cars at night and hide during the day. Even though many were lost due to the working conditions, Black people were in fact constructing the pathways for future Black people to escape the South. And my mother was doing the same for me. Creating a pathway. But so much of her was lost along the way. Today she says, *I hate what that railroad did to me. I hate the humiliation. I hate all the times I didn't stand up and say something. I hate all the times I felt like a sellout. I did my time and got the hell out of there.* But once my mother didn't have her job as her identity, all she was left with was her self.

$\mathcal{M}AD$

When my mother had a weekend off from work, she would cook breakfast for us. The only time we had breakfast on weekdays was in preparation for a standardized test. Usually she'd prepare Malt-O-Meal with sugar and butter. But on weekends, she made grits and eggs with bacon and toasted white bread. She'd holler to my brother and I from the kitchen while she was still preparing the meal. But if we didn't wake, wash our faces, and arrive in the kitchen before she'd finished, a spiral would ensue. She would stomp out to her room and slam the door when we sauntered in, awaiting her audience before the thunderous departure. Shutting us out, emotionally disconnecting. Leaving us to eat alone questioning what went wrong. We became accustomed to this behavior but were still unsure of the cause. Perhaps she felt alone in those moments. She often expressed that we were ungrateful when it came to food. Because she understood what it was like to go to bed hungry. We viewed food as an essential, not a luxury. The kitchen was a space of contention in our home. Even these moments of care ended in a disruption that would echo throughout the weekend. I think what my mother couldn't articulate was a deep and persistent feeling of loneliness.

She resented our childlike helplessness. She was most cruel when we were sick. She would say, *You think I have time for this?* As if we had conspired against her. Once on our annual summer vacation to Mexico, I became sick and Shannon, who was prone to ear infections after swimming, had a fever. She was overwhelmed and furious with us. This is probably why I didn't tell her that the tour guide who had taken us out in the open water to snorkel, while she stayed ashore, had put his hands inside of my swimsuit, and inside of my body, while I looked at the coral below. I didn't say anything to anyone. I knew somehow that it would be my fault. I recently told her what happened that summer under the water, to which she shouted, *What do you want from me? I did the best I could.* And I immediately became that ten-year-old girl in the warm waters of the Gulf, all alone with no shore in sight, and I understood why that girl didn't tell her mother then. Because she couldn't have survived both violations. She buried it, and her body became ill.

We left the trip earlier than planned. Upon deplaning, she said, *Pretend to be really sick so we can skip the line.* I was *really* sick. Once we were moved to the front of the customs line, I was vomiting again, and she said, *Okay, that's enough. Tone it down.*

She refused to speak to us on the car ride home, aside from telling us how ungrateful we were for getting sick on vacation. She iced us out emotionally, and we patiently awaited her return. I received the intensity of her rage, as she felt I'd exaggerated my illness, and Shannon was simply following my lead. She always insisted that he did whatever I did, therefore I was responsible for his behavior. But who was responsible for hers?

As we grew older, we learned to conceal our illnesses.

As she grew older, hers was more difficult to ignore.

Have you ever seen a rock crumble? Or the collapse of a mountain? The sinking of a blue whale? Goliath falling. The snap of an Achilles. A house set ablaze. Nothing is quite like seeing the deterioration of a human soul. It begins slowly, indiscernible. But it takes only that one foundational beam, in that one particular spot, to make the middle fall out the bottom. And only then can you understand all those creaks over the years. They were subtle and so faint that you could dismiss them. It's only when you see the ruins at your feet that it begins to make sense. From grainy to full focus. All the weight and all that water to bear over the years, and one day it becomes clear how fragile that house always was. How much you didn't see because you didn't want to see. Because it would alter who you thought you were. Then you look at the rubble and begin to fear the limits of your own bones.

Not acknowledging mental illness is simply another refusal of pain.

It began with incessant sleeping. If my mother wasn't working, she was sleeping. But she would rarely fall asleep in her bed. She would doze off anywhere, everywhere, but she refused her bed. She feared what awaited her there. The sofa, the table, the toilet, the tub. Disappearing into her nightmares. She would wake up frantically looking for her pocketbook, panting and wide-eyed, staring at me suspiciously. Not at me, *through me*. Even as it became more frequent, it was never less alarming to be accused of stealing. *You been in my purse?* Somehow, I always felt guilty. Her eyes so accusatory that I was compelled to apologize just to break her gaze. After tucking her monogramed bag beneath the blanket, her eyes rolled back, and she would be out again. Perhaps our existence as her children was a threat to this new lifestyle, or maybe it wasn't us that she saw when she'd awaken, but little Black bodies that overpopulated her childhood homes.

Her sisters say she was always like this, tortured by nightmares. I suspect that it began in childhood when someone climbed through the bedroom window where all the children slept, pressed into one another across two mattresses. The window had no pane, it was simply covered by the shingles that would typically protect a roof from the elements. My mother recalls once waking up to the shadow of a man fondling her. She screamed, wakening the whole house on Beulah Street as she watched the man leap back out the windowless frame. Soon afterward, Betty Jean boarded up the window, not only blocking out intruders but also the sun, the breeze, the few pleasures that make a life in poverty bearable. As Betty Jean grew accustomed to urban life, she realized she was in the ghetto now. She was shaken from her country naivete that one could rest soundly and undisturbed with open windows.

The emerald carpet was covered in designer clothes as she removed her garments, her armor, wherever she happened to fall asleep, and they remained there for days, sometimes weeks, until I was summoned to clean. I became the mother in residence, a role that brought me much purpose. I ironed and washed and cooked for me and Shannon. I was being groomed to be a good wife to the wealthy Black man that she imagined would prevent the bloodline's potential backslide into poverty. She'd remind me that she made me beautiful by marrying a White-adjacent Black man with a narrow nose and thin slits for lips. My birth alone left me beholden to her. And I acquiesced.

Meanwhile, she got heavier and heavier. By the time I was ten, my mother weighed more than three hundred pounds. She would eat when she was angry. When she was anxious. When she was tired. When she was restless. When she didn't know what else to do with herself. My father did little to conceal his disgust. She would stuff chips in her mouth in front of him and watch him squirm. He was cruel, and she didn't know where else to put her suffering, so she ate to fill the voids.

Her relationship with food was always complicated by the fact that she didn't have any growing up, and now she could indulge without ceasing. Initially her weight gain was a sign of wealth, because she was no longer the girl they called "skin and bones" or "po." But then it became her comfort. She was at war with her body. When her butt blossomed, at first she was proud to have curves, to be womanly, but then it crossed a line. The line between sexy and repulsive is slight. When Shannon and I were able to shelve objects on it without her awareness, we gave it a name, *the Cahoonta*. We laughed with my father at his vile jokes. My mother threatened, *He ain't gone buy you no Jordans, he broke as hell. So be careful what you laugh at.*

The threat was for us, but the shaming was for him. She was the breadwinner now, and she let it be known. A double-barrel hit.

It was disturbing to watch their marriage curdle. I felt I needed to choose between them. She was not dependable, but more than he. He was not the kindest, but more than she. I would have chosen my father, but he wouldn't choose me back. They had each already chosen themselves. Me and my brothers were standing in the middle of the wreckage, blaming one another for the flames. Trying to salvage what we could from the burning house.

My father felt that she betrayed the life they had agreed upon by becoming fat. They could never reach their opulent pinnacle if she was overweight. Fat was for people out of control. For people without couth. He didn't know that the only way to save their envisioned life together was to love her. That the food was merely filling the void of where the love once was. My father believed that he could shame her out of her funk. (No one would ever say sadness or melancholia or depression. She was simply in a funk.) The only lecture I recall receiving from my father with sincerity was, *Don't be fat like your mother. Slow down at the table. Push back from your plate. Nibble, don't gorge. A girl always holds in her stomach. You don't want lumpy thighs like your mother.*

· · ·

We returned home one day to an empty house. The living-room furniture was gone. My mother's precious emerald set. The étagère, record player and all the records, the fish tank and all the fish. Even the bed in my parents' room. *Junior's* room was cleared out as well. Shannon and I sat together in the middle of the green carpet and wept uncontrollably. "We've been robbed," I said. But all the other bedrooms were untouched.

My mother paced from room to room nodding her head with furrowed brows, taking inventory. Her lips drawn tightly, as if she were holding something there. I remember wondering why she was so quiet. Surveying, but not frightened. There was a silent calm that was unlike her. Sometimes when she awoke in her sleep from nightmares she went to the front door and made sure the deadbolt was secured. Checked every window in the house. Set

the alarm she'd had installed. And placed broomsticks or base-
ball bats in the windows for additional security. Made sure her
children were in their beds. Pulled the covers up under our chins
and kissed our heads before going back to her room. But in this
moment, she was still inside. She was never more terrifying than
when she was in this state. Someone was about to pay, and I
didn't want it to be me.

My father had come while we were in school and my mother at
work and cleaned out the house with the help of *Junior*. He had
made his son an accomplice in ransacking our home in the middle of the day while the neighbors watched. My mother later discovered that the house had been put up as collateral for another
house that he was purchasing across town. The mortgage lender
had somehow gotten her phone number and called to speak with
her about the transaction that she knew nothing of. Both of my
mother's childhood traumatic experiences had been ignited,
abandonment and housing insecurity, by the man she had chosen to marry twice. A man she had known since she was sixteen.
A man she half trusted, because she could never fully trust any
man. *Niggas and flies.*

I was thirteen. This was my parents' second and final divorce.
My mother sank deeper.

Eventually, all the clothes my mother had acquired to exude
wealth no longer fit her. She could no longer shop designer, she
had to settle for Lane Bryant. To which Shannon would say from
the backseat, *Where are we headed, to the big-chick store?* She had
doubled in size, because if she wasn't sleeping, she was eating.
This, too, was a form of vanishing, retreating further into invis-
ibility. Even in her sleep, she would grab handfuls of potato chips
from the pile she poured on the nightstand or armrest of the sofa
or atop her bare leg, and stuff them into her mouth with her eyes
shut. She wanted desperately to be fulfilled. I would stand over
her, watching her chest rise and fall, and sometimes she'd stop
breathing and I'd shake her awake. I found crumbs in the folds of
her sheets, in the crevices of the sofa cushions, wipe them into a

pile in the palm of my hands, throw my head back, and toss them into my mouth like sprinkles. I wanted to feel what she felt. To be closer to her. Sometimes I would tear off pieces of the plastic bags and eat that too.

After my father left, we ate out more. Fast food for dinner. Food for when we felt good, food for when we felt bad. Food for funerals, food for graduations. Food to say sorry, food to stay mad. Food when we were bored and food when we were having fun. Rich food, poor food. Pappadeaux and Pancho's.

Whenever she ate, we ate. She encouraged us to get more. Shannon was considered obese by his pediatrician, and I would have been too, had I not fully invested myself into basketball in middle school. Even when the regular season ended, I would travel with my AAU summer league team. It was my father's favorite sport. I thought if I became an exceptional player, he might come back for me. That he would come to my games. I begged and he said he would. I searched the bleachers for him. When you love a man the way I loved him, you can spot him at the Million Man March. Maybe he was running late, I'd think time and again, and Shannon, who was always there, would tell me tenderly, *Sasha, he's not coming.* And I became so angry with my brother for not allowing me my delusions. If I gave up hope, then there was nothing left to inspire me. It was easier to be upset with my brother than to blame my father. My father never came. And he never called to say he wasn't coming. But at least I was distracted and away from home most afternoons and summers.

When our neighborhood built low-income apartments, we relocated. My mother didn't like that more Black people had been moving in, and poor ones at that. She said she needed to save her children, not from poor people but from the things that poverty can make a person do. This is what humans do, use the safety of their children to conceal insecurities and justify their prejudices. We moved to a grand sprawling house when I was in high school. My parents competed to prove they were thriving independently of each other. My father's new house was lovely, with a garden full of roses, but inside was sparse, having only the furniture he had taken from us. He was eating sardines from a can with hot sauce and crackers whenever we came to visit. He had no laundry detergent or dish soap. Single rolls of toilet paper and no paper towels. The home had no love. But there were curling irons under the sink. My parents had been cheating on each other. My mother's lover looked almost identical to my father, fair-skinned, green eyes, Creole, and bowlegged. He was a railroad engineer. They were engaged for years but when his heart started to give him problems she left him. *I don't do sick.* My father's lover couldn't have been more different from my mother. She was pliant, the type of woman my mother calls meek. My mother supposes that they were introduced to each other through my paternal grandmother, who had never approved of my mother. She was an executive assistant for her entire career at the same oil company and never aspired for more. A soft-spoken, old-fashioned lady who couldn't have children but was content with childlike men. They're still married. My mother never remarried.

My father is a master at making others feel sorry for him when he has betrayed them. Through tears he'd suggest that he didn't spend time with us because he didn't have the money to provide us with the lifestyle we were accustomed to. That it was our fault for shaming him with our needs. And my mother is a master of making others think their feelings are their own, when really she has bestowed them. She never said, *You should hate your father,* but when she would occasionally drop us off at his new home, she'd come inside and look around. They would still behave as if they were married. Kissing without discretion, undressing each other, laughing like teenagers in love. But driving away from him brought my mother a sadness that she refused to acknowledge, so she turned to her old faithful anger. *What kind of man steals from the mother of his children? A real man leaves with the clothes on his back. I'm sorry I chose him to be your father.* It was the only kind of sorry she had to offer. I was sad too. I missed him but I was afraid to say so because I feared she'd see it as disloyal. She still insists that we call *her* on Father's Day. I felt as if a limb had been severed, or numbed. A part of myself couldn't be exercised. Even though I felt he betrayed me by leaving me alone to care for my mother, I still believed in him, that he'd come back for me. Perhaps it is better to never have a father than to have one and lose him. He was my phantom limb.

My father had been the only one who could make my mother laugh in a particular register. Only he could disarm her, even in desperate resistance. With him gone, Shannon assumed some of his responsibilities. He was always the temperature regulator. Guilt was my contribution, I knew we were a burden, my acknowledgment was my way of comforting her, atoning for my birth. He was the funny one, I the dependable one. He always told the truth, and I lied to keep her from disappointment. He chose to forget, while I remembered. He gave her neck massages, and I ran her bath. Because the tub was the only place where she was at peace. All the ice she carried that shielded her heart melted away in the tub. She was soft and tender there. Whenever my mother experiences discomfort, she takes to the water. The water settles her. The ocean, a pool, a hot spring. Often, it's the bathtub. I can't recall my mother ever taking a shower. It is one of her only rituals that must not be disturbed or hurried. Many of our most difficult conversations have taken place with her in the bathtub and me sitting on the floor beside her. She'll send for anyone in our family to meet her beside the tub, she is immodest in her home because she never allows anyone but family to enter. Many of her friends have never been inside. The bathtub is also where she spends time with my daughter. It is perhaps where my mother is most honest.

One day when I was about ten, she called for me to sit beside the bathtub. As I sat on the tiles she was quiet and it was not immediately obvious what I was doing there, but I felt the intensity of the room. Nervously, I scanned my mind for what I could have done wrong. She sat for a while before asking me to pass her a crumpled-up ball of paper that was on the floor beyond her reach. The steam rose from the still water. I asked her what was on that paper as she grabbed the cordless phone from the floor. She ignored me as she dialed the number on the paper. Silence between us was always unsettling because it usually meant something was brewing, the stillness before the storm. Someone answered on the other end of the line. She introduced herself and asked to speak to Joseph. Her tone not dissimilar from the one she used with customer service representatives when she wanted her voice to sound like she was a White woman. They spoke briefly, she listened and nodded, she told Joseph how many children she had and where she lived. She asked him how many he had. The call couldn't have lasted for more than twenty minutes. When she hung up she threw the cordless phone across the bathroom floor and sank down into the water, using her toe to turn on the faucet and allow more warmth in. I asked who she had been speaking to. She said, *My daddy,* and sucked her teeth. *Niggas and flies.* She had somehow been connected with his sister who shared his phone number with her. I don't know what she had expected, but he couldn't give her what she needed that day. That was the only time she heard her father's voice. But she knew the only way she would have the courage to make that call was from the water. With me beside her.

Sometimes she'd ask me about my day, and I told her lies to please her. She told me about the men she was dating, some of them were her coworkers. Or her subordinates rather. One of the men was married and left his wife for her, only for her to dispose of him once he did. She was intolerant, like her mother. I cherished these moments of calm between us. A single mother will sometimes look to her children to fill the spaces left vacant by an absent man. She confided in me when I wasn't equipped to provide support or comprehend the complexities of her experiences. But neither was she. She understood her pain as anger and her destruction as power, thus the remedies were misapplied. What she saw as liberation was avoidance. Her emotional growth had been stunted in childhood, therefore she reacted as a nine-year-old in moments of frustration. And now, as I mother my teenage daughter, whenever she screams and slams doors like my mother would, I cover my ears and run to my closet, turn cold, and retreat into myself, just as I had as a girl when my mother behaved this way. While sitting in the dark, I remind myself that she is behaving like a child because she is a child, and I open the door because I know how isolating it can feel when your mother shuts you out emotionally. As a girl, sitting beside my mother while she bathed, she became supple, she let me in, and I cherished these moments. I tried to repeat to her phrases that I'd heard the women say at 50 10. Tried to mirror the wisdom of womanliness.

The married man she dated when I was in high school had lost one of his friends, another railroad man. He wanted my mother beside him as he grieved. She invited Shannon and I along without context. As we approached the open casket of a man we didn't know, I saw the man from our living room in the front row beside a woman and two young adults. I ignored the dead man and locked eyes with the woman beside the man. Her eyes as she watched my mother hug her husband. I stood behind my mother as she raised her chin with pride as her two youngest children walked behind her to the back of the church. The wife turned repeatedly throughout the service to stare at us. I was afraid to meet her gaze again, it held both sorrow and disbelief. After the service, railroad men came to greet my mother in the back of the church, where she laughed loudly and threw her hair back over her shoulder. She seemed pleased to be the one he had chosen.

When I saw the married man smiling and coming toward us, I asked if we could leave. If I could wait in the car in the parking lot. For selfish reasons, I was always attempting to avoid an escalation. Everywhere we went, when I noticed someone behaving in a way that may upset her, servers, cashiers, whoever, I would interject. It was self-sacrificial, but I would rather her be angry with me than withstand the embarrassment and shame of watching my mother make a stranger cry. At the funeral my mother spoke sharply through her teeth as she smiled and let me know we would not be leaving. I turned to my brother with widened eyes. He shook his head at me, as if to say, this is awful, but we cannot leave her here alone. As if to say, it's either going to be them or us, but somebody's getting hurt today. We knew this wouldn't end well. They embraced, the married man and my mother, and held on to each other. I gave him the scowl I was too afraid to give my mother. When we finally departed, as we descended the church steps, I heard a voice obscured and distant, and then in full clarity. The wife was behind us. Pleading to speak with my mother. My brother and me stood between the two women. I held my breath. My mother looked to the woman, scanned her from head to toe, and paused before saying *no* and turning away. The wife grabbed at the strap of my mother's purse on her shoulder. My mother gave the wife the same look she gave us when we displeased her. It wasn't a look; it was more of a searing gaze. The kind that slices you open without a word. The kind that seems like it could kill a man. Sharp and swift and without a doubt. Like the heat that surrounds your face when you open the oven. You know it's coming, but its intensity still stuns. The woman released the strap and stood with her mouth open. She didn't know she was walking into the eye of a storm. I wanted to say something, but I dared not betray my mother. My brother turned to the wife and mouthed, *I'm sorry.* It was, in fact, her funeral. And we watched a grown woman's lifeless body as we crossed the street to our car in the parking lot. The wife still standing at the steps of the church. She had turned to stone. The entire way home my mother screamed at us. A mind-numbing scream with nowhere to escape to. She'd somehow seen my brother's apology, even though she'd already turned away. She saw me as an accomplice. We were traitors. She would make us suffer.

Whose team are you on? was a question often posed to us. She threatened to abandon us the way she had *Junior*, who she felt had chosen my father's side when he helped him empty out our living room. She seemed more upset with him than with her ex-husband. But he was only a child, caught in the crosshairs of his selfish parents. I guess she thought it was expected of my father, that's a man, but *Junior* wasn't a man, that was her son. *You know I will cut you off. You see how I cut your brother off,* she'd say to me and Shannon with a kind of grunt and maniacal chuckle. *Junior* was away in the Air Force by then, starting his own family and seeking emotional support from his mother. She ignored his calls. Refused him and his growing family. *Junior* is eleven and a half years older than me, so by the time he moved out I was only five or six, I don't have many memories of him, except he and my mother's violent confrontations when he came home after curfew.

After the emptying of our living room our family was divided in two, *Junior* and my father on one side and on the other side me, Shannon, and my mother. *Junior* hates us because it's easier than hating his mother. Once when he came over unannounced, through a back window, and was watching TV on the green leather sofa, my mother snuck up behind him and whispered in his ear, *If you ever come into my house through that window again, I'll mistake you for an intruder and blow your muthafuckin brains out.* She kept a gun in her pocketbook. Another time, years later after he'd married and had a child of his own, *Junior* showed up at our front door and my mother told us to keep quiet. He eventually left, but I'm sure he knew we were home. I never wanted to be the one on the other side of the door, knocking to be let in, while my mother pressed her finger to her lips in hopes that I would go away.

And as for that married man, he left his wife and home and moved into a small town house near our new home. I went with her to visit him when he moved in. I never looked him in the eyes again. Afterward, on the drive home I noted how nice the place was, to which my mother replied that she would never be going back there. So why had we gone to that funeral, why had he left his wife, why had we even met this man? She simply said, *I'm done with him.* Disposed. Maybe she could never trust a man who would leave his wife for another woman. Maybe because men are deemed more powerful than women, she played with them, weakened them for sport.

He, too, was dangerous. Shortly after she dumped him, he came to our house and let himself in. He stood still looking into my mother's eyes, his ego in one hand and a gun in the other. The sentiment was clear. *If I can't have you, no one can.* My mother never looked away from him. Never screamed. Never flinched or shed a tear. Never pleaded for mercy. She simply said, *Oh you gone kill me? In front of my kids?* And that was the end of that. He got in his car and drove away. He went back to his wife and died of a heart attack shortly after. My mother told me of his death, *You know they call me the black widow.* Just as Betty Jean had been called. Their venom of differing formulas, but erotic warfare all the same. I, too, came to know the satisfaction of seducing men into submission, and from the experience I know that the only way to get there is by killing off a part of yourself. He wasn't the first man to die of a broken heart after my mother disposed of him. Nor the last. We did not attend his funeral.

. . .

I was terrified of my mother and her power. And as a teenager I began to see that most people were. Her power grew congruent with her wealth. She felt to me indomitable. It seemed like no one could ever stand up to her. She cowered to no one, except Betty Jean. By the time I was in high school I relied on her less, which she had encouraged but also resented. Not intentionally, I began to exclude her. I was preparing for college, and without any guidance, I needed to figure everything out on my own. Despite being in the top of my class, none of my teachers or counselors took to me. I remember making a perfect score on my English assessment exam and my teacher handed back the tests, acknowledging the high scores of my White peers, none of which were as high as mine, but not mine. After making a perfect score in my Latin class, the teacher said, *Can no one in here beat her?* Both of those teachers were White women.

I knew that I was smart, because the only Black teacher I ever had, an older woman named Mrs. Frasier, had told me so in third grade. I was causing mischief and my parents had come to the school for a parent-teacher conference. Mrs. Frasier told them, "Ain't nothing wrong with this girl here. She just bored is all. She finishes her work before everyone and then starts disrupting everybody else." I was moved to advanced placement courses. I was sad to leave Mrs. Frasier, but I would see her occasionally at church on Sundays, with her long acrylic nails and rings on every finger, sitting in the pew near my grandmother. I wore my new appointment with pride. I was on the honor roll every semester and I pleaded with my parents to put the honor roll sticker on the back of their cars like the other parents, to which they responded, "You can't put stickers on a Benz, babygirl." The stickers piled up on the top of the kitchen cabinets, out of sight. I would occasionally climb atop of the counters to dust them off and count them like medallions. My parents told me I was pretty far more often than I was told I was smart. I never had another Black teacher after Mrs. Frasier, but what she provided was everlasting. It's what my mother had needed during integration. And what every Black child needs, someone to say that the child isn't *bad*, she's just curious.

No one at my majority-White high school was interested in helping a Black girl advance, and I didn't feel entitled to it because my mother had prepared me. *No one is coming to save you. You must save yourself.* Even if my mother didn't have answers, she could always point me toward where to find them. She always told me I could do anything I wanted in life, because I was her daughter. She told me there was no room that I didn't belong in. She told me that everything in life is negotiable, so don't be afraid to ask, so I asked my teachers to change my grades when I felt they were unjust. Her mantra was *God will make people say yes when they want to say no.* She taught me the power of audacity. This was the greatest gift she's provided me. That most of the battle is just believing. But as I began to see intellect as a way to distinguish myself, I could sense my mother feeling she was being left behind.

This shift became obvious to me one afternoon when *Artemis* came to visit us. Our new house sat at the end of a cul-de-sac in a wooded area with a man-made lake behind guarded gates. I was in the study on the computer when *Artemis* walked in to say, *You know that your mother is threatened by your intelligence.* My expression questioned her. My mother isn't threatened by anyone. And now I wonder, what had *Artemis* witnessed that day, had it always been there, shrouded in my mother's largeness? I wonder what happens when a mother begins to feel she is losing her position. Especially when she holds no dominance elsewhere in the world. Would she be willing to sacrifice the expansion of her daughter's growth in service to her ego? There is a tension that tightens between mothers and daughters as they grow older. But to want to flatten the very being that your body helped bloom is contradictory. It's not uncommon, though, especially for those who feel they weren't allowed their own spring season. Their own April, before they decided that making a baby could fill that hole in the dirt where the stem was supposed to be. But how can you water a new seed when you yourself have gone dry?

I remember coming home from college during winter break my sophomore year, the distance had allowed me space to hear myself without the noise. I was sitting in the passenger seat asking my mother why she made promises she couldn't keep. Why had she purchased a car for me only to stop paying the car note and tell me that my boyfriend should be paying it. Why did she want to push me into the arms of a man. A man who was a criminal. At the time I was dating an older man who I'd met at a cookout at *Red's* house, he was a former bank robber. She told me that she had nothing else to give me. I cried not because I didn't already know this to be true but because she had confirmed what I had spent so long refusing to believe.

Sometimes she is cruel beyond measure.

Sometimes my mother's behavior seemed like borderline personality disorder.

Sometimes she seems manic-depressive.

. . .

It wasn't until I began reckoning with my depression that I could see that my mother was suffering from what seemed to me to be her own mental illness. She never expressed shame, or hurt, or fear. She was only capable of expressing anger and rage. In our intimate moments together when I was a child, she had always discouraged any expressions of pain. When she was hot-combing my hair at the kitchen stove, if I winced at the heat biting the tender skin behind my ear as she eased in with the narrow teeth through my hair, she grew frustrated. *I ain't even touched you yet.* But the eye of the stove was flaming red, and the rising smoke reached me before the metal comb. I was praised when I silently endured. Care was never without pain, or rather the suppression of it. These were early lessons of endurance. A child expressing hurt was a nuisance. A girl expressing hurt was not tolerated.

Any confession of pain was considered weak. And weakness can be exploited, making you vulnerable to those who wish to see you sink. She reminded me often, as a warning, *Weakness will get you nowhere in life.* I was too sensitive, like my father. In therapy I had learned that there was a reason there were days when I didn't want to leave the bed or take a shower, days when I wanted to perish. Eventually I had the courage to tell my mother, *I'm sad,* she would say, *Don't speak it into existence, boo.* She wanted me to bury my suffering because there is no well for the tears of a Black girl.

Now I know that behind all the shouting and criticism, she was afraid. My mother feared someone coming to take away her middle-class life. Her security. That one wrong move could land her back in Third Ward. Like a slip and fall. And she would lose her manicured lawn, the diamonds she stored away and wouldn't wear out of fear of losing them, the Jacuzzi she had installed in the backyard under the pecan tree. She didn't particularly get to enjoy the life she built, she enjoyed the respect it yielded, her fear eclipsed the pleasure. Because she knew that if she pissed off the wrong White person at work, the world around her could collapse. She'd seen it happen to others. We still see it happening. This meant that she was constantly compromising herself to stay in the game. A White person with too much time and too much power can ruin you.

In his book *Flyboy in the Buttermilk,* Greg Tate poignantly acknowledges this fatal path that leads brilliant Black minds "down the crossroads . . . undecided between suicide, sticking it to the man, or selling its soul to the devil. The ones who keep up the good fight with a scintilla of sanity are the ones who know how to beat the devil out of a dollar while maintaining a Black agenda." But what about the ones that get out with the dollar but not with their sanity? Like my mother. Or with neither, like our beloved Nina Simone, who grew so weary of the game when she wrote in her journal, "They don't know that I'm dead, and my ghost is holding on."

Perhaps my urge to diagnose my mother is purely selfish. At least then I could say that she was sick and then maybe I could intellectualize the hurt I feel when I'm with her or at least have more compassion. I thought if she got help, or admitted that there was a problem, then the healing could begin and we could be close again. But even then, it doesn't take away the feeling of betrayal. On September 29, 1984, Andy Warhol wrote an entry in his diary stating that he had attended the birthday party of his friend Jean-Michel Basquiat's mother, an Afro–Puerto Rican woman of the water. Warhol describes Matilde as "matronly," which tells me that he was racializing her in a way that distinguished her from his friend Jean-Michel. She was Black, but in his eyes, her son was less so. She was a dark brown, round woman with a forehead that folded in a perpetual scowl of dissatisfaction. Warhol noted that his friend confided in him that he believed his mother had abandoned him when she was institutionalized. In all of his work, Jean-Michel never expressed this directly. But just because Matilde had been diagnosed as schizophrenic didn't mean that the resentment went away. And in my experience, after expressing resentment, the guilt comes in quick succession.

. . .

One morning, I received a call from my mother in the hospital. She had lost control and driven herself to the hospital. She felt like a dozen men were standing on her chest, she couldn't catch her breath. I have always been her emergency contact person; even as a girl, I was her confidante and nurturer. Now she was forced to surrender to her suffering and I was not within reach. Her system was collapsing from a lifetime of repressed rage and sadness with nowhere else to go. At the time I wasn't sure how to process my mother being unwell, as it seemed to defy all that I had been taught about Black women and stamina. Strong, resilient, and unbreakable. When I called, she asked me gently not to pretend to care. Because I wasn't there beside her, I had betrayed her.

I was already seeing the fraying of Connie's edges before my departure to New York, but hearing about her crisis from a distance brought on complex feelings, guilt being at the forefront. When your mother is unstable it changes the way that you interact with the world. Especially if your mother is Black, because there is no empathy for a sad Black woman. There is no language. White women in distress are coddled. Hysterical White women are a kind of helpless feminine ideal. But there is no precedent for how to hold a weeping Black woman. You feel responsible for their suffering, and even if you realize that there is nothing that you can do to reverse it, you try still. You stand by and watch how the ignorance of White people harms your mother, your god, and you become the mender. I recall Malcolm X saying, "We watched our anchor giving way." Left to fight against the raging and unwavering tides of violently racialized America while seeing the one who taught you your bob, your swing, and your defense withering away. You can't help but look in the mirror and anticipate a similar fate.

The effects of Whiteness on the psyche of the Black lived experience goes beyond cold-blooded murder and imprisonment. There is the insidiousness of the everyday maladies. It's the micro and macro aggressions which are then redeemed at home against the ones you hold dearest. Because where else do you put all that rage but into a slap across the face of your children and call it discipline? An authority made pliable by violence.

In his autobiography, when Malcolm X speaks about his mother, who was institutionalized when he was around thirteen, he grasps for ways to help the reader understand the difficulty of witnessing the collapse of your first home: "I can't describe how I felt. The woman who had brought me into the world, and nursed me, and advised me, and chastised me, and loved me, didn't know me. It was as if I was trying to walk up the side of a hill of feathers."

One night in Omaha, Nebraska, while her husband was away corralling others for Marcus Garvey's crusade for a Black utopia, a pregnant Louise Little was confronted by a pack of Klansmen at her doorstep. They probably thought that without the man of the house home, they could elicit the type of fear that would compel a pregnant woman to insist on fleeing. They probably thought she was a wife like the ones that had helped them iron their white robes. They probably thought they could intimidate her with violence. But they didn't know she was bred in violence, the product of her mother's rape by a Scottish man in Grenada. She wore that violence in her skin. They couldn't fathom a pregnant woman with the courage and will to step outside barefoot and weaponless to protect her other three children who peered out the window in terror. Placing her belly between the armed, hooded men and the promise of those waiting for her return inside. She knew they were watching. And sometimes a mother must do the unthinkable just so she can tell her kids that they can too. Shortly after this she gave birth to baby Malcolm. He, too, was with her that night, feeling the pulsing of adrenaline and the ways that the body can digest fear and make rage. He, too, was bred in the violence he would later be equipped to confront on behalf of Black folks. Even if he couldn't recall that evening, on a cellular level, his body could. Louise taught him his first lesson of dignity and will that all of humanity would benefit from in perpetuity. His mother also helped him see the different angles from which the system can throw a lick. Ultimately, White folks took his father from him, when his body was maimed by a train, and they took his mother, when they institutionalized a Black single mother of seven, her youngest just six months old. Spreading the children among different families. There are so many ways to dismantle a Black family.

When such tragedy is replicated in a family from one generation to the next, one womb to the next, I wonder in what ways the human anatomy begins to evolve and change shape. Just after scientists reported that trauma can be genetically inherited, I saw Jamaica Kincaid speak at Barnard College, and when the interviewer asked her thoughts on this discovery, she laughed. She laughed a laugh that felt like it was on the brink of exhaustion. A chuckle and a sigh. She laughed at the knowing that Black women carry but which is disregarded until a White man says it is so.

These traumas may be passed along, but in many ways our bodies are working to protect us. All the women in my family have died of complications of dementia. I believe that the repression of traumatic memories over time, to safeguard the nervous system, can manifest into a kind of rot. Neurological pathways burned out irrevocably over time. A decay of all those dead ends.

The composer and producer Quincy Jones has said that he completely blocked out the day that his mother was taken from their home in Chicago in a straitjacket until during the filming of a documentary about his life at his childhood home. Imagine trying to document your life but you can't even recall the most impactful moment of your childhood. How can you retrace a life of music while excluding the reason you play the piano is because she had played, and in her absence, the piano became your mother? His mother, Sarah Frances Wells Jones, was one of ten children from a family that went up to St. Louis from Vicksburg, Mississippi. She, too, was a striver. She was a freedom fighter. A gorgeous woman with honeyed skin and a storied voice, who spoke many languages and sang to her sons from her piano. He had blocked out that she had thrown his coconut birthday cake out of the window on his sixth birthday but somehow his body retained a repulsion to coconut. Like a short circuit, he forgot going to visit her at Manteno State Hospital, but the feeling of abandonment prevented him from allowing his lovers to get too close. We forget the origin but remember to tend the contusion. Quincy Jones suffered a brain aneurism at forty-one. Because you can only do so much blocking.

My mother has blank spots in her memory where her childhood used to be. When I ask her to recall moments, she is incapable. She disassociates to survive. And when anger just won't do, I suppose one flows naturally toward madness. My mother suffered silently for years as she desperately attempted to contort herself to fit into the ideals of what was deemed respectable in a world that would never accept her. Bending and overextending. That's the thing about respectability politics, the return is never quite what it presents itself to be, just like all the other promises of America. But you still try. If your money was a little longer, nose a little sharper, partner a little lighter, pitch a little higher, then maybe they will see you as equal. I think toward the end of her career at the railroad my mother finally came to see that no matter what she did, or how high she ascended, she would still be treated like a Negress.

With me living in New York, she also came to realize her dependency on me, and she hated the idea of needing anyone, because that meant that she could be abandoned again. And perhaps she felt I had abandoned her by leaving Houston. With all of her children grown and living away from home, she struggled to find reasons to continue the fight she'd been in since she was thirteen. Without the fight, she struggled to find reasons to stay alive.

After my mother left the hospital, she took her first extended leave from work, released what felt like thirty-six years' worth of tears. And rage. *I gave my life to that railroad, and they don't give a damn about me.* It is scary to see the most formidable person you've ever known crumble, because then you must consider that it may come for you. In some ways, survival is surrendering to this reality. And releasing the fear of remembering.

What if you walk right into the past before it comes to snatch you back?

The beauty and elegance of the bayou is often disregarded due to its milky brown hue. You can only arrive at brown when you have absorbed and so shall reflect the color of coalescence. The brown suggests that the water has history; the color indicates memory. Even when there is a quiet collective agreement to forget, the water knows.

Awakening

FOUR GENERATIONS: MYSELF, BETTY JEAN, AND
MAMA CONNIE HOLDING SOFIA, 2017

SASHA

//////////

We are much more than we are told.
We are much more beautiful.

—EDUARDO GALEANO

15

Memory of Fire

"A land condemned to forgetfulness" is what the writer Eduardo Galeano once called the Americas. "A system of power that is always deciding in the name of humanity who deserves to be remembered and who deserves to be forgotten." America insists: Forget where you come from, forget your languages, forget your rituals, religions, homelands. Forget centuries of enslaved labor. But the past is all I can think about these days. I learned to mother through remembering. Motherhood feels like a sequence of confrontations with the past. Difficult moments where I see myself in my daughter's face and I must decide if I want to practice the type of motherhood that I theorize or the type of motherhood that I am familiar with. As a young single mother raising a Black child in America, I am forced to ask, *What do I do when I see myself turning into my mother?* My mother who mothered from, and in defense of, her traumas. What can I disentangle so that my daughter can be a little closer to freedom? I piece together fragments of the past to construct a future that liberates me from it. I feel the tremors in my body, and I look to my mother, and to her mother, and ask, *Can't you see me shaking?*

They deny their pain and I drown in them. They say they forgot the past, yet memories of what my ancestors endured to get me here keep me alive. Teaching me how to keep my head up, barely breaching the surface, to gather and gasp air deeply when provided. It is only here, in the sacred space between aliveness and submersion, that you can be carried. But you must relinquish the fear of being taken under.

This precarity is where Black women have endured, built lives, and even dared to love, with the weight of a nation on their hips. The same nation that is responsible for all this forgetfulness. Telling us we don't live lives worth remembering.

To my mother and to her mother I say: Give it all to me. Allow me to carry this for us. Allow me to disentangle all this beauty that's tethered to all this pain. But even when my mother, and her mother, dare not speak of the past, their bodies are still in conversation with the hurt. When memories become transient, the body holds it to justify the armor you've built that clings like a scab to a wound. Deep down they both desperately wanted someone to ask them, "What is your story?" and then stick around to listen to the answer. But when I ask, the hurt replies first: *Oh lord, here she go remembering again.*

. . .

In 2005 my mother and grandmother drove to Tyler, Texas, where I was attending college as a freshman. I was recruited to play basketball for a Division II university. To get to the small East Texas town they drove three and a half hours north on Interstate 45. The flatlands allow for a clear view of the distant horizon blurred only by the heat waves. On either side of the highway are farms where longhorns graze. Besides the car, nothing moves quickly. You journey through what feels like a sinister land, the breadth of history in the air. You're driving north, away from the Gulf, so the air dries up. You pass through Huntsville, where my father's brother is serving a life sentence in an institution that transitioned seamlessly from plantation to correctional facility. When the light on the top of the tower shines, it signifies that someone is being killed in the most active execution chamber in the country.

My beloved Texas has made a name for itself through its merciless cruelty. There was a grand imposing statue of Robert E. Lee in Tyler, where I was studying, that signaled to me: *You don't belong here.*

Betty Jean and my mother arrived to take me to visit the last of my grandmother's aunts and uncles living in Shreveport, Louisiana. My mother had arranged the journey for her mother and included me because she could sense my distress. I was living in an on-campus apartment where I had my own room but shared the bathroom with my roommate who was also my teammate. When we met, she acted as if she had never seen a Black person up close before. Then she told me that she hadn't. She inspected me. But when my eyes met hers, she'd look down or away, as if I'd just caught her, as if her thoughts had been revealed to me.

One afternoon, my roommate and her boyfriend, who was visiting from their rural hometown, came into the apartment arguing, assuming I wasn't home. He yelled. Threw things. Punched walls. Then the crescendo, "I won't share no shower with no Nigger." I continued reading. I had grown up in a house where I learned to tune out noise, disappearing into the spine of a book. But all this commotion over me seemed excessive. Eventually I came out to use our shared bathroom, their eyes widened before shutting the door. All the noise settled. The next day there were flowers outside my door with a note. I never read the note, and I stepped over the flowers. Our coach called me and my roommate into her office and said we needed to *work out our differences.* I told her the situation had nothing to do with me before exiting. A few days later I returned to the apartment after practice, and my roommate had moved out. She quit the team. The room beside me remained vacant for the rest of the year. The university decided that isolation was the solution for Blackness.

My mother and grandmother came to remind me of who I was and where I came from. To take me back to our ancestral homeland of Louisiana. I was so unhappy in Tyler that I couldn't keep any food down. When we arrived in Shreveport, Betty Jean told everyone we saw that I was in college. For me, this was nothing to note, all my friends went to college after high school. It was just what one does. I was reminded in Louisiana of my privilege. As Aunt Eloise and Betty Jean reminisced about Elm Grove, and all those hard yesterdays, I realized that neither one of them had graduated high school. They were expected to quit to help in the fields. To help feed the men and raise the young. Betty Jean only got to the tenth grade. Aunt Eloise, the third.

I dozed in and out of their conversation. My mother never has liked to see me rest, she sees leisure as a symptom of laziness. But this, I'm sure, is inherited from her mother, whose labors as a girl were in direct correlation to her value. But Betty Jean had softened. She pulled my head into her lap and stroked my hair. Something she had never been able to do with my mother. "Listen here," my grandmother looked down into me, "don't let those White folks take nothing off you. You right where you supposed to be." I didn't have to ask her if she had ever been called the N-word. It is understood that we all had. "They always getting in the way. They'll do anything they can to run you up out of there. Don't let 'em move you, baby."

Don't let 'em move you, baby.

When I returned to Tyler I understood that I wasn't there alone, I was carrying generations with me. My family from all over Louisiana who couldn't read because it was illegal. I say that I carried them, but really, they were carrying me.

. . .

Back in Tyler I remember thinking that racism is draining. I was fatigued because I was pregnant. I also remember thinking that my grandmother must have known, because she had been so tender with me. Perhaps in the way that she wished she would have been cared for. My first boyfriend and I spent the summer together swimming and fucking at the sparsely furnished apartment of my friend who lived on Holly Hall. When I called him to ask him for help paying for the abortion, because I didn't want to alert my mother, he said the baby wasn't his. That was the last time I spoke to him. He doesn't know if I had the baby or not. He never called. We had known each other since I was thirteen. How could the person with whom I shared my first moan be so cold?

Gone's daughter took me to the abortion clinic and cared for me afterward. I didn't tell my mother. I was no longer a passive listener of the stories I had heard in the living room at *50 10*, I was now living within them. I had heard this one before, too many times to count. And I am sure that my first boyfriend, a first-generation fatherless Black boy born to a Jamaican woman navigating migration and motherhood alone, had heard these stories in his living room as well. He was simply assuming his position. Obeying what he had been taught he should be to call himself a man, apathetic.

For childish reasons, I thought those stories from *50 10* would never become my own. But the cycle doesn't stop because you say so. You can't call the game from the sidelines. You gotta get on the board first. Everyone knows you must learn the game before you can break the rules. Before you break it open and investigate its insides. Allow the light to come in. Then a kind of aperture happens. Exposing the beauty and the bruises. And isn't this our deepest fear and our greatest hope as human beings, to be fully seen? Even if it is by oneself. It hurts so bad to be both the seer and the seen. That's why so many of us choose to look away.

I began college pregnant.

And I graduated pregnant.

Motherhood proved inevitable.

16

Sofia

She didn't know what to throw away and what to keep.

—TUPAC SHAKUR, "BRENDA'S GOT A BABY"

I met *the oilman* in Houston early in the summer, when the crawfish was ripe from the bayous. He was in town for a conference. My friend had stood me up, so I ate at the counter and the bartender told me my bill had been paid for by the stranger a few seats away. He smirked and waved to me with his fingers. The bartender, a younger White man, noted that had the older gentleman not paid, he would have covered my bill himself. White male egos jostling before me.

The oilman offered to take me to lunch the following day, at the Galleria, and I agreed. In Houston culture, this was not uncommon. These Southern standards of women being courted in this way still hold true. He told me he loved my smile, reaching across the table to tuck my bottom lip. I was pouty because my laptop had crashed earlier that day while I prepared for an exam in one of my undergraduate courses. He bought me a new one after dessert. He asked me if I could have any car, which would it be, I said something unimpressive, he laughed and said, no, you need a Maserati. When I suggested Gucci, he said Chanel. I wanted crossbody, he said handle bag. He began grooming me to understand that I knew nothing, and he knew everything, and if I was a good girl, he would make sure I had whatever it was that he wanted for me. I was living my mother's dream. She encouraged her twenty-year-old daughter to be in a relationship with a man older than her and praised my good fortune. With all I had accomplished, this brought her the most pride. She had made me beautiful and now it would pay off for the family, even if it meant sacrificing her daughter. It didn't matter how he treated me along the way. And he fulfilled the longing I had for the way my father would treat me before he left, when he still called me *precious one*.

A week later he returned to Bogotá, where he lived alone. He would Skype me from his large empty bed with exposed wooden beams hovering overhead while the maids brought tea to his bedside. I listened from my college dorm, absorbing. With him I was able to rest in the foreign state of helplessness while he got to feel like a big man.

For years we met up in beautiful hotels from Paris to Punta del Este, Tuscany to Mexico City. Way beyond the waters that I was used to. I think people would see a young Black woman with a slight, follicle-ly challenged White man and assume his wealth because even if restaurants were closed, once we walked in, they'd reopen the kitchen for us. My presence affirmed his power. And he was generous with me because of this gift I bestowed.

It would be years before we became intimate, but he frequently asked me if I would give him a daughter. His machismo philosophy was that men, innately, seek to spread their seed and multiply their lineage, while women are simply seeking security. The latter was not untrue from where I was situated at the time. He assured me that all one needs to have a child is love and money; I had the former, he the latter. When I went to the bathroom and I lifted my toes toward God, it was a kind of prayer. That maybe he would keep his promise. That maybe things would be different for me.

I could feel it. I knew I was pregnant before any test could tell me so. But when I told him, he said abort the child or you'll never hear from me again. Because of Betty Jean I had no fear of vanishing men.

. . .

There were a dozen people in the room when I gave birth, none of them the father of the child. My labor was induced a few weeks early because I ridiculously felt better equipped to raise a Capricorn. I was ill-equipped either way. I made the decision without notice and *the oilman*'s passport was supposedly still being processed for renewal, so he couldn't attend the birth of his first daughter. He sent flowers and well-wishes.

My mother looked at me and asked, *What if the baby comes out Black like me?*—as if she was apologizing. I was heartbroken for her. Failing to assuage a lifetime of self-loathing, I replied, *If she is, she will be beautiful.* My aunties, cousins, younger brother, and childhood friend filled the small delivery room while I played Norah Jones on loop for twelve hours. It was the night that Mara Brock Akil's series *The Game* was being revived on a new network after a long pause in production and I heard Shannon whisper to my friend, "Watch she go into labor soon as the show comes on."

I was upset with my mother because she had left me to walk across the street with my cousin to get margaritas and nachos from the Mexican spot. She came back handing out salt-rimmed plastic cups. My pain was muffled by their joy and laughter. I wanted my mother to comfort me, but we have always had different concepts of the word. I wanted her to ask me how I was and stroke my hair. She thought being there and working the room was care enough. Their laughter made me feel protected.

All the women cocooning me were single mothers and no one asked who the father was. Or where he was. They knew not to. Just as they knew not to ask Betty Jean where their fathers had gone. He was where they all were, doing what they do best, getting lost.

My doctor was selected by my mother. An older Slavic man who had delivered my younger brother and many of my cousins, all via cesarean. He was acquainted with the cervixes of many of the women in the room. I didn't see him until delivery. He was on standby, calling in periodically to check my dilatation.

There was no care provided by the medical staff. Often, women in the maternal ward are treated as if they are ill, but being pregnant is not a pathology, and many complications could be avoided if individual care and comfort were provided. I could sense the nurse's judgment, I was a twenty-three-year-old Black woman without a husband. They didn't see me as a person with agency, a person they needed to tell what they were putting into my IV. They were frustrated with my endless questioning about what their plans were for my body.

Like other times in my life, I turned to books for guidance beyond what my mother and grandmother could provide. Books on how to give birth, what to expect, how to prepare, manuals with images of demure White women who didn't gain any weight during their pregnancies standing beside supportive innocent-looking White husbands who held their hands. Nowhere were my circumstances illustrated on the pages. And just like other times, I would have to imagine a life for myself and my child. But the women standing before me—my aunties, my mother, my cousins—were reflections that proved my existence.

The doctor arrived, insisting that I be transferred to the operating room to deliver the baby via cesarean so he could go home because he was tired of waiting. His decision was based solely on convenience. I objected fiercely, but the nurses continued raising the bed railing and rolling me away. I was terrified and helpless. My water had already been broken, I couldn't get up and walk away, or get a second opinion. I was at the mercy of a man who was ready to go to sleep.

My birth advocates were my family. My cousins blocked them from rolling the bed out of the room and my aunt *Artemis*, who was beside my mother when I was born, put on gloves and told me to start pushing, that she would deliver the baby herself. She checked my dilation and said the baby was ready. I hadn't taken any breathing classes, or birthing lessons. As I wept in fear,

I was coached in real time. If these women had grace for nothing else, they respected motherhood and birthing as a sacred act and would not allow my doctor to take me away to the operating room where they couldn't monitor him.

I think my daughter felt the protective circle, because after twelve hours of stubborn refusal she began making her way down the canal. Within minutes I was fully dilated. The women praised my strength because I didn't cry or scream. Shannon fainted. I closed my eyes and pushed as *Artemis* instructed. I felt the shift in the room that night. In those twelve hours, I had earned an irrevocable reverence. I, too, had been delivered. My brother cut the umbilical cord. Later that night, while I struggled to get my baby to latch on, an older Black woman nurse came in to tell me how lucky I was because so many other women left the maternity ward alone. And in that moment, even though my daughter's father wasn't present, I felt so held.

. . .

We called her Sofia because he'd always envisioned that his first daughter would be called Sofia, Greek for "wisdom." He threatened that if I didn't call her this, he would never speak to me again and he would never take the time to meet her once she was born. The only stone he had left to throw. He would wield it for many years to come. If you don't answer the phone, I won't speak to her anymore; if you don't bring her to the airport during my layover so that I can see her for exactly two hours between flights, I won't speak to her anymore. If you don't do as I say, always, I won't speak to her anymore. All of this from a man who insisted on a name that would rarely slip from his lips. It worked. I didn't want my daughter to carry the wound of being a fatherless child. What I didn't know as a young mother was that his actions were entirely beyond my control.

I didn't like the name Sofia. The only Sofia that I'd ever known intimately was the character from Alice Walker's novel *The Color Purple,* and I did not feel fondly about her when I first read the book in high school. I suspect that this was related to my own self-hatred and subconscious anti-Blackness. And I didn't like the way that the character was subjected to the whims of that White woman for the majority of her life. But upon revisiting the book I fell in love with Sofia. She took up space and made every character around her more honest by insisting on respect as her birthright. Unlike many of the other women in the novel, upon our first encounter with her, it is made clear by Walker that Sofia is unrelenting in her pursuit of freedom. One moment has always been seared into my mind upon my rereading as a mother is when she storms up to Celie as she piddles in her yard, one of her eyes fastened shut, shiny and purple, and without shame she asks her why she would tell Harpo, her stepson, to beat his wife. Loosely a query, "You told Harpo to beat me . . . Don't lie," she insists on making Celie confront herself and her reasoning in this moment. And Celie is never more honest than in her response to Sofia: "I say it cause I'm a fool, I say. I say it cause I'm jealous of you. I say it cause you do what I can't . . . Fight."

Sofia softens and delivers a relatable response that many of us can recite: "All my life I had to fight. I had to fight my daddy. I had to fight my brothers. I had to fight my cousins and my uncles. A girl child ain't safe in a family of men. But I never thought I'd have to fight in my own house . . . I loves Harpo . . . But I'll kill him dead before I let him beat me."

Prior to this we knew nothing of Sofia's background, but it was implied, between the lines, that she had fought tirelessly to get to the point where she is when we are introduced to her. Her self-respect had been hard-earned. You can only get there by losing some blood, sinking into some holes, and sitting with your eyes wide open seeing nothing but darkness and no way out. A Black girl certainly isn't born with what Sofia had on her, it is a journey, a journey that Celie had yet to commence. And her initial impulse was not to begin her own but to witness another woman with her head under the foot of her husband, to thwart her progress. Because if they both have black eyes, then Celie could offer her a cold compress and sit beside her, accompanied in her suffering, united in pain. Isn't that what us Black women are supposed to do? Gather in the name of grief and never give it a name. Sofia refused Celie's request and had the grace and compassion to take her hand and gently guide her toward her own path of liberation. "You ought to bash Mr.___ head open . . . Think about heaven later."

I agreed to call her Sofia, with an *f*, just like the character in *The Color Purple*. My wish for her was that she be protected from all that Walker's Sofia endured as a girl child among men. When people assume her name is spelled with a *ph*, she takes it personally, "the *f* is for fire."

. . .

The oilman and I took a road trip to Disney World and the Florida Keys for our daughter's first birthday. On the way back to Miami he drove with one hand on the wheel, the other tucked between my thighs as we spoke. Despite not being together, our familiarity meant that we could always lay claim to each other's bodies. Or rather, he was granted absolute access to mine. He asked me what I wanted to do with my life. I told him I would continue working in communications, writing press releases, just as I had been before giving birth. He scoffed, "Is that what you love?" I wanted him to be proud of me, so I said what I thought would please him. He reframed the question: *What would you do if money didn't matter?* I said I would be a librarian. Stories had long been my escape and salvation. I would steal time between classes and after school sitting in the library. Even today, when I read a book in my mother's presence, she sucks her teeth and rolls her eyes in disappointment, *If I wanted to be alone, I could have stayed home.* I assumed that if I was a librarian, I could read all the books I pleased without interruption. He said he would be a valet, so he could drive cool cars all day. This was already his reality since he collected automobiles and was a member of a racing club. We laughed and looked out into the sunset. Something about the audacity of the sky, painted in pastel ribbons, as we drove back from the Keys, floating just above the water, gave me the courage to say aloud what I was too embarrassed to admit to anyone else, "All I care about is reading and writing in my journal." I gazed out across the water feeling irresponsible for entertaining these desires. After all, I am a mother, I must stay grounded as my needs are secondary to those of the child. He squeezed the inside of my thigh and turned to me, "Then that's what you should do. If you love what you do, the money will come."

17

New York

At twenty-three I didn't know who I was, or exactly what I wanted in life, but I knew I didn't want to be defined by motherhood. I wanted more than that. Even if I didn't quite know what that was. When word spread that I was pregnant, my older brother, *Junior*, a thirty-five-year-old man with his own family, called to taunt his little sister, *Look at you now. I guess you're not as smart as everyone thought you were, huh?* He called to tell me that I was just like all the other unwed single mothers in our family. That I wasn't in fact special or singular in any way. He called to tell me that I was common. And he saw the common outcome for a single Black mother as destitution. He laughed maniacally before I hung up. I promised myself that I would not allow motherhood to consume my identity. This proved challenging, since I became a mother before I could call myself a woman.

When I was pregnant, I was still an undergraduate, but I refused to drop out in fear of never returning to complete my degree. After the awful experience in Tyler, I left basketball alone because I no longer needed to escape my life, I was ready to live it, so I transferred to a university in Houston. I took twenty-two hours in my final semester and walked across the stage weeks before giving birth. My daughter was with me that day. My graduation was held at Hofheinz Pavilion in Third Ward, only a few blocks from where my grandmother raised her children on Beulah Street, near Brays Bayou, just across the way from Cream Burger where Betty Jean took her kids on payday so they could split two burger combos between them while she smoked her Benson and Hedges. My aunties were there, my grandmother, my mother, and Shannon. We celebrated like it was for all of us. My father wasn't there. I can't remember, but I'm sure he probably said he was coming and then something came up.

After giving birth, a discomfort began to creep around inside of me. Like a signal or a siren. Or a whisper awakening me in the silent hours of the night. It was an impulse to run. I could never forge my own path of mothering while still in the familial system I wanted to disrupt.

At a nail salon in Houston, an older Black woman getting a manicure beside me stared at me. I smiled politely and said hello, hoping she'd look away.

"Are you still writing in your journals?" she asked.

I scanned the area to lock eyes with a witness. A teenage boy beside her shook his head, rolled his eyes, and looked back at his phone as if to say, *Here she goes again.*

I pointed to myself and she nodded. And I reluctantly nodded.

"Keep writing in those journals. Your words will heal people one day."

This was especially unsettling since I had no thoughts of anyone ever reading my writing but me. She said the spirits instructed her to tell me.

Before saying farewell, she added, "Get as far away from your mother as you can. She will get in your way."

I spoke with my mother on the phone every day, laughing and gossiping like girlfriends. She confided in me but I always felt the need to hide myself from her. And I would never truly discover myself if I didn't run. Connie is so powerful and unyielding in her ability to influence and coerce, that I had to put the country between us. To untether myself. To cut the cord and develop ideas and explore curiosities that I couldn't if I lived in her proximity. Just like Betty Jean, I chose mobility as a means to build a new world for myself and my involuntary little companion.

. . .

Despite all the books I'd read, I'd never considered writing as something people do for work. My mother suggested that creativity was a hobby for children, and it had been decided that I would be a doctor because I excelled in the sciences and math. I simply did not know anyone who worked for money using their imagination; most of my family had relied on their physicality. After the trip to the Keys, I googled "How to be a single mother writer" and Toni Morrison appeared in my search. *What are the two things I must do or else I will die?* she asked herself. *Write and Mother.* Mother as verb. Morrison wrote in the mornings while her boys were sleeping. I took notes. I googled: "Where can I learn to be a writer." I couldn't see myself in Iowa. NYU focused on fiction, and that somehow felt more frivolous. Nonfiction felt like something my family would feel proud of. My father always made note of people he saw reading novels and decided that they were silly and mindless. The equivalent of watching reality television today. It's funny how you can see your parents' insecurities so clearly as an adult. The ways that their every word held irrefutable validity, only to realize those words were produced by their fears. Especially since my namesake is a Russian novelist. I was still being guided in many ways by the principles of my family. And I desperately wanted to break free, while still desperately wanting to be accepted.

Columbia University was in New York City, the center of the publishing world. And it was in Harlem, the neighborhood many of the writers I loved had written from. I began my application that night while my daughter slept in her crib. Fear and hope accompanied me. The idea that by pursuing my dreams, my daughter might one day feel empowered to do the same. I couldn't sleep, so I started packing. I thought if I went to sleep without starting the process, I would wake up the next morning and talk myself out of it.

Sofia's father initially encouraged the move because he frequented Manhattan for work, before ultimately objecting to the relocation. I had hoped that he would be proud of me, since he had encouraged me to pursue my dreams, but there was an unspoken clause, just as long as they didn't inconvenience him. It's possible that he didn't want us there because his eldest son, a neuroscientist for Meta, was staying in New York with his girlfriend for a brief time and he occasionally visited them. He said that his son's girlfriend saw him as a father figure, and he didn't want to disrupt that image by telling them he had a daughter with a twenty-three-year-old Black girl. I helped keep his secret, and I hated myself for it. I watched their holiday gatherings online, each time saying I wouldn't look, I wouldn't check their profiles, but I couldn't help but watch and dream of Sofia one day being invited. But instead, she spent the week before the holiday with him, a stopover on his way to his sons.

He still hadn't told his sons or any of his extended family about Sofia. He was waiting for the "right time." When they have their own kids, they will understand the impulses of men, he'd say. When they all get together for Christmas, he'd tell them that he had donated sperm to help me, a young Black woman in need. A noble contribution. Or better yet, he'd say he never knew about her and that I'd found him and told him about his child. He had a condo in the Financial District that he purchased while we were together. It was a new development and we selected furniture to be imported from Italy. I'd assumed that Sofia and I would live there when we moved to NYC since he lived between Bogotá and the villa in Tuscany that we'd frequent. But he didn't want his neighbors to see Sofia. To see his face written across hers.

His subsequent girlfriend is a Black Brazilian younger than me by a year, and he kept Sofia from her until she was pregnant with his child. Until he felt that he *owned* her. Only then did he reveal to her that she wasn't in fact pregnant with his first daughter but his second. And he eventually brought us all together, his four Black girls, and he sat at the head of the table, squinting at the menu, and telling us to order whatever we wanted.

I tried to convince him to love Sofia. I tried to get her to be perfect in front of him. Just like I had done with my father. Be perfect so he'll love you and never want to leave you. I wanted her to do what hadn't worked for me as a girl. My daughter was confused by the angst her father brought out in me. When he called, he only wanted to speak with me, not with her. She was a reminder of his failures. I was the salve. He wanted me to stand up so he could see what I was wearing. To pull down my top a little bit. He'd pull out his penis a little bit when Sofia went to her room, bored with him. When strangers and servers praised our daughter for her precociousness, he beamed with pride. In private he said talking to her was like talking to a wall.

He began comparing his new daughter to Sofia. Asking me questions about our daughter as if we were friends at an open house as his new daughter experienced developmental delays. He spoke to our daughter on FaceTime and criticized my parenting. Asked me why she had to be eating a snack every time they spoke. I asked him if he had any other suggestions on how to keep a toddler still in front of a screen while talking to a stranger. He said I pushed our daughter too hard, that's the only reason why she was intellectually advanced. She was a kid who wasn't having fun. "We are happy to have a happy dummy," he told me. Fully aware that I desperately wanted to be a part of that *we*. He called me often to ask, *When did Sofia start reading? When did she learn multiplication?* He couldn't understand why the daughter who lived in precarity was thriving. He wasn't as essential as he'd hoped.

He was tired of being a family man, he wanted to be free. He told me to meet him in Buenos Aires and hire a sitter for Sofia. When I landed in Argentina, a Ferragamo bag and diamond bracelet were gift-wrapped on the bed. He told me he loved me. I wanted him to love our daughter. Before returning home, I left a few strands of my hair in his luggage for his girlfriend to find when she unpacks his bag.

He shared his cowardice with me and shrouded it from everyone else in his life because he felt that no matter how low he went, he'd still be above me. There is no lower rung than a Black woman, and oh what comfort I provided him. Even though our relationship fostered *some* shame inside of him, I provided him a freedom that he wasn't allowed anywhere else. He confided in me his deepest fears and filthiest thoughts without restraint. And isn't that the role of the Black woman in America, to help people's malice feel permissible? To take their dirty thoughts and rinse them clean? To sit silently as they feed, filling themselves with what they need to go out and build empires, or in this case, oil companies and electric cars. There is a moment in Lorraine Hansberry's play *The Sign in Sidney Bernstein's Window* where the White sex worker explains that her attraction to Black men is driven by her desire, not desire for him as a person but desire to feel less shame about her profession. For when she's with a Negro, no matter how many tricks she turns, she's still not Black. And as for me, with my daughter's father, I was simply performing the role I was born to play.

. . .

Within the year, with a suckling infant, I was in New York City, and I hadn't even submitted my application to graduate school yet. I applied to one master's program, and if I didn't get accepted, I would keep applying until I was.

I knew that I needed to live near the water, the island embraced me. With every breath, the moisture and salt in the air felt like home. Equating mobilization with freedom, I left behind the only town I knew in hopes of being released from family cycles. What I didn't realize was that all I sought to escape was already inside me. In my bones. Home is nowhere, but somehow, everywhere you are.

I moved to New York with no promise. I landed in Harlem, comforted by living on the narrowed part of the island, tucked between rivers. I could walk out of my apartment and turn east or west and ultimately arrive at the water. It felt to me like the Hudson's depth held wisdom and the East River told lies. There was a chaos on the east and a calm on the west. So I almost always walked west through St. Nicholas Park down to the Hudson when I felt confused about what had brought me there. I wouldn't receive answers, but I always felt settled when I departed.

I thought that once I arrived in the city and simply breathed the air and walked the streets of Langston Hughes and Audre Lorde that I'd somehow learn to do what they had done. I arrived on 135th Street at dusk. It was the summer that a man was acquitted of murder by a jury of his peers in Florida after killing a boy named Trayvon Martin. One of my mother's ex-boyfriends drove my belongings to New York. He had become like a stepfather to me during my late high-school and college years because he was the first and only man I had encountered who actually did everything he said he would. For this I will always love him. Years later, in 2020, he died alone in his rig of the Covid-19 virus on his sixty-eighth birthday. When I stood in front of his embalmed body to speak at his wake in Tuscumbia, Alabama, expressing my affection for his dependability and belief in me, I felt the gurgling of the familial underbelly. His daughter, his firstborn, ran out of the small funeral parlor wailing. Screaming the unresolved question that often accompanies grief, *Why couldn't he be that for me?* Her younger siblings ran after her, including the daughter whom he had kept a secret for most of her life before showing up with her at a family reunion. His secret daughter wearing his face to the occasion was all that he could offer to his family at the reunion, no explanations were provided, and no questions were asked. This is how it is. Secrets either go with you to the grave or they are revealed without explanation.

I had felt an obligation to speak at his funeral, to provide his legacy some redemption. I flew to Alabama to say that sometimes men are able to be there for children that are not their own because they can start anew, without the past getting in the way. Without all those ghosts and guilt. He saw his firstborn daughter, who had been a teen mother, working at Waffle House for more than two decades, as a failure of his own doing. His son became addicted to OxyContin prescribed by a doctor after a car accident. Their existence was a stain. I was a concealer. With me, he could step in and father me on my journey because we both filled a vacancy. With him, I was admired for every risk that I took, while my own father ignored my efforts to impress him and doted on my cousins and any other young people who were not his own. So, to the daughter who ran out of her father's wake, I could only look to her and give a knowing nod with tears that grieved for us both for all the times that we begged to be chosen by our fathers, only to be left with a hatred for ourselves for being foolish enough to believe.

. . .

My stepfather had yet to arrive when we landed. Sofia and I slept on a pallet on the floor under the moonlight in an empty one-bedroom on 135th Street with only what I could fit in two suitcases. "We did it, Mommy," she said smiling up at me. She was two years old but understood the magnitude of what we had just done. We traveled around the world meeting up with her father when he beckoned us. A slow life where we never had to rush toward anything. Everything would be different now. We held each other and slept soundly on the floor knowing that we would be okay as long as we were together.

My grad school application was due only days into the new year. I spent the fall writing and learning my way around the city and searching for childcare. In Houston, you simply enroll the child in the closest institution to your home, but New York was complicated. When I called or showed up to day cares there were chuckles before referring me to a wait list that usually took at least one year to be called from. I felt ridiculous and childish to think it would be simple.

The oilman funded our transition to New York but still refused to help me beyond the meager monthly amount that he decided on, which fluctuated based on his ego and the amount of attention I extended to him. On his good days he suggested that I move to Italy, and he would buy me a home close to his so he could sneak away from his new family and visit me and Sofia in secret. Other days he'd encourage me to return to Texas to live a simple life beside my mother. Or to a small Caribbean country where we could live well on the US dollar. Meaning, he wanted us to disappear from the worlds he inhabited. I considered all of these options, because I still thought he knew best, but I always came back to the more consistent feeling inside of me that said I was exactly where I was supposed to be.

I could see the Schomburg Center from my living-room window, almost like a north star. The building was illuminated with the names of people I didn't know, and I would look them up and learn as much as I could about their journey, read their books, watch their films, and anything else I could study and devour. I walked to the Schomburg Center multiple times a week with Sofia. The talks were always free, and I had nothing else to do in the evenings and no one to see. I walked across the lobby where Langston Hughes's ashes are buried and into the auditorium to listen to Zadie Smith, Chimamanda Ngozi Adichie, Zanele Muholi, Renee Cox, and other artists I'd never heard of speak on their creative process. Years later, when I was invited by Novella Ford, the associate director of public programs at the Schomburg, to host a conversation with Tarana Burke about her memoir, we spoke about how literature had saved us after abuse, about Maya Angelou and how her story set so many of us free of suffering silently. My daughter and I hugged and cried together over Hughes's ashes because she had been with me all those nights at the Schomburg, while I listened in an attempt to create a life as an artist and mother, not dissimilar from the way my mother had while watching films and television.

That winter I submitted my application to the MFA program and waited anxiously. I grew homesick in those days. I wished for the Houston rain. Prayed for it. It didn't rain that mournful torrential terribly gorgeous rain in New York like back home on the Gulf. The waters blurring the windows always felt like permission

to weep. I love the moody skies. The unmooring of the mundane.
I am drawn to storms just as I am to my lovers, gorgeous in their
fury, and thrilled by the thought that they could kill me.

I missed the chaos of home. The nostalgia for the storms was a
longing for my family. The hurricanes were a kind of homecoming for us. The last family storm I took part in was Hurricane
Ike. Since our home was sprawling, everyone gathered there. The
women cooked together, the dominoes were out, loads of ice and
batteries in case we lost power, the cousins smoked out back, the
kids ran wild upstairs, we watched Tyler Perry plays or bootlegged
comedy specials. When we are all together, the possibility of tragedy feels less significant. Should we die, we die together.

· · ·

I received a call from the essayist Phillip Lopate telling me I had
been accepted. I danced around the living room with Sofia. I was
prepared to apply a million times, but I was grateful to only have
to apply once. My plan was in motion.

At the accepted-students event, I met someone who became my
closest friend and coconspirator, G'Ra Asim, one of a handful of
other Black students in attendance that night. There were three
of us in total for our year. But I knew that I was not like anyone
else there that night, because I had to hurry home to my daughter
who I had left with a new friend in my apartment. As undergrad-
uates, many of the others had attended Ivy League schools, and
I went to a state university. Others had come to graduate school
straight from undergrad, I had taken three years and was therefore
older than most. Others had parents paying their tuition, I was
maxing out loans and grants. Most were White. Most had been
read Marcel Proust for bedtime stories; I had never read *Infinite
Jest*. I tried to maintain my mystery to protect myself from being
identified as other, I hadn't realized that this was my advantage.

The first time I walked into Butler Library I was overwhelmed
by the architecture and the access I had to literature. As I ascended
the stairwell inside the main hall, I met eyes with the larger-than-

life painting of the former university president Nicholas Murray Butler. A White man looking down at me was not unfamiliar. I looked up at the painting and I smiled and said aloud each time I entered, *You weren't expecting me, were you?* Almost every room I enter in New York, I can tell they weren't expecting me. Being a Black woman is both my superpower and my greatest obstacle. The former because they will underestimate me every time. No one sees me coming, their imagined opponents do not resemble me. I slip in under the radar. The latter because anti-Blackness is ever rampant. Although G'Ra told me that I am a palatable Black, the *Black girl starter kit* for White men who have never dated a Black woman. It was hurtful because I knew he wasn't necessarily wrong. This sounds like an insult, but it's a way of negotiating an impossible conundrum. Just like my mother who chose to be intolerable instead of invisible. I've been trying to find a way to be tolerable and visible. And further still, desirable. This is what my mother invested in for me. She was ensuring that I knew how to move in a room full of vultures, but more important, how to move so that White people could feel comfortable in my presence. Ultimately, it all feels like a betrayal.

· · ·

When I graduated from grad school two years later, I begged my father to come. He said he'd come but hadn't booked a flight and the date was approaching. I pressured him, guilted him. I regret this. I regret all the times that I've begged my father to show up for me. Each time I tell myself I'll never beg again. And I've betrayed myself every time. My mother came. *Junior* was there, he said he felt he'd missed out on too much of my life. Shannon had moved to New York and was living with me and Sofia until he found a place of his own. At the graduation ceremony, Shannon rose to the position he'd always had in my life, the person who helped me survive my childhood. He was a kind of buffer. Shannon knew how to speak to my parents without intimidating them. He helped me manage them that weekend. He held

Sofia's hand through the ceremony. He tried to tell my parents how to be supportive, when to keep quiet, and different ways that they could demonstrate that they were proud of me. He asked my father to pay for the graduation dinner and asked my mother to bring flowers. But there's no crash course for something like this. They felt out of place, like they didn't belong there. In the sea of mostly White people in sky blue robes and a daughter who floated fluidly among them. They saw me as no longer of the tribe. They talked about how they couldn't wait to leave. My mother refused to be introduced to my friends and treated everyone with contempt. She could never say she was intimidated; her way is to reduce others to soothe her fears. We argued over dinner. They said that I'd been reading too many books and that I thought I knew every damn thing. I had spoken to G'Ra about my family, but he'd never seen them in action until he joined us for dinner. He hugged me afterward and I knew what he meant. I thanked him. They departed the next morning on the earliest possible flight.

Sofia cheered for me. Congratulated me. She'd been beside me, bearing witness, and she told me what my parents couldn't, that she was proud of me. We spent the night at the Standard, a hotel in the East Village where Shannon worked at the time and had gotten me a room for graduation night. Sofia wore my cap, and we jumped on the bed and ordered room service. She took photos of me, and after I put her to bed, I took a bath to try to wash away the day. I cried and chanted quietly, *I will never let them hurt me again,* until I fell asleep.

18

That's Not How That Went

they ask me to remember
but they want me to remember
their memories
and i keep on remembering
mine.

—LUCILLE CLIFTON, "WHY SOME PEOPLE
BE MAD AT ME SOMETIMES"

I am asked to remember myself as a girl in therapy (the first in my family to do so). What that girl needed and what the me of today can offer her. I was never a girl. Or at least I never felt like one. I never felt protected or childlike. I was never called sweet. I was called thick, I was called redbone, I was called big-boned, I was called stallion, I was called to fix plates, I was called to raise boys, I was called into the kitchen. I was a woman among women even when I was a child. And like any fruit that ripens too soon, I hardened before I could arrive at my robust optimality. This was not a choice. It was an expectation. It was a forced quickening. At ten my body betrayed me. At ten my body shifted terrains without my consent. From flat plains to rounded peaks and deep valleys. I remember the world around me adjusting to this shift as well. My thighs and ass emerged, in the same way a peony opens, a swift rupture with no possibility of returning to its previous form; away went my aspiration for innocence. I developed a deep fear of being seen while also being titillated by the newly found attention.

Even my father, whom I treasured most in this world, insisted that I hide. I was no longer allowed to wear my favorite denim shorts that I suddenly had to wiggle into, or play outside alone, or ride my bike beyond the railroad tracks. My new body felt like a punishment that I had to live within for eternity. And I dreamed of transcending my fleshly form. My parents intended to shield me from predators, but this only introduced me to the many restrictions my body would eventually yield to. Besides, it had already begun in our own home. And would carry on for years.

I began being abused so young that I can't even remember the first time it happened. My earliest memories of sexual abuse are in preschool, when I was three or four years old. A cousin, who was being abused, would stay in our home for respite, and thus the cycle of pain untreated proliferates. My cousin's mother had been abused. And although she never told me, I can assume that Betty Jean was abused too. Abuse is insidious; difficult to detect or trace or contain. It moves through our family undetected, people reenacting their hurt on those closest to them, those they love and trust will keep their secrets.

Some days I cannot trust my memory. Some days I feel as if it was my fault. Maybe I asked for it. I can't recall ever being treated like I wasn't guilty of something despite never knowing entirely what I was guilty of. It's such a strange feeling as a child to always have the impulse to beg forgiveness for existing. I carried my body like an apology. As if I needed to hide so that others were not suspicious of me. The abuse left me repulsed with myself. Especially when my parents preached "your body is a temple" or "your body is your virtue." They didn't know that all of that had already been taken away from me, leaving me worthless while also understanding that my body was my only access to value. And without it, I felt there was nothing left of me to hold as precious. When you are a girl and you recognize that your only value is associated with physical elements of your being, you internalize this as your potency. Skewed formations of self-worth begin to rise on the soft spots that have yet to determine its final shape. Like the supple crown of a newborn's head that everyone avoids in fear of irreversible damage due to its malleability. Ego is molded from the remnants of racialized fragmenting of the Black girl's existence, and you begin to subjugate this as your power, because above all else, you must survive by playing the hand you were dealt. And the hardening begins.

This new body produced suspicion from my mother and aunties. When they called me fast, they didn't mean the urgency in which my body developed. How could flesh alone suggest deviance? They had internalized what Black women had been told about themselves since slavery and passed from one generation to the next. It is here, in the home, that racism begins to infect the most intimate corners of the Black human experience. At ten years old, I was five foot eight with fully formed breasts. While my friends still wore children's clothing, I came to obtain an authority that I did not earn nor desire, granter of masculinity. Allowing grown men to fondle me, I fumbled my way through adolescence making no attempts to reclaim control over my body, but rather using my body to bend others to my will. This is far too much power for a girl.

I remember reading the memoir *I Know Why the Caged Bird Sings* by Maya Angelou in high school many times and each time being struck by her reaction after being sexually assaulted by her mother's boyfriend, Mr. Freeman. Even as an adult she references him with the article of respect, *Mr.,* a derivative of master. Initially, before being capable of processing her pain, she is thrilled with the attention and began to invite his fixation on her by sitting in his lap while her mama was away at work. As a small girl, she is not yet able to differentiate tenderness from terror. (Many of us will spend a lifetime trying to make this distinction.) She knows only that she has the magic to make his flesh stand erect like "an ear of corn." After she confides in her mother, Mr. Freeman is murdered by her uncles. Young Maya stopped speaking for several years in hopes that men would forget that she was in the room. Sometimes power is not force, it is refrain.

. . .

When I began writing this book, I knew I wanted to write about Black womanhood, but I kept being pulled back to motherhood and I couldn't understand why. The same way I couldn't write about Black motherhood without writing about America. I wanted to disconnect from that part of the story of Black women, but that was the story. That is the main artery, the main body from which the rivers and tributaries are formed. They all somehow connect to motherhood.

I also had to question why I wanted to avoid motherhood. Because I assumed there was no power in that identity. But there is only power there. I began to understand the ways that my body was hypersexualized when I was thirteen and men, almost compulsively, told me what they would do to my body. One consistency across racial lines were comments about childbearing. It didn't matter that I was still a child. My body excited and provoked the idea of reproduction. If the men say it enough, and society tells you this enough, you begin to see it as your value. And then you begin to exploit it and embrace the degradation. This way you can get ahead of the pain, disarm it. Desensitize yourself. Claim it as a type of power. Or you could dismiss this and reject the concept of motherhood altogether. But even those who don't have babies can embody motherhood and be treated as such. The hypersexualization and the identity of motherhood are in tandem.

Shortly after the emergence of my hips, my father disappeared. I began to disassociate from my body. As I reflect on what that little girl needed, I am reminded that I learned so young how to hate myself from my family. It wasn't until I was a mother that the unlearning began. Because I saw this beautiful human and thought, *If she's beautiful, what does that make me?* I saw her as precious and in need of protection from all the pains the world is sure to bring to the mouth of a young Black girl and force her to swallow. I struggle to ever think of myself as a girl in need of protection. But in raising my daughter, I can see that it's what I needed most. In my daughter I can see that she feels safe, allowing space for her young mind to process and imagine otherworldly things, not just fear and recoiling in anticipation of agony.

I remember constantly trying to work out ways to shield myself and perhaps this was being misinterpreted by adults as arrogance. I suspect that there was a power or presence that I possessed that the adults around me experienced as a confrontation. Beauty is often experienced as a confrontation. Without saying a word, a symmetrical face that aligns with the standards of beauty can induce surrender and subsequently shame and uncertainty in the viewer. As a girl, I was unaware of these responses, but as a *Black girl,* everyone seemed to think I understood them and was playing a game of ignorance. Trying to get over in some way. That I walked and carried my body in a particular way to invite these feelings. That my ass and hips moved not from joy or function but for the deliberate consumption of others. I shrank further into the depths of myself.

So to that little girl, I don't quite know what to say, and it feels strange to unearth her, but I wish I could hug her and protect her and listen to her and believe her. And when I struggle to access that part of myself, I practice all the care that I needed as a girl on my daughter. I listen to her, I trust her, I try not to allow my fears and insecurities to shield me from feeling when I am challenged by her. Like when she was three and had a tantrum in the middle of an uptown 3 train full of Black women, who all cut their eyes between my daughter and me. One of them shook her head and looked away. The looks said, *Your child is out of control, you should be ashamed,* and I was. Once home, I called my mother asking for her help on what to do with a three-year-old having fits in public. "None of my kids ever fell out on me in public . . . you know what you gotta do." I spanked my daughter's backside for the first time and her brown eyes filled with disbelief. She cried tears of betrayal. I, too, cried afterward, because I had done what I said I never would, all because I felt ashamed in front of elders on the train. I vowed to never hit her again, to not betray us both again. I apologized to my daughter. I was tested again recently when Sofia, now thirteen, shouted at me over dinner at home and told me to *shut up*. One part of my brain said, *This is wild behavior, don't let her get away with this, do something dramatic to get her attention and scare her into submission.* Another part of my brain empathized, *She must be really overwhelmed.* I sat quietly stunned while Sofia began clearing our plates from the table and I wasn't even done eating. I went to my room and called my mother, ashamed to recount what had just happened. She gasped, *"That's that White shit,"* she said. *"You know what you gotta do . . ."* After a long pause she continued, "Break her." I said, "Mama, that's that slave shit." My mother was suggesting I perform a calculated series of actions to dismantle my daughter's spirit, her confidence, the essence of who she is. My mother's voice dropped to a sinister tone when she said, "Break her," and my brain scrolled through memories of times when my mother tried to break me as a girl. To do what the whole world was already trying to do to me. And I began to cry for that girl. I thanked my mother for providing clarity on exactly what *not* to do. I went to my daughter's room and gave her a hug and she apologized. She told me that she didn't know what to do with her anger, that she repressed it at school. "But at home, I know you're going to love me no matter what." In that moment, it was clear to me that my daughter felt safe. She was saying that she knew I would never abandon her, even when she's at her worst. The usefulness of fear in a family is perhaps the same as in our country, to impose a will that solely benefits the iron fist. Even without the presence of fear, I think Sofia understands not to try that again.

I'm acutely aware that failure in motherhood is inevitable, especially when you're still trying to reconcile your own terrors, but this was one of those affirming moments. One of many moments when the little girl in me helps do the steering toward a path that's not always visible.

19

Conjure

From Latin *conjurare:* band together by an oath, conspire

My friend Mengly introduces me to her friend: *This is Sasha, she has a mom like ours.*

Somehow, we always find each other. Us women with the open wounds. In the poet, warrior, mother Audre Lorde's "The Master's Tools Will Never Dismantle the Master's House," she states, "Interdependency between women is the way to a freedom which allows the I to be, not in order to be used, but in order to be creative." Initially I saw motherhood as a hindrance to a creative lifestyle, but community has opened up new forms of mothering, new forms of care, that make a more expansive life possible. In moments when responsibility debilitates me, these women come to feed me, to nourish me, to make the load lighter.

My relationships with Black women were complicated by my relationship with my mother. I saw her in them, both beckoning and repelling me. My first girlfriend bore great resemblance to my mother while also sharing her explosiveness, and for this I was fiercely attracted to her and equally distrustful. I called her *Rocket.* Her emotional instability felt thrilling, like home. A place where I could pull my bra off through my sleeve and let all my imperfections hang buoyantly. Where I could be my lowest self without consequence. Because healing is hard and sometimes it's easier to give up, but then you have to deal with the painful come-down. She reintroduced me to old wounds and we dwelled there together. I manipulated her to see how much she could endure, tolerance as a measurement of devotion. How can you say that you love someone without fastening your hand around their neck and seeing how tight you can squeeze before they yell for mercy? She once confessed that she wished I was her mother and at night she needed to suckle my nipples like a newborn before falling asleep. We looked to each other to correct our mothers' neglect, and we failed miserably. She reminded me often that she wasn't my mother, and I wasn't hers. I refused this truth, and her, because I couldn't be with someone who didn't allow me to rest, as I wished, in repudiation. I held her accountable for my unresolved pains and said to her what I was afraid to say to my mother. When she broke up with me, it was a clean, swift sever. She disappeared. And I felt abandoned again. We both knew it had to be done that way, or else we could have stayed in that cycle forever.

I am drawn to women, as friends and as lovers, who under-stand how to move with pain and still, miraculously, make space for love. There is a way that one can decide to lead with our anger and distrust. And this anger is warranted. Anger is a necessary armor, our body's natural responses to centuries of terrorism that's infiltrated the Black family. We have every right to be angry, but I've seen how that anger can erode your insides, while still offering no justice for your circumstances. But the anger can be harnessed and become a source for a kind of essential joy. As if your life depends on it, because it does. I remind myself that I can choose. Nature's defenses create its most glorious reverberations. A shifting of an element. Like the way that ice becomes a stream. Or the way that lava turns to stone and provides the rocks of our shorelines.

My friends are these shorelines. Pressure turned to precious stone. A soft landing space between me and the world. Like my mother, we learned to love through lack. When I look into the eyes of my Black women friends, I see their beauty and yearning, and when I look a bit deeper, I see myself. That their beauty is my own. And we mother each other, and we daughter each other. I still feel a bit like a burden, afraid to inconvenience others, but less so.

. . .

After being in New York City for a few years, I began to realize the domestic space as both domicile and studio. A space to create and host and cook, while still being a controlled and safe environment for Sofia. I could put her to bed and continue my evening among other writers and artists whose minds sharpen my own, encouraging me to keep going.

In 2017 I visited an exhibition at the Brooklyn Museum called *We Wanted a Revolution: Black Radical Women, 1965–85,* co-curated by Rujeko Hockley and Catherine Morris. The show featured Black women artists, many of them mothers, who were fighting collectively for the right to create and exhibit their work. There were archival letters from notable museums that politely told them that Negresses had no place in American institutions, and it is essential that they remember their place, which was to visit the museum on Negro nights and be sure to enter through the back door. These experiences were so recent that these women were still alive to speak about it. They were from Betty Jean's generation, and I tried to imagine my grandmother walking into a museum; she wouldn't have bothered to try. I don't think my grandmother ever visited a museum. Her creativity was actualized in how she chose to live.

One particular self-portrait, *Flower Sniffer,* from 1966, by Emma Amos, stayed with me. A Black woman seen bent and uncertain in her body through a circular frame like a lens or porthole, with her nose in a bouquet, peering out as if she's been caught in a moment of pleasure. Amos was the only woman member of the Black artist collective Spiral, formed in 1963 to create visual contributions in response to the March on Washington for Jobs and Freedom, where Dr. Martin Luther King Jr. delivered the "I Have a Dream" speech. Despite studying as a serious artist at NYU, Amos was expected to be the secretary of the group and bring coffee to the men, which included the artists Hale Woodruff and Romare Bearden. Black women were at war with not only White supremacy but also the fragility of Black masculinity. They needed to feel like men, so they invited Amos to soothe their egos. But she refused all roles except artist and equal amongst the men. "That was one of the most political things I ever did," she later said.

In the summer of 2017, I reached out to Amos's studio for an interview, I needed to understand how she built this life for herself. I leaned toward work opportunities that could sustain my life financially while also feeding me new ways to live as an artist and a mother without compromising either. I was living off the rental income of a condo *the oilman* had purchased for me in the South earlier in our relationship and the fluctuating child support he provided for our daughter. When I wasn't stroking his ego to survive, I was writing freelance art criticism for magazines and newspapers.

I had been commissioned by a literary journal to write a profile on Amos. When I went to her studio on Bond Street, it was my first time being close to a working artist and experiencing the space where she processed and built worlds. But Amos was suffering from dementia and spoke only of her mother and her childhood home in Georgia. In her mind, she was a girl again. I am still stunned by how the brain clings to memories of childhood even in its deterioration. I remember when May was dying in the study in our home in Houston, and while my mother cared for her she told stories of her own grandmother, the enslaved woman who had been freed by Union soldiers at Milliken's Bend in Louisiana, and how they would sit under the shade tree together at dusk. Perhaps we never really stop being these girls, we are just forced to conceal them from harm, the only protection they ever receive is when we start to call ourselves women. In many ways I feel I am still that girl from my childhood, seeking someone to come in and mother me. My therapist tells me *I* have to mother that girl now. But I don't want to be the one. I'm already mothering so many—my daughter, my younger brother, my mother—I don't want to mother myself too. I search for mothers everywhere, in everyone. Like the book I read to my daughter as a toddler about the baby llama going around asking animals of other species, "Are you my mother?" Each time, each one said no. I was happy to collect shards from broken women who were seeking daughters to water and fill the voids of the ones they had birthed and left mangled. We always find each other.

The studio manager recommended that I speak to Amos's friend and fellow artist Camille Billops, who lived only a few blocks away in one of those sweeping SoHo artist lofts from the '70s that no longer exist at that price point. I recognized the name from the Brooklyn Museum exhibition. Billops answered on the first ring and invited me over that same day, as if she had been expecting my call. And then nothing was the same for me. I went to Billops's loft expecting her to share stories with me about Amos, but I left with the understanding that if I did not pursue my dreams, I would resent my child, and she would be left holding my bitterness. I left with more empathy for my own mother. I left with more than I could carry. So I came back again and again for weeks. And she greeted me each time with the same question, *Are you thirsty?*

Camille Billops

CAMILLE BILLOPS AND CHRISTA

I

In 1961 at six o'clock on a spring morning in Los Angeles a group of Black women convene at the middle-class home of the family matriarch. There was probably tea and hushed whispers so as to not wake the child who rested in the next room. With all of their morning responsibilities abandoned and hair still tied back in rollers beneath silk scarves, they've gathered to convince one member of their tribe not to give her four-year-old child up for adoption. As they heard a car door shut in the driveway, one of the women peeped through the closed curtains to confirm the arrival of the member in question. Twenty-seven-year-old single mother Camille Billops entered, stoic and searching for her daughter, Christa Victoria. If, in fact, she housed any shame or doubt inside of her, there was no evidence of this on Camille's being. The women—her mother, her mother's sisters, and a few cousins—all made dibs on the child, as if she were up for auction. The strongest offers were that of Camille's sister Billie and her mother, Alma, who had raised the child up until this point while Camille studied art and childhood education for physically handicapped children at Los Angeles State College at night and worked at the local bank during the day. Alma, too old and too tired, and Billie, married to a man whom Camille was suspicious of being unpredictable and unfit. "I'm going to take her. She's mine," Camille said, "and there's nothing any of you can do about it." Known for her smart mouth and uncompromising nature, Camille woke Christa up and walked her to the black Volkswagen Beetle and drove directly to the Children's Home Society of California. She let go of Christa's hand and told her to go to the bathroom; when Christa returned, searching for her mother, she looked out of the window, grasping her small teddy bear, and watched the black Bug drive away.

Camille had met Christa's father, Stanford, through a mutual friend and their brief yet intense courtship ended abruptly. Stanford, a tall striking lieutenant in the US Air Force was stationed in California. A few months into their relationship Camille was pregnant, despite her realization at the age of ten that she didn't want to be a mother, but abortions weren't legal in California until 1969. If they were going to do this, they had to do it traditionally, and Stanford consented. Five hundred shotgun-wedding invitations went out and before the guests received them by mail, he was gone. Camille called around searching for him and the Air Force informed her of his military discharge. When Christa was born on December 12, 1956, Camille received a postcard, "Wishing you well, Love Stanford," with no return address. He continued these cruel communications for years until he mistakenly wrote his return address; he was living in New York City on Pitt Street. With three-year-old Christa on her hip, Camille booked a flight across the country and sat on the stoop waiting for him to arrive home. Stanford pulled up in a Cadillac convertible, wearing sunglasses and a slight smile. He greeted them like old friends. Invited them in for beverages and shortly after showed them to the door, wishing them both all the best. Camille never saw him again. Christa reunited with this stranger three decades later and asked him if he was her father, and he replied, "I suppose so," to which she said, "I'm glad we got that squared away."

II

Was it in this moment that Camille decided to abandon motherhood? Or was it many moments that led to her dropping Christa off and speeding away? Christa, along with Camille's family, believe it was an affair she was having with a White man named James Hatch. Her stepsister Josie was his student at UCLA in the theater department in 1959, and she introduced Camille and Jim. Knowing that Camille was single, she said, "He's ready." Camille was teaching then in the public school system and making ceramics at home. She asked Hatch to come over and take a look at her pots and he asked her to audition for a play he cowrote with UCLA colleague C. Bernard Jackson inspired by the Greensboro, North Carolina, student sit-ins, *Fly Blackbird*. She was never quite as good at acting as she had hoped and was selected for the chorus, but she was onstage at the Metropolitan Theater in LA. Jim was the first person to tell Camille she was a good artist. "I will always love him for that," she says. His support provided her with permission to be whoever she pleased in any given moment, even if that meant not being pretty, what her family said a woman must be at all costs. This introduced Camille to a new way of being. A world of artists and activists, organized by the American Civil Liberties Union, who began protesting school segregation and Black oppression. At the height of the Civil Rights Movement, Camille was the mistress of a White man who believed in her, and despite Los Angeles being on the precipice of the Watts Uprising, she was not deterred by the vile language and glares thrown at them by strangers. Camille began slowly shedding the cultural influences of middle-class Black America. Her parents had come to California during the Great Migration, like many Southern Blacks who moved west in search of opportunity and the possibility of providing their family with security from the violence inflicted on Black bodies. In LA they worked in service to White folks, therefore it wasn't necessarily work that they couldn't attain in the South, it was their dignity. Her father, Luscious, from Texas, was a cook and her mother, Alma, from South Carolina, was a domestic and seamstress. However, escaping the South in physicality doesn't remove the emotional traumas of being Black in America; their White ideals were held firmly intact and their Southern traditions folded neatly within. Whiteness was still seen as superior in eloquence and refinement and the Billopses would emulate this in their home, for appearances' sake, but when the burlap curtains closed at night, Luscious drank like a fish until he passed out and his wife carried him to bed each night. Alma bestowed these beliefs of Black female servitude on her two daughters, and they consented, but the youngest child will always rebel, and for Camille, Jim was the catalyst. She had been taught that motherhood and womanhood were inextricable. If you were not a mother, then what would you be? Mother is to be a woman's highest title, and anything that takes precedence, even your own dream, is deemed selfish. Images of Camille with baby Christa show a polished and respectable young lady with permed hair and slicked-down edges. But in the images with Jim, you can see the physical transformation. She cuts off her permed roller-set curls and has a small perfectly picked Afro. The hairs along her top lip thicken and grow wildly, untamed. Camille preferred to be called artist, not mama. She had never allowed Christa to call her Mama, she was to call her Bootsie, like all of her closest friends and family. Jim also suspected that Camille was giving up Christa for him and offered just enough discouragement to absolve himself of responsibility, "Don't give Christa up for me." When Jim was offered a Fulbright appointment to teach at the High Institute of Cinema in Cairo, Egypt, the center of the 1960s Pan-African movement that brought over many young American artists and activists like Maya Angelou and Malcolm X, he asked Camille to come visit before his wife and kids arrived, and without hesitation she went. But before departing Cairo, she told him she would not return unless he left his wife and children. "He met me at the airport and his wife left," she says, "we chose each other and entered into another life. That's when the world opened."

In Cairo, Camille began experimenting with sculpture and her first solo exhibition at Gallerie Akhenaton was a small collection of ceramic pots and sculptures of those close to her, like Jim, who would serve as her constant muse, benefactor, and advocate. Their intimacy and artistry were to always exist intertwined given the racially charged political unrest that they protested in their life and through their creations. They dared to love each other in a time when interracial relationships were still considered criminal in the United States. Their first collaboration was a book of poetry called *Poems for Niggers and Crackers,* published in Cairo in 1965, with poems written by Jim and American poet Ibrahim Ibn Ismail; Camille created the illustrations. Driven by all that she had sacrificed, Camille explored any medium she could get her hands on, photography, painting, printmaking, and eventually film, which would be her most critically acclaimed work. She spent many years creating and showing work in Egypt, Germany, and China before returning to her homeland after John F. Kennedy's assassination, to find her own countrymen not so welcoming to Black women artists. They settled into New York City's East Village where the Armenian American English professor and author Leo Hamalian helped Jim secure a teaching position in theater at City College while Camille taught ceramics there. As with all great artists, there comes a time when you must turn inward and begin dissecting yourself, to become the subject of your own examination. This led Camille into filmmaking.

III

Camille tells me:

"I was with all of the various Nigga bitches. Emma Amos, Faith Ringgold, Elizabeth Catlett. They had Black night at museums like the Whitney where they would let us in the building but not show our work. We were fighting so hard to get into the Brooklyn Museum and they wouldn't let us in. So we said, well fuck you and the horse you rode in on. I said, you know what, I'm making my own way. So we bought this big-ass loft a long time ago when it was cheap. I told Jim, why don't we buy a loft, and we did it. Jim had most of the money. I had a little something to contribute. I told him I wanted my name on it, and he said okay, so we got married. We are all we have. I would have never ended up being a working artist if it weren't for him. His favorite words were 'Why not?' and 'Yes you can.' We created a library space, a studio in the back, an archive, and the dining area is where we host salons for our publication *Artist and Influence*. Every Black artist of our time has sat right here in this living room, and we recorded it all—bell hooks, Julie Dash, Amiri Baraka, all the Niggas. We invited everybody here: friends, students, and White gallerists and curators. We sold art right off our walls. I stopped begging a long time ago when I discovered I could sell art without having to kiss booty. These alternatives made it possible. Bob Blackburn was very helpful, he taught me printmaking. There were many artists that I met at the print shop while I was working, like Romi [Romare Bearden]. This is what you do when people don't let you into their playground. We did it out of defiance. I always did whatever I wanted to do.

"In the early '80s Christa found me. It was a great shock to me. She sent a letter and a cassette tape with a song, asking me if I would see her. She was twenty-something. I was scared because I had already learned how to live with my guilt about giving her up. I wasn't trying to come out from beneath the water. I was never a very good mother. I did what was best for both of us. I was twenty-three and I hardly saw her when she was little, she was always with my sister Billie or my mama. Mothers are supposed to protect, and the only way I could do that was by giving her up. I didn't see this as feminist then, I just knew I wanted to reverse it, I wanted to be free of motherhood. I agreed to meet with her. Jim really liked her, and they got on. Naturally, she was an artist like me, it's in her blood. When I started making films, she helped us. You can hear her voice singing on the opening scene of *Suzanne, Suzanne* about my niece's drug addiction and her abusive father. People wasn't talking about domestic violence back then. Our films had a tendency toward dirty laundry, they say it like it is, not like it's supposed to be. It was hard enough being Black so everyone wanted to appear perfect, keep up appearances, you know. My sister wanted to take Christa but I didn't trust my brother-in-law, Suzanne's father. Her adopted mother, Margaret, was fabulous, a jazz singer. She was the little ship that helped me sail the dangerous night. Then we made the film *Finding Christa*. Christa stayed here with us for a while when we were making the film and then she moved to New York to study, so I could help her become a singer. We were always fighting because she wanted me to feel guilty. She kept asking me why I gave her away. It was always verbally violent, and guilt-ridden. I was all kinds of bitches to her. She wasn't easy. I tried to explain to her that I didn't want to be a mother. But it was complicated. Jim says we were too much alike. She's a Sagittarius and I'm a Leo, too much fire. She was a star in *Finding Christa*. People say I show no remorse in the film, they say I'm cold, but if I had to do it again I would. I know I made **the right decision, wouldn't change a thing.** Well, the only thing I would do differently would be to give her up earlier. But it was hard. Her father disappearing on me was a gift, otherwise if he had stayed, I would have just endured, that's what Black women did in my family, endured. Christa was a very good actress, and this was a part of our competitiveness. She took up space in a way that was threatening to me. This caused a big friction when she was staying with us. Adoptees have what they call 'the great wound,' and it would always come back to, 'Why did you throw me away?' She would come and stay here and see everything that we have built and turn to me and ask, 'Why wasn't I here? Why wasn't I a part of this?' Jim welcomed her with open arms. But I didn't like her taking up so much space here. I would correct her and let her know, 'This ain't your place. You don't own this.' She was even beginning to claim the film, saying it was her film. I said, 'Now wait a minute, you didn't shoot that film. I shot that film. I cut that film.' She wanted to be a filmmaker but want and spit are two different things. Yeah, so I suppose there was some essence of competitiveness. She was difficult, I was difficult. We had an argument and then she walked out one day. Then one day she returned. It didn't last. It became argumentative again. Then she left again in 2013. We didn't talk again. I let it go. She had become ill and had to have an operation. Then she needed another one and she said she wouldn't have it. She killed herself by not taking that operation. I wasn't invited to the funeral. When she died somebody called to tell me. Who was it that called me? I don't remember. It was early in the morning. Like a blast from the furnace. You have to stand very still and face it. Then I had to bury it. Jim and I both. And that was it. It has to have a place. I've accepted the guilt. I will carry it with me forever. Sometimes I feel her when I am working."

IV

Before Christa's death she shared a letter on her Facebook page in 2014 titled "Given up Twice—Is It All Worth It?" In the letter she speaks about calling her stepfather, Jim, on Father's Day 2013 and Camille also picking up a receiver in a different room and abruptly hanging up when Christa announced herself. Half an hour after the call Christa receives an email from Jim stating that she should never call or visit their home again. Christa suspects that this email was written by Camille, as it contains a "callous" brashness that isn't indicative of Jim's character toward her. The email stated that both Jim and Camille were "cutting all communications" with her, including "telephone, letters, on the internet and personal appearances on the tai chi court," as she was causing too many disruptions in their lives. The email was signed by Jim and sent from his account, but the statement "four-year-old child continues to protest her mother's decision for giving her up" were words that she had heard endlessly from her biological mother. Christa never spoke to Camille again, but after seeing a therapist, she concluded that Camille was uncomfortable with Christa's intimate relationship with Jim. Thirty-two years after reuniting, Christa was dismissed. This three-thousand-word letter is filled with discreet anger, confusion, hurt that reads like a muffled scream into the abyss of social media. She signed the letter, "Christa Victoria (my name since birth)."

In the film *Finding Christa,* which won the Grand Jury Prize at Sundance, making Camille the first Black woman producer/director to be awarded this prize, Christa says that she felt like an octopus, wanting to extend all parts of herself around the woman who birthed her, but Camille felt like a cactus, sharp and defensive. Christa also states that meeting her birth mother and biological family saved her life, but one may consider their final split to be the event that led to her demise. Camille challenged assumptions about what a Black middle-class woman had to be and chose her artistry above all else; despite her family's beliefs that she chose Jim, she was choosing herself. To assume that Camille prioritized her relationship with her life partner seems misplaced and in contradiction to her radical act, which was to choose herself even when everything around her said that her purpose was to serve, soothe, and comfort, a rejection to the concept of Mammy.

Camille's genius lay in her ability to imagine Black futures in a country that did not value Black life and the expression of that life through art. Before *Roe v. Wade*, before the *Loving v. Virginia* ruling, she made decisions that seemed improbable.

The future that Camille envisioned was one that benefited the well-being and advancement of not just one individual being that she birthed but an entire generation of artists and scholars who were nourished by her contributions as an artist and archivist. Christa, unfortunately, was a casualty in Camille's ambitious defiance.

. . .

Camille reminded me of my grandmother in many ways. Ulti-mately, I think it was their commitment to selfhood. The fire and generosity in their spirits; they'll give you all that they have, as long as it doesn't bring them to their knees in the process. They woke up each day and chose themselves. And what a revolution-ary act when you've been conditioned to sacrifice your*self* in ser-vice of the nation.

I wondered about the women like Betty Jean, who never had the choice of being an artist. Who had nowhere to put the rich intensity of her interiority, not even in an ear. Motherhood was where she created. And years later, in grandmotherhood, she would be heard. All those strange spiritual stories that her grand-mother shared with her as they hung sheets on the line, harvested the yams, canned the peaches, shelled the pecans, and scaled the drum that ignited her imagination but had no place for release. I wonder what she may have created if given the chance. If all the Negresses of Elm Grove, Louisiana, had been given the chance, what would they have made?

I think all mothers have considered, late at night, what it might be like to disappear and leave motherhood behind. To just walk out the door with nothing but your pocketbook and never return. And for this reason, and because many of us stay and define ourselves by our sacrifice, we condemn those who do leave. Because the measure of a woman is defined in the ways we martyr ourselves for men and children.

. . .

I knew I had to find a way to be an artist and a mother. Sacrific-ing my child would make it impossible to work through the guilt. Sacrificing my work would make me resent my child. For me, one could not exist without the other. And in many ways, Camille's sacrifices and insistence that the art institutions of New York City take her and her fellow Black women artists seriously allows me to do so. I gather elements of different women's stories and try to build a life of my own. Feeling my way around and learning to trust my intuition. One missing element from many of the lives of the girls in my family was the ability to trust our intuition. So much of that is discouraged in lieu of yielding to the adult in the room. But what about when the adult is just a fully grown child reenacting their traumas? Every time something awful happened to me as a child, I felt uneasy just prior, but I followed what I was *told* to do. And continued to do so as a woman. I began to consider what it may be like to teach my daughter to follow her instincts. Many of the rooms my daughter occupies are full of adults. My friends are only now beginning to have children, and mine is thirteen. I replicated the communities I read about in Maya Angelou's autobiographies. I returned to Toni Morrison's mothers: There's the matriarch Eva Peace, in *Sula,* who burns her son Plum alive to release him from his demons after he returns from war riddled with PTSD and the heroin addiction needed to soothe the ghosts at night. Sethe in *Beloved* slit the throats of her children before she'd hand them over to her slavers. Sethe followed the water to freedom, only to find her past on the other side, awaiting her. I wanted to be in charge of my life like these mothers and live inside of them. The loss of my child would be a grief as heavy as the loss of writing, so I found ways to nurse them both.

The power of the Black single mother is that she does not see herself reflected in the familial paradigms and therefore is not restricted by the adherence to them, leaving space for alternative families to be built through community. The most resourceful and imaginative women I have encountered are Black single mothers. And isn't this the actual American dream, building something gorgeous out of an array of opposing pieces available to you? By creating innovative ways of not just surviving but thriving in a single-mother household? A bricolage of a life.

Around a quarter of American children live in a one-parent home, more than in any other country for which data exists. A report by the sociologist Christina Cross of Harvard University finds that the consequences of single-parent households in the Black community are largely mythical. The Black American divergence from the nuclear-family norm of two parents in a household has historically been the source of attribution for poverty and lack of education in the Black community, just as Daniel Patrick Moynihan suggested in his discredited 1965 report. As with most American political narratives, when you peel back the thin superficial layer, you find that the center does not hold.

The problem with this widely accepted theory is that it fails to specify racial differences. Much of this theory holds true for White families with single-parent households, but Black families have different experiences. Cross finds that Black children raised in single-parent households are less negatively impacted than White families in similar economic circumstances and family structures. A child raised by a Black single mother is just as likely to graduate high school and attend college as a Black child raised in a two-parent home. The reason is overwhelmingly clear—community support. The grandmothers, the aunties, Sister Mary Clarence at the church, the lady down the block who feeds you when Mama is working late, the cousins and the blood memory that says swimming isn't the only way to cross the river. Or what Cross refers to as "extended family embeddedness." By looking beyond the members of the household, Cross identifies that support doesn't always live under the same roof but provides nourishment all the same. A single mother's home is not lacking in care simply because it can't be found beside her in her boudoir. Supported by the many communities of which I am a part, I have come to see motherhood as an incubator for a radical imagination. It is through the power of the collective that we continue the fight for the future of all our children. For me, creativity and motherhood are not at odds; they are, in fact, in tandem.

In New York City, I depend on a queer community, a family I have chosen, to help me raise my daughter. There is my friend Chaz, a chef, who takes the M4 bus across town to pick my daughter up from school when I can't. He teaches her how to prepare homemade pesto for dinner. She calls Shannon *Guncle* when he comes to sleep on my couch when I am creeping out to visit a lover. Daryl, the Olympian, introduced Sofia to saber fencing at the Peter Westbrook Foundation. When Camille breaks down the significance of Picasso's *Guernica,* Sofia seems to only half listen, but it shows up later in her English essay. Courtney gave Sofia her first job, paying her in cash to train her puppy. In Brussels, Adeola introduces her obsession with mussels, Ivo keeps her in touch with her Croatian heritage, and in Berlin, Kevin and his partner take her to see *The Lion King.* A friend at Condé Nast knows she loves science and invites her to have a conversation about gravity with the astrophysicist Janna Levin for *Wired,* and G'Ra features her in his punk band's music video. She's introduced to places within the world and within herself that are beyond my reach. One of the joys of meeting new friends as a single mother is that I meet a certain unshielded version of the person. My mothering of Sofia seems to disarm. Each of them eager to share what they wished someone would have taught them as kids. So I not only meet them where they are presently but also, in their interaction with Sofia, get a glimpse into their past. When we gather for holidays, and birthdays, and piano recitals, my daughter's friends are confused: "So which one is your father?" To which my daughter says, none of them, and *all* of them.

· · ·

Over the years Sofia spent weeks with her father in the summer, or he would steal time in New York between business meetings. He never took an interest in her life. Sometimes I had sex with him if I was especially desperate. I told myself, *It will only take a minute, and it will be over.* I had become comfortable since childhood with betraying myself in service to the greater cause. This was my contribution to the tribe. But I wasn't that twenty-year-old girl anymore, and our daughter had been raised to speak openly in times of discomfort. She no longer enjoyed spending time at his house because she was mostly left alone with her younger half sister and the maids. She could sense the resentment as he found ways to belittle her precociousness. *Why can't you just be a kid?* he'd say when she started listing the animals that live in the ocean's midnight zone. *Why don't you like roller coasters?* when she'd ask to go to the National Geographic underwater experience after he'd already purchased tickets to Warner Bros. World Abu Dhabi. He showed no interest when she said she wanted to be a marine biologist but encouraged her half sister when she said she wanted to be a strawberry farmer. She was beginning to realize her insignificance in her father's presence. A feeling she was unaccustomed to anywhere else in her life.

Each time Sofia returned home from being in Italy with her father, she told me she didn't want to go back for a while. It took me some time to see that what I had been compromising myself for was not actually beneficial for my daughter. She had shaken me out of a delusion that he was what she needed to be made whole. Similarly to my relationship with my mother, I accepted that he could never be what she needed him to be. And once I accepted this, the fear gave way.

He had always threatened that if I ever took him to court for child support, he would never speak to her again. I took the risk because he owned a European electric car company and an oil company in South America, and he refused to contribute adequately. Unless of course I met up with him on a trip where he would give me thousands in cash for child support so the transaction wouldn't be traced by his girlfriend. He was taking care of her family back home, and her brother worked as his gofer. He didn't know how to be in love if it wasn't transactional.

I hired the attorney who had worked for the mother of Mick Jagger's child and Robin Givens when she divorced Mike Tyson. He had spent his career tracking down powerful elusive men who didn't take care of their children and holding them accountable in court. I had been connected to him through another woman who had a love child with a notable musician who was evading support. Once *the oilman* was served at his newly constructed residence in Abu Dhabi, he never spoke to Sofia again. And in some way, it was a relief to be confronted with my greatest fear. The inevitable had happened, and all I could do was surround her with the love and tools she needed to move through the bottomless void of abandonment. A wound I've spent a lifetime trying to heal.

Like my mother had done with me, I enrolled Sofia in a predominantly White school in hopes of her receiving a rigorous education. But in New York City, I felt most of the academically challenging schools were private, and since I am a single mother, I make nearly all the decisions on my own. On some days I was grateful for this, on other days I wish I had someone to share these mundane moments with. *The oilman* decided that private school was not a necessity in America and refused to help with tuition because in the '70s he had studied in the States as a foreign exchange student in the Midwest and felt it was an adequate education.

When I met *the oilman,* he had recently divorced his college sweetheart, a South American woman with whom he had two sons, both millennials a few years my senior. I believe he craved the soft ignorance of youth and the Blackness he had been denied in high school as a foreign exchange student in the rural Midwest. His host mother had forbade him from dating a Black girl from a neighboring school. He still remembered her name. I once tried to help him find her online so that he could separate the two of us, his fantasy from his reality. They met at a school game; she was a cheerleader for the opposing team. They crossed paths at the water fountain. While hydrating, he watched her. He had never seen a girl so beautiful, he says. He took her number and attempted to call her on the landline at his hosts' home. It was attached to the kitchen wall and there was no privacy. This is when his host mother decided it was her duty to protect him from the Black girl from the neighboring town. I am still unsure how she knew that the girl was Black. Perhaps because the neighboring town was predominantly Black, as many schools were still segregated at this time. Whatever the case, his host mother forbade him from seeing her. In his mind, I was *her*. And nothing swells desire quite like forbidden flesh.

At my daughter's private school, White women tell me plainly that they could never invite me to their home around their husbands. "He wouldn't be able to contain himself." They confuse me for the nanny at pickup: "Tell her mother she is such a great scientist." They try to hire me because I'm so good with "the girl." A natural reaction to the discomfort of my presence is to invite me to work for them. How distinctly American. "Oh, I didn't know you were her mother, you're *so* young." They can't help themselves. I can feel their eyes consuming me, taking me in sip by sip, their mouths filled with the bitter zest of awe, confusion, and disdain. I imagine my grandmother and my mother knowing these looks all too well. I now understand why my mother never wanted to socialize with other parents at open house or with the White ladies on Pfeiffer Drive. Somehow, in spite of all the scorn, we keep finding ways to survive. It is my community that has both inspired and enabled my life as a writer and single mother. For a long time, I asked myself if it was sustainable, and they kept showing up to tell me it was.

Betty Jean's aspirations for liberation were realized in motherhood defined by her own terms. My mother tried and failed to achieve peace through a financially stable middle-class life. My understanding of motherhood draws inspiration from both women, combining their desires and pushing them further still. Through history and imagination, my generation of Black mothers is taking the shape set forth by our foremothers to build familial structures—and communities—that allow us to live, presently, creatively within a wounded body, and multiply through a wounded womb, while recognizing the beauty from which we are descendants.

My aunts, and any woman within arm's reach, had the authority to instruct and discipline me if my mother wasn't around. *The*

Baby worked as a dental assistant, and when she lived in our guest room, she urged me to floss as if my life depended on it because a girl's smile is a reflection of the value she places on herself. It is an intimate space of the body that we share with lovers, yet it is exposed to strangers upon our first encounter. If you have a yuck mouth, then everyone knows your house is trifling. If your breath is sour, then everybody knows your na-na is too.

Red introduced cleaning as a form of meditation and self-soothing. She showed me the places where dust settles and goes unnoticed. That the unseen is no less significant. Her home was designed with elegance and adorned with flowers despite financial precarity. She said the home is where one creates the beauty they want to see in the world, and that it is our birthright.

Artemis told me that while in the break room among colleagues, her White best friend said that her husband would never date a Black woman. When my aunt slept with said White best friend's White husband and he left his wife for her, she moved into best friend's home with her two small Black children in tow, the same home she had helped select the drapes for, and the kids began to call best friend's husband Daddy, only for *Artemis* to dispose of him shortly after; she taught me how to sing a siren song to turn subjugation into power. She taught me that White women can never be *fully* trusted. Even when they love you, your position is fixed beneath them. And it ever shall be, in their eyes. I had a similar experience in graduate school when a friend stated firmly that her boyfriend would *never* date a Black woman. I stayed in the friendship far too long because there was a twist, my friend was Chinese and her boyfriend Black. However, the sentiment stood all the same when it came from a person of color with White aspirations and an affinity for proximity to Blackness. But, *Artemis* assured me, revenge can be healing.

At the root of each of these lessons is control. To harness the kinetic energy of your anger and generate enough power to make things move.

Even with all of these contributors to my daughter's life, I still

wished I had one of those mothers that I could depend on to help me be a mother. But I knew that if I called on her, the mother that I needed would *not* answer the phone. Still, I kept breaking my own heart. Desperately hoping that one day she would pick up. The mother that answered was the mother of the girl inside me that I was trying to mother, the one who dangles her help as collateral for dominance and control. To isolate me and render herself irreplaceable. The one who says I shouldn't trust my friends with Sofia because all of them are jealous of me and secretly despise my daughter. The one who criticizes and plants doubt instead of flowers about everyone who helps me bloom.

Community parenting has become more widely practiced, especially after the legalization of same-sex marriages and many people choosing to have babies without partners, a familial queering that was largely adapted from the imaginations of Black women. Stigmas persist but women are shifting toward more creative and varied ways to mother that were imagined by Black women for survival. They suffered the consequences of subverting norms and now non-Black mothers benefit from the groundwork laid by them and think that it makes them progressive when they call themselves *baby mamas*.

$\widetilde{V}iral$

One night G'Ra invited me to a vigil at Columbia University for Black women who had been killed by police in the United States. I wasn't sure what to expect. My daughter and I walked fifteen blocks hand-in-hand to a small room inside the Law School that was covered in poster-size images of Black women and girls who looked like us. Who looked like my family members and neighbors. Kimberlé Crenshaw, law professor and cofounder of the African American Policy Forum, asked us to line up and each of us received a woman's name that had been typed, printed, cut into a small rectangle, and glued to a skewer stick. We were to say that name into the microphone. Once you said the name you then circled the room to hand it over to a group of women dressed in white, like Ifá priestesses.

The name I drew was Korryn Gaines, who had been murdered by police in her home in 2016. Her young son watched his mother's blood spill out on the carpet. Video footage shows Baltimore County police shooting into her home while Korryn made her children sandwiches. A stray bullet punctured and permanently wounded her toddler Kodi. Or maybe it had been caught in the flesh of its intended target. This wouldn't be the first time Korryn's children were harmed by the police; she miscarried twins while being held in police custody having never been charged for any crime. Just for being a Black woman who refused to be quiet.

Though Korryn streamed the violence in real time, so much

remained unseen. You can't see all the loss she experienced that brought her to the moment where she sits armed in her home as police invade. You can't see the residue that forms after carrying dead waters in your womb. To push two lifeless bodies from your own. It's always more difficult to move those without souls. She wasn't only protecting the living children but avenging the dead ones. Behind that door weren't just a couple of eager White cops, it was generations of White men coming into a room and taking Black babies from their mothers and walking away to the rhythm of their wailing.

. . .

My daughter, who needed the microphone lowered for her small voice to be heard, said the name Charleena Lyles, a thirty-year-old mother who was shot by the police she had called to report an attempted burglary. Many of us began to weep. Perhaps because we knew that, ultimately, there is only so much I can do to protect my daughter from having her life taken by the state. Or maybe it was the thought that each of these women were once girls. That some of the names drawn were girls who never had the chance to become women. Their mothers had once hugged their daughters the way I hugged mine after she stepped away from the microphone. And worse, the mothers who hadn't taken the time to hug them. For fear of making them soft and dependent on love for survival, when it is all that is keeping us alive. For fear of getting too close to your own child, knowing the fragility of Black life, rationing care as preparation for the inevitable. Or for fear of doing it wrong, because it's not easy to summon what you've never held. There are so many ways to die.

On February 19, 2020, at 4:56 a.m. Breonna Taylor tweeted, "Why do I feel like all my life Since I've been able to work I've always been the one making sure folks straight & nobody has ever looked out for me the same way."

Many Black women stay up late worrying about loved ones, and wondering, *Who is protecting me?*

Less than a month later, Breonna was murdered in Louisville,

Kentucky, as she lay dreaming in her bed. She knew what we all know: That we are not safe here. Breonna's life had no value in the eyes of the state of Kentucky, where her killers went home before dawn, climbed into their beds, and slept.

I have had many restless nights pondering the question Breonna asked. I have never felt protected. Breonna reminds me of the limitations of my own power to protect my daughter. This has been one of the most challenging parts of parenting a Black child. And more still when they are grown. My mother worried more about her sons than about me when it came to police violence. She was a teenager in 1970 when she heard the shots fired and subsequent riot after Houston police shot Carl Hampton of the local Black Panther Party's offshoot, People's Party II, on Dowling Street. She remembers the snipers on the roof of St. John Missionary Baptist Church. And she wondered how her God could allow that to happen. But the police chief, Herman Short, was known as a Klan sympathizer. This memory stays with her but she doesn't carry concern for me. It doesn't matter how many Breonnas she hears about. There is a theory that we'll be *okay*. That *we got it* and don't need guidance as girls. Especially girls like me, Breonna, and *Righthand*, firstborn daughters. My mother was more concerned with me not becoming pregnant prematurely. The protections are gendered but the violence, in all its variations, is distributed equally.

You can google Black girls and women being beaten by police and even school security guards to dispel the myths of gendered violence. I struggle with how to raise a child when the lynchings are online. When my daughter can find videos of Black death before she knows how to interpret them, and thus begin to identify herself as a problem. The gender discussion my mother argues doesn't hold weight because Black women, trans women, and girls are masculinized in a way that assumes their impenetrability and doesn't afford them the consideration of plausible harm. What confuses me about this is that Black mothers are women who were once Black girls. Shared circumstances between us doesn't necessitate empathy.

Connie and Betty Jean inherited tactics of discipline internalized by enslaved mothers and inflicted them on their children—inducing a fear that they assumed would help keep them alive. If a child sees a cop breaking a Black person's body because they are racist, and then sees her mommy breaking her body in the name of love, can a child differentiate the motives? I realize that my mother's discipline was a form of care, but it sets the precedent that a love that doesn't burn to the touch isn't worth holding on to. The fluttering in your stomach is not butterflies, it's fear. They're actually flies, alerting you of the rot.

In her book *Black Meme*, Legacy Russell identifies that the viral circulation of violence against Black people originated in the era of lynching photography. Postcards of Black people dangling from trees were sent via mail to loved ones, both domestically and internationally. Intimacy fostered by a shared lust for blood. While I naively thought that reposting Black death on my timeline would prove what Black people already knew to be true, that White folks are killing us in innumerable ways, it only satiated this old familiar thirst. American history is on loop. But social media can also serve as a tool of collective mourning—and protest and commiseration. Where Black memes are shared that validate our experiences and we laugh together at the depths of our despair and insistence on staying alive. Memes about Black mothers make me feel as if we all had the same mother. They were all born from the histories those postcards captured.

My mind often drifts to Diamond Reynolds's daughter, Dae'Anna. The way she sat in the backseat, watching blood slowly bloom across her stepfather's white T-shirt. Her calm almost terrifying as her mother recorded Philando Castile's last breath amid the erratic shouts of a cop in the background. It tells me that her mother had taught her how to behave in moments of terror. I wonder if she has nightmares, ducks down during fireworks, or winces at the sight of blood now. How does she think about life when she witnessed how quickly it can be taken? One moment you're driving home from school and then a forty-second encounter with a police officer can rupture your world. Does she see herself as a person? Or an object—her mother's purse on the floor of the car that she picked up as her mother is handcuffed. "It's okay, Mommy . . . I'm right here with you." She pleads to her mother to keep quiet: "I don't want you to get shooted." At four years old she was not mature enough to understand conjugation, but she's in the back of a police car with complete comprehension of her place within the racial order of her homeland.

Reynolds's decision to document as her fiancé's lifeless body slumped behind the wheel on Facebook Live is not dissimilar to Mamie Till's decision to have her son Emmett's open casket published in a magazine. She documented the crime—to tell us, *This is not my burden to bear alone.*

. . .

Just a few blocks from where protests erupted in honor of George Floyd, a Black trans woman named Iyanna Dior was brutally attacked by more than a dozen predominantly Black men. The attack was filmed. The outrage was footnoted.

On April 2, 2019, hip-hop artist Meek Mill (@MeekMill) tweeted: "Can you imagine tryna fight for niggas that you know will kill you?"

To which the queer civil rights advocate Preston Mitchum (@PrestonMitchum) replied: "Black women and Black LGBTQ people can."

During the summer of the pandemic, the author Kiese Laymon wrote about Black boyhood in *The New York Times* "we tried to humiliate Octavia in the lunchroom to make ourselves feel harder, impenetrable, like men." The group of Black men who hurt Iyanna Dior wanted her blood to make them whole. They were not entirely dissimilar from the officer who kneeled on George Floyd's neck. Fiona Apple's 2020 album, *Fetch the Bolt Cutters,* has an entire track dedicated to Shameika, a Black girl she never took the time to get to know, who told her back in middle school that she had potential. This country owes itself to the Shameikas, the Iyannas, the Octavias, the Breonnas. And if you consider the cultural impacts that America has on the world, perhaps the debt extends even farther. A debt to all the Black women whose backs have been bent into bridges so that you can be raised. Then, when we erupt, they call us angry, and we are. But we are angry and we are soft, we are formidable and we are tired, strong and vulnerable, essential and forgotten. We carry all these ways of being at once.

. . .

At the end of the vigil, we were each given a tulip seed, buried beneath soil and tucked into a mason jar, with the name of a woman murdered by the police hovering over it like a flag. Only then was it announced that the women who were handing out the seeds were the mothers of the slain women and girls. When she gave me a seed, I looked into the eyes of Korryn Gaines's mother and I wanted to say something, my lips parted, but nothing came out. I held my breath, searching. Sometimes there are simply no more words. She looked into my eyes before embracing me. Still, she had more love to give.

The tulip seeds never bloomed, but Sofia and I keep the tiny flags tucked in the soil of our plants, to keep them alive in our home. And when we water the succulents and the aloe, we are watering a hope that our daughters are allowed to grow. Or at the very least, that somebody remembers our daughters' names, and speaks them aloud.

Recy Taylor

MRS. RECY TAYLOR, 1944

On September 3, 1944, Recy Taylor was walking home from church at night when she was spotted by a group of White men who had circled the small town looking for a Black woman to consume.

They had gathered in the town center and piled six-deep into a pickup truck. They had probably had dinner, perhaps a few beers, and maybe some ice cream before they decided what they would have next, Black flesh. They drove around Abbeville, Alabama, for hours. They accosted a Black girl outside of her home, but her mother and auntie fought them off, though they didn't bother to report this predation to local authorities. The men continued their pursuit until they settled on twenty-four-year-old Taylor, with whom they were familiar, as the town held less than two thousand residents. It didn't matter that she was a wife and the mother of an infant child. To them, she was a place for throbbing masculinity to culminate. She was a place of arrival, a place where those young boys could be transformed into men. Decades later they openly admitted their guilt, without fear of consequence. They were never taken to trial.

Rosa Parks was the NAACP sexual assault investigator for this region of Alabama, and she came to visit Taylor in Abbeville. The deputy sheriff of the town shared Taylor's maiden name because his ancestors owned hers as property, they were kin. But that didn't stop him from heaving Parks down the steps of Taylor's porch and demanding she never return. She came back. Again and again. Until Parks, Taylor, and dozens of other women fled to Montgomery, Alabama, and formed the Committee for Equal Justice, which helped to instigate the Civil Rights Movement. Formed by Black women banded together in the name of racial and gender equality. Nearly a decade before the bus boycott in Montgomery, before Parks sat down on that bus, the revolution had already begun.

In many recorded speeches by Dr. Martin Luther King Jr., when the camera pans to the audience, it is Black women filling the pews and the collection plates. Black women organizing and elevating and centering Black men because there was an understanding that a man needed to be the front-facing figure. Even in the Civil Rights Movement, the rights of women were sidelined in the name of progress. *Sit down, ladies, we'll get to y'all in a minute.* Stokely Carmichael once allegedly stated that *the only position for women is prone.* The idea was that once the men were free, they would liberate us, the trickle-down effect. But freedom don't drip. It's snatched and dragged upward, against a steep tide.

21

Witness

Betty Jean eventually married Pops after all eleven of her children were born. She married a man who had fathered none of them. A man ten years her junior with no children to call his own, and by the time they met Betty Jean's tubes were tied. He resembled her grandfather whom she had left behind in Elm Grove.

Pops is the kind of man who collects. He knew every one of Betty Jean's lovers in Third Ward, he was just waiting on them to ask him what he knew. And no one ever did. Except for me. He observed Betty Jean for years before she even knew his name. He preserved her history while she avoided it. Patiently waiting for her to notice him.

He remembers all the places she lived around Third Ward. He remembers the spot on Alabama where she stayed when she first moved to the neighborhood with her two daughters and her mother. The four of them sharing one bed. Children at the foot. Mamas at the head. He remembers when she left and lived in the Smith Addition. Then she came back and lived on Cleburne Street. Then moved over to Hadley Street. He watched her family multiply and all he ever said when she came to the corner store where he would stand outside drinking all day was, "Hey there, how you?" She didn't speak to drunks, so she paid him no mind. Then he remembers when she disappeared. Left the neighborhood and moved over to where those White folks lived in South

Park. He didn't know where she was. But she'd cross his mind from time to time. He missed watching it all unfold.

Then he got a job at the police station downtown. And there she was. He almost hugged her. But he knew better. He was grinning and going on and she didn't recognize him.

"You don't 'member me?" His open-faced gold tooth shimmering.

"I don't know you," she said, and carried on.

She was his supervisor at work. They worked nights together as janitors cleaning up after the lawless and the profiled at the police station. There was no extravagant courting. She had no time to date with the kids ever in need of attending to. Her youngest still crawling. They were bonded by working together, pushing brooms and emptying bins. The day passed faster when they were beside each other. It wasn't more than a year before he moved in to *50 10,* and another before they married. He did what no one else seemed to even come close to accomplishing, making her laugh. And oh, when she laughed, she shook the room. Like thunder coming from a deep place inside that caused her body to reverberate. And once she was done, she'd cut her eyes to look at you like, *Now look what you've made me do.*

They got a dog called Wendy, which Pops loved like his child. This was the only way that she could enter such a union: without feeling like she was *owned.* But she still reminded him that *50 10* was her house. In the beginning of their marriage, Betty Jean forced Pops to sit on the floor when he returned to *50 10* from work, so as not to soil her sofa. I remember her once snatching the Sunday paper from him, reminding him that he couldn't read. As if he had forgotten. She recognized the power of literacy because she had grown up around family members who had died without understanding the written word. A not-so-subtle reminder that she was superior, should he choose to momentarily forget. Her children, many of them teenagers by the time he came along, disrespected him just as she had. But he stuck around.

While Pops retained all of Betty Jean's history, he drank himself sick to forget whatever he had come from. He was hiding from something in that bottle, until Betty Jean told him, "Listen here, if you ever show up on this porch drunk again, you may as well turn round and go right back where you came, 'cause you ain't getting in here." He knew, like everyone else, she wasn't the type of woman who wavers. She took consideration before speaking and never betrayed herself. Pops never drank again after that day.

That's when he started collecting things in the ways that he would collect memories. The toys from McDonald's Happy Meals. The California Raisins figurines. VHS tapes, then DVDs, then Blu-ray. Comic books. He was an archivist. He piled them on top of one another, but in Houston, the water makes it challenging to keep anything too long. The water disavows preservation. The humidity and the hurricanes forced their way into *so io* without much resistance. It was accepted as inevitable, so the water flowed and rose where it wished, leaving much of his collection molded and invaluable. Betty Jean allowed him to build a house out back where he could play with his collections.

When I asked Pops what made him fall in love with Betty Jean, he smiled and pressed the pads of his fingers together with the opposing hand into a small circle, "Her waist was 'bout this big." Betty Jean looked up over her glasses at him and gave an affirming nod that said, *He ain't lying.* Not as if she were pleased, just an approval of the validity of his statement. I never saw her proud of anything except her grandchildren. She didn't get caught up in the ego of her beauty. It was irrefutable, and she knew this, so she took no joy in discussing the obvious. It simply was. I do wonder if she missed the attention as she started aging. If perhaps this was part of the reason she decided to marry in her late thirties. That maybe the thrill was gone once she was no longer in her childbearing years.

Betty Jean married Pops at the courthouse downtown. She wore a crisp white blouse with iridescent buttons and high-waisted trousers with her hair pinned back from her face. He wore a dark suit and tie. The photos are black-and-white, but there is brightness in her. She smiles through a pinched mouth, pushing her dimples to their depths, like she just might burst if she releases what she is holding back. She says she only married him so that she wouldn't be a burden to her children. She was thirty-nine years old. I believe it flattered her that he had watched her all those years in Third Ward. That he had deemed her life worthy of witness. Not spectacle. They worked beside each other until they retired.

Eventually, it was Pops who began helping Betty Jean's kids locate their fathers. He knew where their mamas stayed and where their grandmamas stayed. He knew their friends and their wives. The kids they had in their marriages and the kids they had on the side. Pops drove a few of Betty Jean's girls right up to the door in his American-made sedan, rolled down his window, and pointed the house out. He'd wait for their return, and they'd drive in silence back to *50 10*. He wouldn't ask any questions. He is considerate in this way. He never pushes past limits. It is easy to forget he is there.

He couldn't help me find the midnight man because he was in California. It wasn't until I was grown that my mother began referring to Pops as her father. She had always just called him by his name in a tone that one says unsavory words, like *piss* and *spit*. His name came off her mouth like a swear. But then one day I heard her call him Dad and my face questioned her without a word, and she hunched her shoulders and tilted her head sideways as if to say, *I might as well.*

I had gotten an ancestry test and was searching for my mother's father and his family. To which she confidently told me, *He's already dead.* When I asked how she figured as much, she simply said, *I can feel it.* She had a spiritual tethering to the midnight man, the kind of sensitivity you gain only through the dormancy of another. Like when your eyesight goes, your hearing is heightened. She hadn't ever touched her father or laid eyes on him, but she tapped into another kind of connectivity. A sensation that can't be explained. What it feels like to lose someone you never really had. Maybe it's the fantasy that you lose. Ghosts are difficult to release. Sometimes ghosts can keep you alive. Even a void with no bottom can grow deeper still. Perhaps that's why my mother resigned to Pops.

I connected with the midnight man's family through social media. My mother was right. He'd been dead for years. I think she found peace in seeing her face in his. Tears collected in the corners of her eyes as she studied a single photo of him for hours: *This is where I get my style from.* As May had told her, he was indeed *sharp sharp sharp.* She had his deep smooth skin tone, eyes like slits when she smiles, his broad shoulders, and his perfectly cut white teeth. Perhaps the greatest grief of the Black people of America is not knowing where we come from while living in nations that don't claim us as their own. Placelessness.

When I connected with my mother's paternal family in Grand Coteau, Louisiana, I felt I'd unlocked another portal when I located the first of our lineage to arrive on the shores of New Orleans at the top of the nineteenth century. Her grandchildren recorded a family oral history of her story before she died. Her name was Carmelite. It's said that she arrived by boat from West Africa to Algiers Point, just across the river from the French Quarter. I wondered if she had considered jumping overboard, like those women who jumped off the *Galathée* into the Mississippi River in 1728 as they approached Algiers Point, certain that the water shall set them free. But she couldn't have, as she was only weeks old when she arrived, she had been born on the Middle Passage. My great-great-great-grandmother was born on the Atlantic Ocean. She was born in the in-between part. That part of the water where *Blackness* was born. If she had a birth certificate, it would read:

PLACE OF BIRTH: Atlantic Ocean / The Belly of the *Barracoon*
LEGITIMATE: No

If we knew her mother, she might be called Yemoja. And if we knew her father, he might be called Poseidon. Her mother was thrown overboard due to illness after childbirth. She gave birth with her ankles chained to the ankles of dozens of other unfortunate souls in the bottom of a ship. Her mother, who was chained to her, helped in delivering baby Carmelite, who was rocked from the womb by the swaying sea. Carmelite's grandmother knew she wouldn't see her daughter again when they handed the baby to her and took her up above to the deck. Mother Yemoja was given to the sea, sacrificed so that her daughter may live to be purchased in the French Quarter. Carmelite was sold while strapped to her grandmother's chest as she wept when the White men made her dance and jump and open up wide so they could check her teeth. All the baby knew was grief, inside the womb and out. They were sold as *one* to a French family, where their tongues were broken to curl around French words. But it was in her mother tongue that Carmelite's grandmother cried out each night, *I want to go back across the big water.*

Carmelite went on to birth twenty-one children on that Frenchman's plantation in St. Landry Parish. And he owned every last one of them. Twenty-one children born from a womb carrying the history of the Middle Passage and all that was lost there.

The United States of America owes its existence to the Black mothers who birthed the nation. There would be no empire without Black women. America introduced the industrialization of the womb. The Black woman's body became an entire industry, a mill. Through rape and forced intimacy, Black children were born to multiply the labor force that benefited the expansion of the empire. America may very well never have gained independence from England without its reliance on and the proliferation of slave labor. Without the Black womb, there is no nation. Much is *owed.*

This is the lineage from which I come. So when I tell you I come from the water, this is what I mean. All the Black people of the Americas come from these troubled waters. No one is untouched by these terrors. Even when they try to erase and revise the past, even when these histories aren't recorded in documents, they live in our bones. In the marrow. They live in the in-between part.

here, hold these

I never located Betty Jean's birth records. In the state of Louisiana, her life was not worth recording. I still don't know where Lilly came from before she landed in Elm Grove. I can't find the names of the slavers who gave Rose's husband those green eyes. There are some parts of my family history that may never be revealed. Some records destroyed by storms, some never digitized, some never created. In Bossier Parish the county clerk asked me why I was looking for *all that mess from the past*. And besides, in Bossier they only digitized property records. But enslaved people were property. By the time digitization was introduced, slavery was long gone, and they saw no reason to keep those records. Only the land and real estate records were preserved. Louisiana is one of the most challenging states for archival research. Some records are sealed by the estates of the slavers whose heirs still benefit from the profits of yesterdays but don't want their family name traced to those tragedies. Concealing history is another kind of violence that goes unnamed. All the paths lead to nowhere. Those records could never give me what I'm actually seeking, *belonging.*

. . .

When words get lost in my throat, I turn to visual imagery to see where I end up. I've begun collaging as a meditative practice to understand the origins of my fears. I dig into photocopies of family images to remind myself that there were others before me who willed me here.

I sit on the floor in the living room with my daughter and cut along the edges of faces, tracing their lines to focus on their individuality. There are the faces of my family in the country, standing grounded and barefoot on dirt roads and at the edge of some body of water. Standing at the shoreline, at the precipice of something. My face as a girl racing against the Houston heat to consume a melting ice-cream cone wearing nothing at all, moments of joy captured in faces I do not know but recognize all the same. We cut these faces out and put them in the wild on mountaintops, in riverbeds, the sky, and gardens where they exchange breath with the trees. Using faces of the past, my daughter and I become the architects of Black futures because there are some parts of our past that we will never know. And perhaps on some level, parts of ourselves. But when I sit really still, I can find everything I'm searching for inside me.

Thinking in the cumulative brings into focus the multiplicity of being. We are each the sum of many moments, of all the care and cruelty we have absorbed. We also carry the moments that those before us have endured. I think about the ways that rivers are always moving, pulled by gravity, but all the time taking with it remnants of the past as it cleanses itself. The ways that water can be traced to its origin by examining the elements within it. When I was pregnant, I read in one of the pregnancy books that a child with a uterus is born with all the eggs that they will ever have in their lifetime. No more will be created after departing the womb. Millions of eggs preserved, in waiting. Which means that at some point, some part of me lived inside of my grandmother as she waited at the 44 bus stop beside the midnight man, in those dim moments just before dawn when everything shimmers with the promise of renewal. Young lovers with hope of a new existence. I was riding along as she traveled from Acres Home to the hotel downtown with my grandfather. I was with my grandmother when she moved to Third Ward. And traces of her can be found inside me. These complicated women who passed on to me compassion and fury and tenderness. I am grateful to have been chosen from those millions.

Ancestry tests tell me what I already knew to be true, that my body bears witness of the past that my homeland wants me to forget. The enslaved Africans (East and West), each of the original European colonizer nations, and the Native Americans they murdered all show up in my bloodline. How am I supposed to sleep soundly at night with this history pulsing through me? Seeing the percentages divided cleanly in this way made me feel like I could say that I was American without wincing. And because of my mother, I know what it means to hold dear a complicated love and the despair of trying to reshape it into what you need it to be through protest, while still clenching tight through failure.

Whenever we visit Houston, my mother picks me and Sofia up from the airport and our first stop is *50 10*. The little blue house tinted by the dust of the earth. The floors cracked from the floods that disintegrated the tile. We peer through the screen door to see my grandmother looking over her readers at a crossword, while Steve Harvey's voice blares from *Family Feud* on the TV. She takes my daughter in her lap and kisses her and tells her how much she loves her, and I watch my mother smile, because her mother never said this to her when she needed it most, but she understands that she hadn't quite learned how. Sometimes it's easier to begin anew than to change direction. But when my grandmother tells my daughter that she loves her, she really means she loves me, and she loves my mother, and we each consider this sufficient.

Forgiveness between Black women feels more knotted. Between the creases that fold around a firmly held grudge is the idea that the other woman, or girl, *knew better.* These codes are implied but never entirely explicit. The standards between Black women are a tightrope so fine and so high, that we are unable to recognize one another's humanity as we struggle to maintain our own balance. Of course, this is merely our own dehumanization of ourselves.

I remember the day when my mother decided to forgive Betty

Jean. All my life it was only thinly veiled that she hated her mother for the neglect of her childhood. I was in high school, and I sat at the breakfast table in our home. An uneventful day not unlike other weekend mornings. My brother and I were only half awake and the silence between us was punctured as my mother placed the pot of grits in the middle of the table with a cube of butter melting in the center. The yellow and the white distinct and contained. After carefully placing the pot, she raised her gaze toward the ceiling and said to no one in particular, *I'm going to forgive my mother today.* My brother didn't react. I am still unsure if she was even speaking to us. It seemed deeply personal. We were overhearing a private conversation that needed a witness. I impulsively shouted, *WHY? Why today?* Why was I so upset? In some ways the only time my mother was soft was when she spoke about her mother's neglect. Bonded in our dissatisfaction. Sometimes her sorrow for her childhood was where we were able to relate the most. Those tender moments when it felt like my mother understood me, even though I didn't have the courage to share my inner thoughts about her mothering, it was comforting to listen to hers. Betty Jean never says she is sorry, just like my mother is incapable of saying so. But when you understand what these women have endured to keep themselves and you alive, a kind of knowing grace is born. *It's time,* my mother finally said. Before leaving it right there. The butter pooled at the center of the pot, sinking deeper into the white mass.

. . .

Betty Jean loves a departure. Even more than an arrival. Propelled by an uncompromising autonomy, undermined only by the consequences of aging. She was prepared to not live if it meant not living on her own terms. When dementia caught hold of Betty Jean, she spoke of her girlhood beside Grandmother Rose while my mother and I brought water with lavender and eucalyptus to soak her swollen feet. Both of us on our knees, while we listened to her as she was transported. Taking us with her back to Elm

Grove. Her thinking the water was the edge of Lake Bistineau and not just a small soaking tub with oils and salts. Me and my mother were preparing for the inevitable but attempting to make it less painful for her along the way. I asked her once more for her blessing to write about her life. Our family. She sucked her teeth, "I done already told you." I began writing this book in the present tense and ended in the past. All I have now is the *was*. That place within my body that opened, allowing her light in to loosen me up, allowing me to unfurl, that place is closed. That place went with her.

At Betty Jean's funeral, there were only three two-minute spots allotted for speakers. I was hesitant to ask, but an empty spot lingered. I called *The Baby* who was coordinating with the church to ask if I could say a few words at the service. She told me she would think about it and get back to me. I respected that this was her mother. However, this infuriated mine. *She's the baby, she ain't running shit.* The hierarchy of age was firmly in place in our family. Even as an adult, I felt the older cousins should have priority in speaking about our grandmother. Two of my cousins who had lived with my grandmother at *50 10* during intervals of their youth had taken the first two slots.

The Baby called me and said she would allow it. *But it needs to be respectful.*

I assured her that there wasn't a human being who I respected more.

Yeah, well, in the past you've said some things that were inappropriate.

She was referring to my grandmother's eightieth birthday party, when I read an excerpt from an essay I'd written in one of my creative writing workshops. I remember only the last line: *She still maintained the confidence of a tight-rimmed virgin.* Betty Jean beamed. *The Baby* scrunched in shame. Betty Jean's church lady friends came to me afterward to embrace me for speaking so honestly about my grandmother. It seemed to me that they were saying that there is a dehumanization that happens when a woman becomes an elder, a grandmother. They are stripped of complexity. They become a monument devoid of all the warm fleshy suppleness. What my grandmother loved most about that day is that she was depicted as both a saint and a sinner. The poison and the cure.

Betty Jean never concerned herself with heaven or hell. Right and wrong. She was more interested in the in-between part. Rather than assessing all the ways that she could die, she experimented with different ways to live. And only when she had exhausted all the possibilities did she slip out of her body as smooth as silk. Without notice or fuss, like a snake sloughing off a skin that no longer served her. In the middle of the night, she let out a single howl, *Owhhhhhhhhhhhh*. As if she was snatched from this life unexpectedly before quickly resigning. All seven of her daughters gathered around her bedside. They attempted to revive her, until *Artemis* demanded they "stop messing with her" and just "let her go." They took heed. And the wailing commenced. In a piercing crescendo that seemed to open up the sky, as they mourned our matriarch. On that spring night, the air hanging heavy with moisture, they howled toward the waxing moon, guiding their mother into the next realm. And once that was done, we were all forced to reckon with the silence. It's the end of a story that brings attention to the gaps. Grief often feels like a series of queries set in motion by the gravity of death. The questions that you assumed would be resolved in the unfolding of a life. But a ghost can only live in the wake of death. And ghosts must be tended to.

My aunt wanted me to go up in the pulpit and hide. To brush away the footmarks of the path Betty Jean had chosen. Meanwhile, Betty Jean wanted it to be known that she was a woman who *chose*. That everywhere she ended up it was because she chose the bridges, she chose the pivots, she chose her own shade tree. Even if the path led to nowhere. But especially when the path led to water.

None of Betty Jean's girls spoke at the funeral. Only two of her sons attended. I wrote my speech over coffee and a cigarette only moments prior. I feared saying something that might be deemed untrue by the people who knew her in different ways than I did. As if my experience could be invalid and another's more true. I felt she belonged to all of us, or rather we all belonged to her, and I wanted to get it right. Each of us was left holding a different fragment. Left to carry one end with no one to hold the other. Each of us left splintered. She had been the one to fill in the space that our mothers couldn't reach. It comforts me to think that just as she loved each one of us in different ways, with each maybe she was able to explore different parts of herself.

As I stood onstage and looked around the church, I locked eyes with Sofia and became overwhelmed with the size of our tribe. An entire sanctuary filled with her children, her grandchildren, her great-grandchildren, her great-great-grandson. I thought of little Betty Jean burying her grandmother as a girl and being left to feel her way around in the darkness. Of her grandmother never getting the chance to meet any of her eleven children. Of how Betty Jean believed there wasn't a person alive who loved her after Rose died. And the only way she knew to satisfy the grief of knowing love and falling from its grace was through her womb.

I started from the beginning . . .

It's easy to forget that she was born on a cotton plantation. It's easy to forget that she was forced to drop out of school to help with picking the crop and keeping the house after her grandmother Rose died. Easy to forget that she left the only home she knew to move to a new city with no promise except sorrow. It's easy to forget that she learned how to love without a blueprint. She learned to love from nothing. Everyone criticized her for having babies, for being reckless, and then they took her babies from her.

And still she stayed true to herself . . . Look at us, she willed us here, we are her legacy.

. . .

Grief is our unifier. Each time we lose someone, the fibers of our tethering congeals. The way that we relate to one another and build intimacy. There is always something or someone to grieve between us. We gathered like mourning doves when *Daddy's Girl*'s best friend, Louisiana, was killed by her ex-boyfriend while walking home with her new one. We were there when *Artemis*'s second husband died of pneumonia. We came when the 911 operator told my cousin to push his fingers into his brother's brain to stop the bleeding. We are grieving still when we refer to this moment as *the accident* instead of what it was, a suicide. When we say, *He was just playing around with the gun as boys do,* we don't want to confront our grief and call it by its name. When *Gone* got the call about her son, she was at work, driving a city bus. She finished her bus route before going home that day. It could wait, I guess; she knew the grief would be there. It is one of the few certainties. It gave her sisters time to deploy their kids to the scene to clean her son's blood and brain bits from the wall and comfort her other one. One tragedy becomes all of ours to carry. We pile it on and admire one another's strength. We weep for one another and somehow know exactly what to do: show up with tin pans full of food, keep the young children occupied, even the kids know to keep quiet, and we always bring in *The Baby* who leads us in prayer. Don't burden the aggrieved with questions on what to do, just intuit. Call Pyburns for the dirty rice, call Paradise to prepare the plot, call the church, call *Loos-iana*. We do grief so well that perhaps we do grief better than we do life. Or life is just a series of grief spells that builds stamina until the next loss. The grief seems to never cease. I assumed this was normal until I was well into my thirties and was surprised when a friend told me her grandmother died and it was the first funeral she had ever attended. I'd been to more funerals than weddings, christenings, and baby showers combined. It clarified for me that everyone isn't as intimate with death as some Black folks are. Death is our gathering ground because it is true. Funerals are the only time we are sure to all show up, wide open and vulnerable, without fear of refusal.

The Baby approached me at Paradise, the burial grounds, and placed her arm around my waist. "I hope we can develop our own relationship together," then she paused, "but not like the one you had with Mama." And even in our grief, or perhaps because of it, we laughed and gathered into each other's arms.

. . .

The last time I spoke with Betty Jean was on a FaceTime call. Sofia and I sat on the sofa at our home in New York. As Betty Jean stared into the rectangular frame and turned to my mother, who sat beside her at *50 10* holding the phone up, she asked, "Is that me?" before quickly asserting, "That's me!" And in many ways, it was. *I am.* I was trying to find myself in her and she was seeing herself in me. Love is merely a mirror in which another reflects to us versions of ourselves that we've missed or perhaps overlooked. They take in all of us and reflect back all that we cannot see.

In the end, her mind was withering. Each day, like grains of sand carried away by the wind, her memories drifted. Memories she'd kept buried for so long. Where do those scattered grains of sand eventually settle, and what new shores are built upon their arrival? Some of them I'll never know. Some of them she shared with me, and no one else, over the last decade as I sat with her in her living room. Necessity more than desire. Like a levee gone weary, they poured into me without probing. As if to say, *Here, hold these.*

WATER IS A BODY TOO, SASHA BONÉT, 2020

ACKNOWLEDGMENTS

Thank you, John Freeman. The most sensitive, most thoughtful human being, with the sharpest instincts. Somehow, you always know exactly what to say, precisely when I need to hear it. I couldn't have dreamed of a better editor to work with on my first book. Alice Whitwham, my ambassador of kwan. Thank you for believing in this book and recognizing its potential. For advocating for me from conception to completion. I'm so lucky to have found you. Whitney Peeling, for your enthusiasm in ushering this book into the world. Thank you, Jordan Pavlin and the entire extraordinary Knopf team, for believing in this project and bringing it to life with such precision and care.

Hilton Als, I am ever grateful to you for always answering my calls and for reminding me of my responsibility to truth. Your mind is a national treasure.

Thank you to Anita Punch, historian of Trinity United Methodist Church of Third Ward, the archivists at Houston Freedmen's Town Conservancy, Dave "Bayou Dave" Rivers, Brady Mora and Naomi Carrier for inviting me into your homes to discuss your research on the Emancipation Trail over sweet tea, Katy Morlas Shannon for assisting me in navigating Louisiana's archives, and everyone in my hometown who helped me find my way.

The University of Chicago practitioner program provided me with brilliant research assistants: Sarah Hopkins, Kina Takahashi, Stephanie Olluo Sahagun, Ayomide Badmus, Shira Silver, and Nina Dolenec.

My beloved friends, I cherish you:

Cortnie Vee, Vernon Bryan, Chaz Williams, Danielle Rosales, Adéọlá Naomi Adérẹ̀mí, Armanda Estrada, Tiana Conyers, Ampah Edwards, Ivo Rovis, Carina del Valle Schorske, Geneva White, Mengly Hernandez, Elizabeth Perez, Kevin St. John, Carolyn "CC" Concepcion, Mickalene Thomas, Camille Okhio, Elliott Jerome Brown Jr., Tschabalala Self, Céline Semaan, Legacy Russell, Sanya Kantarovsky, Daryl Homer, Alexandra Bell, and Courtney Willis Blair.

G'Ra Asim, friend of my mind, thank you for reminding me that it's more important to be brave than perfect. Heather Radke, for reading every page with care and helping me nurture a sustainable practice. Loryn Lopes, my first and final reader, for laughing and crying with me until we couldn't tell the difference.

Monique Turner, William Davis, Carolyn Owens, Roxell Richards, and the rest of my many many cousins who grew up beside me at *50 10. Pops,* for remembering and telling it like it is. My nieces B & B. All my beautiful Aunties who were courageous enough to determine their own lives and generous enough to share them with me. This book couldn't happen without you. Thank you for supporting me and trusting me with your precious stories.

Shannon, thank you for affirming my memories and for being my first friend.

My parents, thank you for teaching me the game. Bobby T., for your encouragement, sensitivity, and ability to create and identify beauty in the mundane. Mama Connie, I am in awe of your will and insistence on living a life of dignity. I'm grateful for every sacrifice, the ones I witnessed, and the ones I'll never know. Thank you for telling me that anything is possible.

Sofia, my greatest teacher, my inspiration, thank you for choosing me. I appreciate your grace while I was living between worlds. I will choose you every lifetime.

My beloved Auntie Vermal Hondras for loving me and cheering me on for hours over the phone. Loving me from this side while her sister, my grandmother Helen Ruth Shannon, loved me from the other.

Betty Jean, my anchor, there will never be another.

And all the women before me who carried me here.

ILLUSTRATION CREDITS

Lorna Simpson

Waterbearer, 1986

Silver gelatin print, vinyl lettering
Overall: 53½ x 81½ x 2¼ in (135.9 x 207 x 5.7 cm)

© Lorna Simpson. Courtesy the artist and Hauser & Wirth

Photo: James Wang

. . .

Betty Davis, 1974, Ronnie Scott's, London, © Derek Ridgers. Courtesy of Unravel Productions Ltd.

. . .

Iberia and Fred Hampton, 1957. Courtesy of Tanetra Smith of the Hampton family.

. . .

Camille Billops and her daughter, Christa, in *Finding Christa,* 1991. Courtesy of the Hatch Billops Collection.

. . .

Mrs. Recy Taylor, 1944. Courtesy of *The People's World/Daily Worker* and Tamiment Library and Robert F. Wagner Labor Archives, New York University.

. . .

All archival family photographs provided courtesy of the author.

A NOTE ABOUT THE AUTHOR

Sasha Bonét is a writer and cultural critic based in New York City. Her criticism and essays have appeared in *The Paris Review, Aperture, New York, Vogue,* and *BOMB,* among other publications. Bonét is a professor of creative writing at Columbia University and Barnard College.

A NOTE ON THE TYPE

This book was set in Legacy Serif. Ronald Arnholm (b. 1939) designed the Legacy family after being inspired by the 1470 edition of *Eusebius* set in the roman type of Nicolas Jenson. This revival type maintains much of the character of the original. Its serifs, stroke weights, and varying curves give Legacy Serif its distinct appearance. It was released by the International Typeface Corporation in 1992.

Composed by North Market Street Graphics
Lancaster, Pennsylvania

Book design by Pei Loi Koay